W9-BKW-522

The Art of Oriental Embroidery

The Art of Oriental Embroidery

HISTORY, AESTHETICS, AND TECHNIQUES

Young Yang Chung, Ph.D.

Drawings by the author

Photographs by Jung Ae Lee, Yoo In Soob, Michael Uffer, and Richard L. Stack

CHARLES SCRIBNER'S SONS / NEW YORK

Frontispiece: Detail from "The Sea," Color Plate 34. Fish in multicolor satin stitches, water plants in four shades of green done in continuous darning stitch on blue silk background.

Copyright © 1979 Young Yang Chung

Library of Congress Cataloging in Publication Data

Chung, Young Yang
  The art of Oriental embroidery.

  Bibliography: p. 175
  1. Embroidery—East (Far East) I. Title.
NK9282.C49   746.4′4   79-18142   ISBN 0-684-16248-2

This book published simultaneously in the United States of America and Canada.

Printed in the United States of America.
Color section printed in Japan.
Designed by Bobye List.

1 3 5 7 9 11 13 15 17 19   QD/C   20 18 16 14 12 10 8 6 4 2

For my husband with love

CONTENTS

ACKNOWLEDGMENTS

In addition to the publishers, museums, and other sources I want to thank for the use of quoted, photographic, and artistic material, I gratefully acknowledge my debt in general to the many friends, associates, and officials whose cooperation helped to make this book possible, in particular to my editor, Miss Elinor Parker; to Ms. Jean Mailey, Curator of the Textile Study Room at the Metropolitan Museum of Art, who very kindly suggested material for this study; to Ms. Barbara Teague, who also assisted greatly in the Textile Study Room; to Dr. Money Hickman of the Boston Museum of Fine Arts, for his assistance in studying Japanese kimonos in the museum's collection; to Mr. John E. Vollmer, Assistant Curator in Charge of the Royal Ontario Museum; to Ms. Jeanne Harris, Associate Curator of Oriental Art, Nelson Gallery–Atkins Museum; to Dr. H. A. Crosby Forbes of the American Museum of the China Trade; to Mrs. G. W. Barker, for valuable information and photos of the modern Soochow Embroidery Institute; to Mr. Jae Won Lee and Mr. P. H. B. Maltby; and finally to the staff of the Photographic Services Departments of the Metropolitan Museum of Art and the Victoria and Albert Museum.

I am grateful to the following for permission to reproduce material and for their other valuable assistance and information on Oriental embroidery:

In Korea, to Mr. Chung Yang Mo, Chief Curator, National Museum of Korea; Mr. Huh Dong Hwa, the author of *Korean Embroidery;* Dr. Joo Sun Suk of Dan Kook University, Seoul; Mr. Lee Kang Chil, Curator of the National Bureau of Cultural Properties; Korean consul Kwang Sik Kim; Rev. Young B. Oh; Mr. Noh Suk Kyung, Director of the Korean Folk Museum; Mr. Park Byung Gwan; Mr. Quae Jung Kim; Dr. Yu Hee Kyung of Ewha University, Seoul; Mr. Zo Zayong, Director of the Emille Museum, Seoul; Miss Lee Yang Sook; Mr. Young Doo Chung, director of Korean cultural research; Mr. Jong Huh, art critic; and my sister Jee Yang Chung, poet.

In Japan, to Ms. Mutsuko Imai and Mr. Yawara Ishide of Mainichi Shinbun-Sha.

In Taiwan, to Dr. Ho Hao Tien, Director of the National Museum of History; Mr. Ang Kien-tsai; Mr. Liu T'ang-ping, of the National Palace Museum; and Professor Y. C. Wang, for material from *The Research and Examination of Chinese Women's Gowns in Successive Dynasties.* I am also grateful to the Peking Press of the People's Republic of China for their permission to reprint photos from *New Archaeological Finds in China.*

FOREWORD

The Korean author observes at the start of her introduction, "The heart of Eastern culture still remains obscure to many people of Western civilization today." This will always be true, fortunately or unfortunately, but we of the West have always dreamed of the East, and are indeed fortunate that Dr. Young Yang Chung decided to write this brilliant book on an important and seldom explored aspect of Eastern culture—embroidery. A Western reader, in enjoying it and absorbing its fascinating detail, may perhaps come a little closer by this novel route to the heart of Eastern culture.

Dr. Young Yang Chung is a scholar, an artist-craftsman, an enthusiast and connoisseur, and, above all, a Far Easterner. From her doctoral thesis, recently published by New York University on "The Origins and Development of the Embroidery of China, Japan and Korea," comes the sound, carefully detailed historical framework, probably accessible in full only to one who reads easily all three Eastern languages. The clarity and enthusiasm of the writing reflect the fact that the author has loved embroidery all her life and has studied it with various Eastern masters since childhood. She has designed, worked, and exhibited many pieces of major importance in traditional and modern Eastern styles and made her own collection of historical pieces. All types of Eastern embroidery are included in her appreciation and connoisseurship—courtly, ecclesiastical, and secular. Her analysis of design and stitchery is unique in scholarly studies of the subject and far more specifically graphic than that of most how-to-do-it books. From her own deep attachment to her Eastern background comes the instinctive understanding of Far Eastern religion, philosophy, and aesthetics that so enriches this book and makes her discussion of Eastern symbols so authentically informative. Among Far Eastern textile arts, those of Korea have been least available to Western study and appreciation, partly because few examples exist in Western collections and partly because most of the literature on the subject is in Korean. Dr. Chung covers this subject very fully.

It is wonderful to hear such an informed voice from the East speak on Eastern embroidery and on the world from which it comes.

—Jean Mailey, Curator, Textile Study Room
Metropolitan Museum of Art

PREFACE

The purpose of this work is to show the importance of embroidery as a major traditional art form in Asia, to describe its development, and to provide some idea of the rich cultural heritage that surrounds it. In order to give the reader the broadest possible understanding of this comparatively neglected subject, I found it necessary both to set certain limits on the research and to expand the study in places to include related fields. While the study of Oriental embroidery is uniquely both historical *and* artistic, my predilections naturally led along those lines for which my experience and training in art had prepared me, and so the study is essentially a historical outline with a definite artistic emphasis. Additionally, archeological and anthropological references were important sources of information in an artistic subject that has firm roots in prehistory and, as in the case of China, in one of the world's oldest cultures.

Although the research of photo examples in many cases could no doubt have been pursued for its primary historical significance, I have concentrated instead on those pieces that offered special artistic interest and high aesthetic quality. With the same main artistic emphasis in mind, technical demonstrations were focused on craftsmanship rather than on historical importance. Further, sheer limitations of space precluded exhaustive technical demonstrations on every example. Instead, such demonstrations were provided only where it was felt that the reader would gain optimal knowledge of stitchery techniques.

Finally, the use of technical terms in three Oriental languages would have proved hopelessly confusing even for the knowledgeable reader, and I have therefore restricted these to the most important aspects of each nation's embroideries. For example, the simple term *satin stitch* translates in Chinese to *t'ao-chen,* in Japanese to *sashi-nui,* and in Korean to *pyung-su.* Generally, I have tried to use Western terminology in naming stitches, except in those cases where Eastern styles showed distinct variations of Western stitch forms, and for these new terms in English were formulated.

CHRONOLOGY

B.C.	CHINA	KOREA	JAPAN
1523–1027	Shang	Neolithic	Mesolithic
1027–249	Chou		
481–221	Warring States	Nan-shan period	Jomon period
221–206	Ch'in		
206 B.C.–A.D. 220	Han	Lo-lang period (c. 8 B.C.)	Yayoi period

A.D.			
221–589	Six Dynasties period	Three Kingdoms period (Silla, Paekche, Koguryo) 57 B.C.–A.D. 668	Kofun 200–552 (Great Tombs) period
581–618	Sui		Asuka 552–645
618–906	T'ang	Great Silla	Nara 618–906
907–960	Five Dynasties period	668–935	Heian 794–1185 Fujiwara
960–1279	Sung		
		Koryo	Kamakura 1185–1333
1280–1368	Yuan	918–1392	
			Muromachi 1392–1573
1368–1644	Ming	Yi 1392–1910	
			Momoyama 1573–1615
1644–1912	Ch'ing		Tokugawa (Edo) 1615–1868
		Chosen	
1912–1949	Republic		
		Republic of Korea	Meiji
1949–present	People's Republic of China		

INTRODUCTION

The heart of Eastern culture still remains obscure to many people of Western civilization today. Few realize, for example, the importance of art embroidery and the fiber arts in the Orient or how those media are closely interconnected with the history, culture, customs, and fine art of its countries.

It may be surprising to learn that embroidery is ranked among the most important art forms of the East. The tradition reaches back into remotest antiquity, back to the China of prehistory, back to the simple village communities of the Neolithic Yellow River Valley, before the fabulous kingdoms and empires of the great dynasties began. It may be more surprising to discover that when one of the oldest known European embroideries appeared, the Bayeux Tapestry (which is not a tapestry at all, but embroidered linen), in A.D. 1070, silk embroidery had already been practiced in China for at least 3,000 years!

Because of this, many authorities have attributed the origin of the embroiderer's art to China and surmised its spread from there to other parts of the world, although there are Egyptian examples that are extremely early. Certainly early China was one of the first countries to develop embroidery into an advanced art form, and this creative upsurgence was naturally an outgrowth of the Chinese discovery of silk.

To understand how embroidery came to be so important in Asia, we must consider some of the historical and artistic features that are unique in the East. These features were really a synthetic blending of ultimately homogenizing factors: the development of a strictly stylized art (based on the needs of early textile design), linked to a prehistoric custom of costume decoration rooted in primordial shamanism and animism; the discovery of silk, and

its use as a medium of exchange and a symbol of prestige; and finally, the isolation of Oriental civilization from European art influences. Each of these factors contributed significantly to the growth of needlework as a major Eastern art form. Separated from Western and Indian art by the Gobi, the Ural Mountains, the Himalayas, and the Pacific, embroidery became the Chinese equivalent of Western oil painting, the national artistic expression. And even though watercolor painting was developed during the Chou dynasty (1027–249 B.C.), it never fully replaced the rich tradition of embroidery design that had preceded it and that had been its mentor and the first arbiter of artistic values in early China and, later, in Korea and Japan. When the first Chinese embroidered silks reached Rome in the third century, the Romans, amazed at their beauty and magnificence, aptly described the art as "painting with the needle."

As silk production gave China tremendous economic and military power, the tradition spread from the cultural womb of ancient China to its neighbors, Korea and Japan. With it came the resplendent world of Chinese culture and its great creative heritage, art embroidery. The use of embroidery in the decorative tradition highlighted the dynastic era, and it even remains as important today in the traditions, national customs, and art of the people. In the historical period, luxuriant silks and satins, and, later on, cotton, came to be the media upon which the polychromatic colors and matchless designs of the skillful embroidery masters appeared. No cultural aspect of the old dynasties was without embroidery. It was used everywhere, on every type of garment, accessory, and room decoration—temple robes and religious banners, wall hangings and scrolls, bridal robes, costumes, screens and accessories for the home, the imperial robes and accoutrements of the court—all bore the rich opulence of an advanced embroidery art. Embroiderers were honored professionals, and the imperial family alone employed thousands. Embroidery had become a fine art, a tradition that was inseparable from Oriental culture itself.

Thus it is that the story of silk and silk embroidery is the story of Chinese history, and of a major segment of its art. From the earliest dynasties, the Shang and the Chou, up through the peak textile industries of the T'ang and Sung dynasties, and into the final maturation of the art in the climactic Ming and Ch'ing dynasties, the history of embroidery is, literally, the history of China: If it was silk that made China economically powerful, so also did the decorative embroidery industry that was its adjunct.

And in Korea and Japan could be found the same vital ties to history and culture, in the lovely court dress of Korean empresses, in the richly embroidered kimonos and kosodes of the shoguns and the Noh theater.

The crafts enthusiast or collector can find much in this rich tradition to both thrill and satisfy. The same basic stitches and methods used in the historical Orient are still used today and still lend themselves to ever new fields of experiment and creative exploration. It is hoped that this book will provide both an inspiration and a stimulus to further study by modern readers, as we proceed, step by step, through some of the interesting history and exciting artistic techniques of one of the world's oldest and finest art forms, Oriental embroidery.

1/ THE FOUNDATIONS OF ORIENTAL SILK EMBROIDERY

HISTORY AND AESTHETICS

In the Neolithic world, simple embroidery decoration was customarily worked on wool, linen, and hemp cloth beginning almost with the invention of the loom, but the development of silk weaving in prehistoric China was an event that changed the entire course of Chinese history. It was destined also to provide a marvelous new medium of creative possibilities for the embroiderer.

Chinese tradition assigns the discovery of silk to Empress Si-ling, in 2640 B.C. The latest evidence shows it was produced much earlier, and was probably adapted to a backstrap or bow-type loom, which may have been in use for hemp weaving in China as early as 4000 B.C. Once discovered and cultivated, silk became the new ground for a prehistoric custom of self-adornment and shamanistic costume decoration which actually predated weaving, far back into Mesolithic times. It was this custom that grew into embroidery on hemp cloth once Neolithic times began, and embroidery on silk fabrics was a natural progression.

The earliest Chinese civilization that sprang up in the Yellow River Valley deltas had its origins in a northern cultural tradition, numerous scattered bands and tribes of Asians who had inhabited the area around Lake Baikal in southern Siberia (which was warmer then) from at least 8000 B.C. These peoples were Mesolithic, living primarily by hunting, fishing, and gathering; game and fish were abundant in the steppe forests, or taiga. They lived in tent or cave dwellings, made chipped-stone tools, used the bow and arrow and boats, practiced a shamanistic religion, spun yarn on polished stone spindle whorls, and practiced off-loom weaving and braiding. Their clothing was fur and hide garments.

The Lake Baikal peoples, and those who lived in settlements along the nearby Shilka River, pursued a typical Mesolithic way of life, with two extremely unusual features; the practice of a crude metal craft, in which various simple ornaments, utensils, and needles were cast in bronze; and the painstaking, elaborate decoration of their hide aprons, onto which drilled, oblong-shaped plaques of shell and mother-of-pearl were sewn in rows of decorative designs, the forerunner of what was to become the practice of embroidery. This kind of activity has been dated at between 5000 and 6000 B.C. (See Fig. 1-1, a modern aboriginal example of the Goldi tribe of the Amur River region, in which the designs resemble rows of shell plaques or disks).

This appearance of proto-embroidery was apparently part of a widespread, much older custom that had been practiced by prehistoric peoples as far back as the Lower Paleolithic. In 1964, at the Sungir site near the city of Vladimir, Russia, the fossilized remains of a Cro-Magnon hunter, dating from 30,000 B.C., clearly showed that his arctic fur garments, boots, and hat had been richly decorated with running horizontal rows of ivory beads, which had been applied with needle and thread.

By 6,000 B.C., the severe arctic winters that are now typical of southern Siberia had begun to sweep over the Lake Baikal area as a result of the final Pleistocene. Game probably became more scarce, and the Mesolithic tribes began a general southerly and easterly movement over the next two thousand years. By 4000 B.C., there were settled pockets of people in various areas of northeastern Asia: along

Fig. 1-1. Bridal robe for a bridegroom. Scalloped appliqué designs on upper body; peony and butterfly designs in long and short, satin, and stem stitches on sleeves and collar, dragon designs on shoulders; couched appliqué and whippings on birchbark paddings on lower body; scroll and wave motifs in satin and stem stitches; some Chinese edgings and Chinese influences. Goldi Tribe, southeastern Siberia, early twentieth century. Courtesy of the American Museum of Natural History.

the Amur River and in Maritime Siberia; in northern Japan (the later Ainu); in Manchuria, Korea, and the Gobi; and in the Yellow River Valley of northern China. The Siberian, Amur River, and Ainoid cultures remained largely aboriginal and Mesolithic, evolving into the modern Tungusic peoples (the Goldi, Yakut, Gilyak, Yenisei, Chukchi, Koryak, and other peoples) and carrying their prehistoric cultural traditions largely into the historic period. But in Korea, Manchuria, and especially China, the nascent development of agriculture was causing a new revolution to take place: the Neolithic.

The fertile valleys along the Yellow River (or Hwang Ho) were ideal for the growth of agriculture, the beginning of which was really an adaptation to more southerly living, scarcer game, and changing geological conditions in the Old World. Along with agriculture came the invention of the bow loom, for as more reliance was placed on cooperation, settled community living, and farming rather than hunting, clothing needs arose, and the production of cloth fabric to replace the use of fur and hide became a necessity. Before the discovery of silk, the pottery cultures of the Yellow River Valley produced cloth from hemp, and there is much evidence that they wore tailored and fitted robes and garments made from this cloth. Upon such cloth there can be no doubt that the Mesolithic, shamanistic, northern tradition that was the origin of the Chinese Neolithic simply continued its custom of costume decoration (previously done with shells, beads, and mother-of-pearl plaques) in a variety of colors on cloth, with needle and hemp thread, and the art of Chinese embroidery was born, at about 3500 B.C.

The Yellow River Valley cultures are divided into three successive stages, identified by their pottery artifacts: Yang-shao, Painted Pottery; Lung-shan, Black Pottery; and H'siao-t'un, Gray Pottery. Various authorities have established definite connections between these cultures and the traditions and cultures of the Mesolithic north, through the various lithic and bronze industries. One factor, however, points most importantly to the linkage of the northern proto-embroidery custom and the growth of the embroiderer's art in northern China: the attachment of spiral-shaped ornaments made of mother-of-pearl to garments, both alone and in combination with embroidery. H. G. Creel, in *The Birth of China*, makes a note of this important fact:

> That clothing was a matter to which the ancient Chinese paid great attention and in which they took great pride we know from the literature of Chou times. In connection with finds even of Neolithic date, Andersson mentions "about twenty globular buttons, in most cases cut out of marble. It strikes one that these buttons are very small (diameter only 4.5–11 cm.), and it seems probable that a people who used such small and neatly made buttons must have worn clothes made of fine material and of highly developed shape." Among the Shang finds there are small spiral-shaped 'buttons' with three points, made of mother-of-pearl, but it is doubtful that these were actually used to secure clothing because the points would have made them very troublesome and fragile. They are drilled for sewing and threading, and are probably ornaments to be worn on clothes.

It has also been clearly established that the Shang

culture was inherited from the Neolithic cultures that preceded it, and that the same combinations of embroidery and proto-embroidery were found in the Neolithic, as Professor Cheng Te K'un observes in Volume 1 of the *Archaeology of China:* "Furs and textiles were both used, and the garments were adorned with embroidery, pendants and buttons made of jade, bone, shell, and stone."

Silk was in its earliest cultivation during the Yang-shao Painted Pottery period, probably by 3000 B.C., since knife-cut silkworm cocoons were found among their artifacts. We can have a fairly good idea of what the Neolithic embroidery and textile designs were like from examples on Yang-shao pottery. Figure 1-2, which depicts a shaman wearing a tiger mask, shows complex sawtooth and zigzag designs on the shoulders, chest, and high Chinese-type collar of his garment: These were probably typical Yang-shao embroidery or weaving patterns. That silk embroidery was certainly in progress is also evidenced by the many Yang-shao needles found, which were made of bone, ivory, and bronze. Undoubtedly, linen or hemp cloth embroidery continued alongside silk embroidery, perhaps for hundreds of years.

It is noteworthy that most of the designs of the Chinese Neolithic were abstract geometrical symbols; this is consistent with the artistic usages of most of the northern aboriginals of today, who use figurative designs only on the shaman's costume, where they are symbolic of the spirit world. Possibly the remainder of the shaman's costume in our Yang-shao example would have shown more figurative designs.

The zigzag bands and lozenge designs of the Chinese Neolithic era were also found in the early Shang dynasty (1523–1027 B.C.), for evidence of the continued tradition of Neolithic silk embroidery was discovered in Shang tombs. Fragments of plain-weave embroidered silk were stratified beneath the patina of Shang bronzes found at Anyang in 1929. Soft silk threads used in these embroidery fragments were fine, loose, and flat-lying (as in satin stitch), the patterned outlines of the pieces being edged with twisted silk thread in Z-shaped designs, similar to the Yang-shao Painted Pottery motifs. It is highly probable that both the Painted Pottery designs and the forms that appear on the Shang bronzes were used in costume embroidery and textile design, and may even have been derived from the latter. Although none of the original embroidery works have survived, these finds clearly

Fig. 1-2. Pottery lid in form of costumed shaman with tiger mask. Designs of straight and staggered lines, scroll meanders, and serrated circle in paint on fired clay. China, Yang-shao Painted Pottery Culture, Neolithic, c. 3000 B.C. Courtesy of the Museum of Far Eastern Antiquities, Stockholm.

show that embroidery was a well-established art form and cultural activity as early as the Shang dynasty, and was inherited from the Neolithic cultures of the Yellow River Valley.

Highly perishable and destructible, the embroidered silks of the earliest Chinese dynasties have not come down to us. The oldest example presently known is a carefully preserved fragment of patterned work that dates from the Eastern Chou dynasty (sixth century B.C.), discovered in a tomb near Ch'ang-sha, China. Its complex design, similar in style to later Han examples, clearly indicates a high degree of embroidery skill and advanced silk-weaving techniques.

Also dating from about the time of the Chou are the Pazyryk tombs in Outer Mongolia, discovered in 1929 by Rudenko, Griaznov, and others. Brightly dyed felt appliqué and embroidery on costumes and other textiles indicated a long Central Asian tradition in these arts. Colorful jackets, horse trappings, belts, boots, leggings, elegant wall decorations, vests, gilded tunics, and even woolen overcoats were all embroidered in a dexterous array of sophisticated designs. Two pairs of embroidered boots found alongside a woman's costume in the

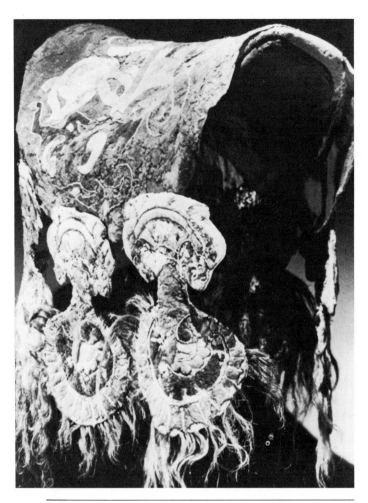

Fig. 1-3. Decorated saddle. Design of combating ibexes, grififns, tree and leaf forms in felt appliqué and embroidery. Mongolia, Altai Region. From the Pazyryk tombs, c. sixth–seventh centuries B.C. The Hermitage Museum, Leningrad.

Fig. 1-4. Bird on a Flowering Twig. Chain stitch embroidery on silk ground, after Rudenko. From the Pazyryk Tombs. China, Chou dynasty, c. sixth century B.C. The Hermitage Museum, Leningrad.

tombs were decorated with great finesse in a variety of designs and materials: felt, silk, and leather. Surprisingly, the soles of these boots were uniquely embroidered with delicate plant forms and silver-thread scrolls, intended to be seen when the lady sat cross-legged. Their arch and instep were appliquéd in feathery scroll designs as well, and over-embroidered with graceful aquatic birds in gold thread. Upon the upper legs and backs of the boots were finely stitched lotus designs, showing Chinese influence, with glass beadwork trimming.

Very richly colored felt appliqué, combined with embroidery, was also evident on horse and saddle decorations at Pazyryk (Fig. 1-3); such lavish trappings, associated with the ancient burial rites, were made for the funeral horses that were buried in the tombs with their masters. Embroidered wall hangings in the same brightly colored design

techniques, showing Chou and Scythian influences, and woven, embroidered silk saddle cloths and embroidered caparisons were additional finds. Another rare example of early Chinese silk embroidery (Fig. 1-4), now in the Hermitage Museum in Leningrad, dates from about the sixth century B.C. (Chou dynasty) and shows a bird on a flowering twig. This interesting piece demonstrates some typical devices of the early Chinese talent for design and stitchery, although it seems deceptively simple, even naive. The dynamics have been very carefully worked out to serve an artistic purpose: This can be observed by laying a ruler over the design and noting the strong vertical balance obtained through placing the various upper elements of the design directly over underpinning elements in the lower area.

Subsequent to the Shang and Chou dynasties, the production of luxuriantly embroidered silks continued as a growing art form that kept pace with the rapidly burgeoning silk industry, an industry that became the major hub of Chinese commerce and a pervasive feature of Chinese culture. This process was an ongoing evolution. An imperial proclamation during the Ch'in dynasty (221–206 B.C.) stated that all the people would be "compelled to work in the basic occupations of farming and weaving; those who produce a large quantity of grain or silk will be exempted from forced labor." Typically, China transferred its cultural heritage from one dynasty to the next, and this was really one of the secrets of the long survival of the empire and of the steady endurance of its crafts traditions.

By the time of the Han dynasty (206 B.C.–220 A.D.), the silk industry was well established and embroidery was solidly entrenched as a fine art. A series of remarkable discoveries shows the sophisticated embroidery expertise achieved in the Han. In 1907 a variety of Han dynasty textiles, silk fragments, and other woven and embroidered artifacts were discovered at T'un Huang by Sir Aurel Stein. A later expedition, led by Kozlov in 1926, located many other pieces of the same period at Noin Ula in Siberia, slightly south of Lake Baikal. In 1972 the most important discovery of all, the tomb of Lady Cheng, was opened in China. Surprisingly, the Stein and Kozlov examples (which are nearly 1,900 years old), revealed eight kinds of stitches that are exactly the same as ones used in modern times. The Stein findings showed only the loop, or chain, stitch, but the Kozlov group exemplified a number of silk embroideries in knot stitch, couched loop, appliqué, satin stitch, and stem stitch, as well as the use of buttonhole and quilting stitches. Still to come was the Peking knot stitch (French knot), called the seed stitch (ta tzu) in China. Legend describes this as the "forbidden stitch," for its tiny size and meticulous execution were believed to cause blindness in the operator who used it constantly. It was further said that this circumstance caused the Chinese government to pass legislation against the use of the stitch, but there is no basis in fact for this suggestion, and none of the Chinese annals mention such a law.

Satin stitch was in use long before the Han dynasty. It is the most commonly used Oriental stitch, appearing constantly on robes and screens, although the chain stitch and couched twist (Pekinese stitch) were also used extensively. After the Han dynasty, no new stitches appeared in China until the Ming and Ch'ing dynasties, when the first counted stitches (Florentine and petit-point) were used on gauze fabrics and costumes.

The Han dynasty was the great epoch of Chinese expansion. It was during this time that China sent visiting armies to Korea, and with them went the entire heritage of Chinese culture. Ultimately, the impact of the Chinese arts spread to Japan also, by way of visiting Korean craftsmen, who by A.D. 300 had brought Chinese methods of sericulture and silk embroidery to Japan.

It was also during the Han that the Old Silk Road, a perilous trade route to the West via Samarkand and the Pamir Mountains, was opened by Emperor Wu Ti. Many glowing references to Chinese embroidered silks appear in Old World Western literature after this time. Chinese silk embroidery was in such demand that Roman nobles paid staggering amounts of gold and silver to obtain it. And silk itself became a medium of exchange equal in value to gold. Han emissaries reached Syria, Parthia, India, and Chaldea, as well as the Roman Empire and most of Central Asia and Siberia, so that by the first century B.C. Chinese silks and their embroidered designs had spread throughout much of the known world. The wealth of the Han Empire grew enormously through this trade, multiplying the riches of the dynastic rulers and setting the stage for the might of imperial China.

In 1972 a very important archeological discovery, the excavation of a Han tomb near Ch'ang-sha, China, revealed abundant examples of the highly beautiful and sophisticated Chinese embroidery of more than twenty-one hundred years ago. The tomb enclosed the perfectly preserved body and textile artifacts of the wife of the wealthy Marquis of Tai, Lady Cheng. Splendid specimens of embroidery, in excellent condition, demonstrated the highly professional mastery of the Han textile and needleworkers, and provided new evidence that practically all clothing and costume decoration of the time was either embroidered tabby or woven silk brocade.

These textiles provide us with an intimate look at the elegant court and upper-class life of the Han. Small wood sculptures of court musicians (Fig. 1-5) show flowery embroidered designs on their colorful robes. Another carved statuette depicts an attendant with embroidered floral motifs on his robe also. The sides and lid areas of Lady Cheng's elegant casket (Fig. 1-6) were finished in appliqué on handsomely designed warp-patterned silk, framed by borders of satin stitch embroidery in lovely

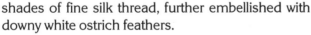

Fig. 1-5. Carved wooden tomb figurines. Costume designs of flowering scroll and cloud forms with geometric borders. From the tomb of Lady Cheng. China, Han dynasty, Western period (206 B.C.–24 A.D.). Collection of the People's Republic of China.

Fig. 1-6. Decorated coffin. Designs of scrolls, bird-wing figures, and arabesques, center panels in chain stitch embroidery; appliqués of warp-patterned silk and ostrich feathers. From the tomb of Lady Cheng. China, Han dynasty. Collection of the People's Republic of China.

shades of fine silk thread, further embellished with downy white ostrich feathers.

Very striking was a painted silk funeral banner that covered the casket (Figs. 1-7 and 1-8), in its center a portrait of the Marquise herself, obviously wearing a silk robe embroidered with typical Han designs, as she is paid tribute by two courtiers, while three ladies-in-waiting, with less ornate robes, stand behind her. The banner is an allegory of the great lady's life, but that she was an important personage and a prosperous landholder in her time we know from the fact that her husband collected taxes from seven hundred families. In general design

the banner is a fantasy, almost a dreamlike vision, and is thought to portray Lady Cheng's passage from this world to the next. Beginning from the bottom, it frames views of the nether world, glimpses of human life (the middle area), and the heavenly sphere (the upper third). Some of the scenes are taken from Chinese traditional legends; others are typical of life in contemporary Han society.

While some of the design symbols on this fabulous banner are obscure, most are characteristic motifs of Chinese origin that appear repeatedly throughout historical Oriental design iconography. The stylized dragons, for example, which intertwine

Fig. 1-7. Detail of painted funeral banner (center portion). Design of Lady Cheng and servants in decorated costumes with kneeling courtiers, surrounded by bat and dragon motifs, on pedestal of thunder line and leopards. From the tomb of Lady Cheng. Color on silk. China, Han dynasty. Collection of the People's Republic of China.

Fig. 1-8. Painted funeral banner. Overall design of dragons, bats, horses, leopards, tortoise, raven, human figures, scrolls, thunder line. Color on silk. China, Han dynasty, from the tomb of Lady Cheng. Collection of the People's Republic of China.

along the left and right sides of the center and upper third, are frequently seen symbols of imperial authority.

An ancient design figure, the thunder line, figures in a simplified form (beneath the white area on which Lady Cheng stands, and the orange section beneath it). Called the thunder line because of its

The Foundations of Oriental Silk Embroidery 13.

derivation from the pre-Shang character for thunder, this classic Chinese motif was borrowed by many cultures and is found in many designs throughout the ancient and modern world. In Europe and America it is an architectural motif known as the Greek key, as contact with China brought the design originally to Greece, where it was slightly adapted to the Greek form. (See Appendix: Design Symbolism.)

Other typical Chinese designs in the banner are the bat symbol of happiness (upper portion, center) and cloud designs in the Han manner (lower left corner of the upper area). The extreme bottom portion shows tortoise figures at both sides of a contemporary event, possibly a banquet commemorating an important day in the Marquise's life. The tortoise was a traditional Oriental symbol of long life. Beneath the tortoises, in the lower corners, are the legendary hares of the moon, mythical creatures who were said to prepare the elixir of life. Influences of the Central Asian "animal style" are present in the writhing leopards beneath the white platform. The remaining design elements seem brooding and eerie in keeping with their other-worldly symbolism, for example, the ominous raven enclosed in an orange sun in the upper right, whose meaning has been lost to time.

Fig. 1-9. Embroidered hat. Chain stitch embroidery in reds, greens, and browns, of cloud scroll and leaf designs; crown of undyed plain weave silk, brim of red lined silk with lozenge pattern. China, Han dynasty. Courtesy of the Sinkiang-Uighur Museum, Peking.

Fig. 1-10. Imperial theatrical costume. Design of dragons, fowl, peacocks, clouds, Buddhist symbols, waves, mandarin square, in couched gold thread; edgings in *k'o-ssu* tapestry weave. China, Ch'ing dynasty, nineteenth century. The Metropolitan Museum of Art, Bequest of William Christian Paul, 1930.

The Art of Oriental Embroidery

The real textile treasures of the tomb were beautifully embroidered pillows, embroidered mittens, embroidered cases for musical pipes, silk slippers, over fifty pieces of embroidered robes, and fifty pieces of special silk embroidery done on patterned gauze and damask yardage. On the whole, the discovery comprises the most important, well-preserved collection of pre-T'ang textiles ever found. Chain stitch embroidery was well represented in the collection, worked in marvelous examples of typical Han design: stylized cloud scrolls and modified cloud motifs, stylized bird-wing and animal figures, as well as flower and lozenge lappets, all in a scintillating variety of rich colors.

The fabled Land of the Seres—the silk people, as the Romans called the Han Chinese—produced an immense body of embroidered masterpieces, of which only a comparatively small number are extant today. With their lovely pure white silks, icily glowing and translucent, gossamer gauzes of cloudlike sheerness, and the fine damasklike weaves that are synonymous with the Chinese ideograph for "beauty," it is not difficult to understand why the people of China have always compared the beauty of their land to that of embroidery and brocade.

Fig. 1-11. Bridal coat. Embroidery of dominant dragon, waves, peonies, mountains, lotus, butterflies in couched gold and shades of blue floss silk on red satin ground. China, Ch'ing dynasty, after 1875. Royal Ontario Museum, Toronto, George Crofts Collection, gift of the Robert Simpson Company.

FOUNDATIONAL METHODS, MATERIALS, AND TECHNIQUES

Yarns

Early Oriental sericulture was a much simpler process than the vast industrial methods used today, but it was still the craft and the science that carefully and patiently made the silkworm cocoon yield a vast supply of durable silk yarns. The production was probably inefficient by modern standards, yet the silk that was produced was of the finest quality. Sericulture shops were small in the early dynasties, and the work was usually done by women. Sometimes a single operator manipulated thousands of silkworm trays and did all of the steaming and reeling alone; sometimes families had their own silkworm farms and produced silk for their own use or sold it on the great markets of the ancient cities.

The quality of silk was carefully managed by the assiduous sericulture process, for poor care produced poor silk. Study of the proper climate and the type of soil used in the cultivation of the mulberry trees (whose leaves are the silkworm's favorite food), the proper harvesting of the leaves and their spreading in the silkworm trays, the industrious methods of raising the silkworm cocoon, steaming, reeling, and finally spinning—all these steps were first originated and mastered by the Chinese. The dyeing process was also very important, as improper dyeing could radically affect the strength, tensility, and sheen of the yarn.

In the historical period, spun silk yarns were always twisted by hand in preparation for sewing. Today we have machine-twisted yarns that may be purchased commercially, but the finest textural gradations have been lost to some extent by mechanical methods, such yarns being generally too tight for the stitchery of fine embroidery on delicate fabrics. Hand twisting of the yarns was necessary to obtain greater or less delicacy, according to the shape and size of the design. Varying thicknesses and, consequently, varying techniques of twisting were required. Hand-twisted yarns also lent themselves to greater facility in threading and easier handling of the fabric when sewing.

The ancient methods even had more practical and artistic value. Hand-twisted yarn was much easier to control apropos the thickness of the yarn, the size of the needle eye, and the thickness of the fabric. Ideally, silk yarns were twisted to the same thickness, or slightly less, than the needle eye to be used, for it was found that thick yarns made unsightly, larger needle holes in the silk. Manually twisted yarn was also more effective in terms of finishing: Embroidery done with it had considerably more glossiness and uniformity of textural surface. Multiple-color yarns were obtained easily by hand twisting also.

Gold and silver yarns for metal thread embroidery were made by pounding gold stock into leaf, which was then sliced into very narrow strips and rolled or twisted into the yarn. Gold paper, or gold-painted paper, which was more economical, was also used for this purpose, and threads were wrapped in it in the same way. Such yarns were always couched on the fabric, using a hidden stitch, since the stitching-through of metal threads would have caused the gold or silver to fray and fall off onto the fabric.

The Roller Embroidery Frame

The embroidery frame in traditional use in the home and by professionals was square or rectangular (see Figs. 1-12 and 1-14), in contrast to the Western embroidery hoop. Although the hoop was also used in the East, the rectangular frame is still preferred today. Round hoops are lighter, easier to handle, and useful on smaller pieces or with cotton or linen, but the rectangular frame offered more advantages in less wrinkling, greater stability, and the accommodation of larger fabrics. The clamping and wrinkling caused by a hoop can tear or damage delicate silk, and size was important too, the hoop not being convenient on larger pieces, such as screen panels. Probably rectangular frames were used exclusively in most of the historical period of China, Korea, and Japan, a number of paintings

Fig. 1-12. *Girl seated at an Embroidery Frame.* Hanging scroll, color on silk. China, Ming dynasty. Courtesy of the Smithsonian Institution, Freer Gallery of Art, Washington, D.C.

Fig. 1-13. Tracing and transfer tools. Left to right: dusting brushes, ruler, drawing brush, stencil knife, fabric brushes, oyster shell block, oyster shell powder in dish. Collection of the author.

giving evidence of this, for the Western embroidery hoop may not have arrived there before the British trade that began in the eighteenth century.

Embroidery frames could be any size and were usually constructed proportionately to the size of the design project undertaken. A representative, medium-size, adjustable roller frame of the Japanese type can be reconstructed through the following methods and materials. A smooth, hardwood lumber suffices for the major components.

> 2 sidebars: 1 × 2 inches, 28 inches long (2.5 × 5 cm., 71 cm. long)
> 2 braces: 1 × 2 inches, 18 inches long (2.5 × 5 cm., 45.7 cm. long)
> 2 rollers: 3/4 inch (1.9 cm.) doweling, 18 inches long

With the following construction, this type of frame can accommodate any length of fabric, up to eighteen inches in width, through the use of roller tension.

Sidebars

The sidebars each need one 3/4-inch rectangular slot on each end, 1 1/2 inches (3.8 cm.) from the end. Two inches from each slot, drill a hole 3/4 inch in diameter on each end. Beginning one inch inside the rollers, drill needle holes 1/8 inch (3 mm.) in diameter, one inch apart, at a 45-degree angle, in the entire length of the sidebars.

Braces

Cut the braces down 5/8 inch top and bottom, five inches from each end. This leaves a 3/4-inch slot bar on each end, and an 8-inch (20.3 cm.) expansion bar in the center. In addition, drill a 3/16-inch (5 mm.) hole one inch from the end, on both braces.

Rollers

In both rollers, drill a 3/16-inch hole one inch from each end. Center 1/8" fabric slot, 12 inches (30.5 cm.) long, in each roller. (Additional rollers, of varying length and with wider fabric slots, can be made up and kept in stock for fabrics of greater width.)

Additional Materials

2 bamboo chopsticks (or similar material)
3/16-inch nails or wooden pegs

Fig. 1-14. Detail from *Palace Ladies* by Chiao Ping-chen. Hanging scroll, color on silk. China, Ch'ing dynasty. Courtesy of the National Palace Museum, Taipei.

2 6-inch (15.2 cm.) picks (tapered or square) used in twisting yarn
darning needle
darning thread

Setting Up the Frame

When all the lumber is cut, slotted, and drilled, lay out the sidebars 18 inches apart, with one brace and one roller at each end. Insert the 3/4-inch slot key of the right brace into the 3/4-inch slot on the right sidebar; follow the same procedure on the left

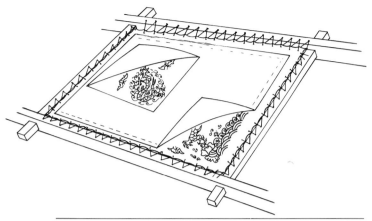

Fig. 1-15. Design on masked fabric stretched on rectangular embroidery frame.

Fig. 1-16. Fabric rolled on embroidery frame with blocking material in place for widening.

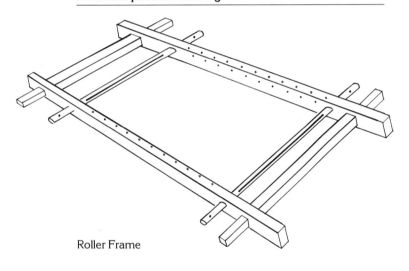

Roller Frame

brace and sidebar. Inside the right brace, slide the right ³/₄-inch roller through the ³/₄-inch hole on the upper sidebar to the opposite side, and through the same hole on the lower sidebar. Repeat the same operation with the left roller. The frame, with its stretched fabric, is shown in Figure 1-16. (The braces may be widened up to an additional 6″ on each side through the use of blocking sticks—chopsticks or similar longer material—wedged between the braces and sidebars. See Fig. 1-16.)

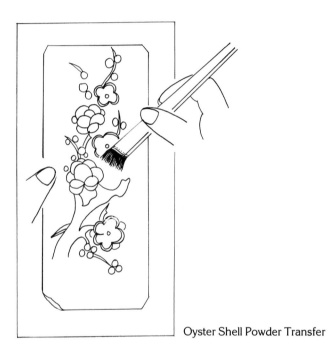

Oyster Shell Powder Transfer

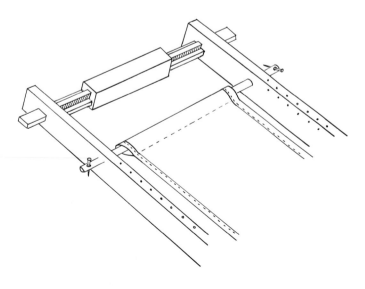

Stitchery on the Tracing Transfer

Design Transfer Methods

Several traditional methods were used almost universally in the Orient for transferring the master design to the fabric: powder and paste transfer; window tracing with paste; transfer stitchery with tracing; and outline stitchery on the tracing. Through the simplest materials, the most intricate designs could be accurately copied onto the fabric. The striking dragon robes shown in Chapter 3 were probably transferred onto fabric with one of these methods. In the prehistoric and dynastic periods of China, natural resources were exploited in a variety of ways. For example, oyster shell mounds that collected outside the villages and cities were for a purpose: they were handy drinking and scooping utensils, supplied the mother-of-pearl material used so often in decoration, and could be ground up to yield a fine, very white powder used in embroidery tracing.

Powder and Paste Transfer

1. The master design was drawn on heavyweight drawing paper.

2. A stencil was made by cutting the design out of the drawing paper, using a very fine, sharp blade.

3. The cut-out stencil was then laid flat on the unstretched silk fabric and either basted, pinned, or held with clips. The design was dusted through the stencil onto the fabric with oyster shell powder, using a small, fine brush or a gauze bag filled with the powder. After dusting, the stencil was removed from the fabric, leaving the powdery outline of the design.

4. A moist paste was made by mixing the oyster shell powder with water. With a fine watercolor brush, the powdered design outline was reinforced with the moist paste mixture. When thoroughly dry, any residue was dusted from the fabric. The design applied, the fabric was now ready for stretching onto the frame for embroidery.

Window Tracing and Paste Transfer

1. The finished design was executed on thin, very fine rice paper.

2. The rice paper master design was then taped onto a window, its reverse side facing in. With moist oyster shell paste, the outline of the design was traced onto the back of the rice paper and allowed to dry.

3. The traced design was removed from the window, turned over, placed back side down on the fabric, and clipped into place.

4. The entire design was burnished over its surface with a wooden spatula, with a medium pressure, to avoid crumpling. The tracing was then removed from the fabric, and the piece was ready for stretching and sewing.

Transfer Stitchery on the Tracing

1. In this method, the rice paper design was placed on the stretched fabric and anchored around the edges with a well-spaced running stitch.

2. The transfer was made by sewing *through* the rice paper, covering the design with the stitchery in the desired colors. When the design was entirely covered with its stitchery (long and short stitch or satin stitch, for example), the rice paper areas bordering it were stripped away, leaving the finished piece. (The underlying layer of rice paper left beneath the finished design served as a protection against moisture and acted as a backing finish.)

Outline Transfer on the Tracing

The rice paper design was basted onto the edges of the stretched fabric as in the above method, but instead of covering the entire design with the finished stitchery, its *outline* was merely sewn through the rice paper, using a running and/or outline stitch in the color of the area outlined. Once the outline was stitched, the rice paper was entirely stripped away, leaving the stitched outline as the guide for subsequent finishing.

Fabrics

As mentioned earlier, silk weaving in ancient China was preceded by a long history of the production of other fabrics on the bow loom, and felting, an import from Central Asia, was also extensively practiced. Quilted garments for the cold Chinese winter and hemp cloth for summer were produced, the latter in plain, tabby, and twill weaves, as early as the Yang-shao Painted Pottery cultures (c. 4000 B.C.). Natural fibers were always used, since there were no synthetics yet invented, and these fibers were derived from animal and plant sources. Animal fibers came from sheep (for wool), goats, camels, rabbits, dogs, and later, horses, for hair fibers. Plant fibers, either stem or bast, were obtained from flax (for linen), jute, hemp, and ramie, a plant native to China whose special linenlike bast fiber was very useful in the production of cloth. With the discovery and cultivation of silk, the rugged bow loom was available to produce it in both tabby and twill weaves.

Plain weave silk was thus soon made in many different textures and weights, but great variety and wide subtlety of color may not have been available much before the Han. Subsequent important advances in dyeing during the T'ang and Southern Sung dynasties probably allowed unlimited variety of color from those eras onward. The thickness of weft and warp threads was what created the weight and texture of silk, then as now. Oriental silks were traditionally prepared in extra-fine, fine, rough, and extra-rough grades. Generally, silk embroidery yarns were used, which were appropriate to the texture of the fabric. Fine fabric required the use of a finer yarn; conversely, rough silk required a correspondingly rougher yarn.

Complicated designs usually show a fine grade of fabric and fine yarn. Since silk embroidery is smooth and delicate by its nature, rough design textures (such as rocks and trees) were achieved sometimes through rough fabric, but more characteristically through the preparation of the yarn by a special twisting method. The accompanying reproductions show some of the varied textural effects that were obtained through the combined use of rough-twisted yarn and varied stitchery, as in floral textures, rocks and trees, and bird feathers (Fig. C-36).

The draw loom was invented in China and was in use there by the Han dynasty. With its development, other fine silk fabrics, such as warp-patterned, weave-patterned, gauzes, and floral-patterned weaves could be produced, and these lent themselves to innovative embroidery effects. (On silk gauze a very short stitch, such as the diagonal or half-cross, and brick stitch were used.) Damasks, a later development, are reversible, warp-faced designs on a weft-faced ground, or vice versa. They take their name from the ancient Near East city of Damascus. Available in various weights and textures, damask is used in the West for tablecloths, drapery, and upholstery, but in the East it was often the ground for beautiful robes and other textiles upon which polychrome embroidery was executed. Brocades have designs inlaid as the weaving pro-

gresses. They are especially handsome and rich when done in silk, and the treatment is found on damasks, twills, satins, or plain weave silk. Both brocades and damasks were embroidered with the same stitchery that was employed on plain weave, the former simply providing a richer, more varied ground.

Stretching Fabrics

In cutting fabrics, at least a one-inch margin was allowed on all sides away from the design. This margin allowed for stretching and attachment to the frame. Any frayed fabric edges were secured with a basting stitch to protect the piece from further fraying before stetching and stitchery.

Method 1: Stretching on the Roller Frame

After the design had been transferred, and the fabric was cut, the first preliminary step before stretching was to attach a backing. This was necessary on the side edges to prevent the silk from tearing away from the roller frame sidebars. Ideally, backing material would be heavier and stronger than the silk. Either thin flannel or double-faced muslin was used for this purpose.

1. Two pieces of backing material were cut, four to six inches wide, the same length as the fabric. The backing material did not lie beneath the design at any point.

2. The backing was basted to the edge of the fabric, on all four sides of the backing material itself.

3. The backed fabric was wrapped around the right roller from the bottom up, toward the inside of the frame, then was lapped about 2 1/2 inches (5.8 cm.) around the roller and basted horizontally across the fabric. This procedure anchored the fabric firmly on one end of the frame.

4. The opposite end of the fabric was guided through the left roller slot, and gently drawn up, by twisting the roller from right to left, the same way a roll of film is tightened. The material was stretched until it was perfectly straight and flat, but less than drum-tight. The 3/16-inch stopper nail in the left roller was inserted into the left brace hole to act as a temporary stop. The fabric was now ready for attaching it to the frame through the use of the needle holes.

5. With a darning needle and thread, the first needle hole was entered from the top, and the thread was secured by tying a knot at the end. The needle then entered the fabric again from the bottom, approximately one inch from the end, and would enter the second needle hole from the top. Pushed through the second needle hole, the needle would come up again from the bottom, one inch from the previous stitch. The same process was continued down the length of the sidebar. The row was finished by securing the last needle hole with a knot, as with the first. The same procedure was repeated on the opposite sidebar. After completion, the frame and its stretched fabric would look like Figures 1-15 (page 18) and 7-9 (page 134).

Although the roller frame method was versatile and practical for many pieces of varied size, it was used primarily by professionals. It had the hazard of possible damage to delicately embroidered areas as the fabric was rolled, even though the work was protected by a felt padding. Also, the complex procedure of achieving correct tension on the fabric during the sidebar stitchery required expertise. On pieces that remained relatively stable—such as the Japanese obi—and that did not require excessive rolling, the roller frame was excellent. It was the only alternative to larger, more cumbersome stationary frames, again, as for the obi, which was six feet long.

Method 2: Stretching on the Rectangular Oriental Frame

A simpler traditional method of stretching fabric was the use of the rice-glued frame. The glue method obviated the need for rolling. It was also superior to the roller frame on rich designs that covered all of the fabric, and where there was much raised work. It was more secure and sturdier, and it stored easily, so that the operator could return to the work at intermittent intervals. It had its liabilities also: The preparation of the glue took time and patience, troublesome wrinkling of the fabric could occur while stretching, and the danger of splashing glue on the fabric required the use of friskets and more care with handling. These drawbacks were minor compared with the advantages of simplicity and facility of procedure, and I have often used this method in my own work.

1. To prepare the glue, Oriental white rice was cooked to a wet, mushy state. It was then removed from the heat and a small amount transferred to a mixing bowl, where it was mashed into a paste, soft and fluid enough for easy manipulation.

2. As an optional protection of the fabric against spattering of the glue, a frisket of rice paper was cut,

a half inch smaller on all sides than the fabric. Laid on top of the fabric and basted loosely around the edges, this masking offered protection while the fabric was glued in place. After gluing and stretching were completed, the design was cut out of the frisket, the remainder being left to maintain cleanliness while doing the embroidery.

3. A frame similar to an artist's canvas stretcher, squared and joined, was laid flat on a table. (Fabric cutting allowed for a one-inch overlap on all four sides of the frame in this method.) Rice glue was applied thoroughly along the entire outer edge of the upper stretcher, then the stretcher was raised, and one inch of the fabric was affixed to the glued stretcher edge and rubbed vigorously until it adhered and was free from bubbles. The same process was repeated on the left side, and the frame was then put aside to dry, usually overnight.

4. When the top and left side were completely dry, a tack was placed in the center of the top stretcher and the bottom stretcher was then glued, and the fabric applied to it, in the same process as above: stretching it from the top center toward the bottom center, and adhering. If the piece was to be remounted after finishing—as in wall hangings or screen panels—the material was stretched almost drum-tight. Other pieces, such as costumes or accessories, were stretched less tight. After pulling the fabric down toward the center of the bottom stretcher, a tack was placed in the center to hold tension while drying. Then all four corners were tacked. The fabric was stretched again toward the bottom stretcher, halfway between the center and the left corner, and tacked at that point. The same operation was repeated on the right, tacking and adhering at the center, then halfway again between the center and the corner, and so on. One whole day was allowed for drying before commencing stitchery. Any spots of glue that had spattered or fallen on the fabric were not removed with water, but rather whisked off with a small, stiff brush after drying.

The glue method was excellent for use in the home and is still readily adaptable to home or classroom work. Many of my students have come to appreciate how the careful preparation of the frame and the stretching of the fabric were important aspects of Oriental embroidery craftsmanship, the prelude to further creative work. While preparing the materials and gluing the fabric, the designer could study the design and plan the finished work further, noting such points as the texture of yarn to be used, types of stitchery, color tonalities and overall color harmony, places stumping would be prepared, basic perspective of the composition, shading, perspective, how the various forms could be modeled, and so forth.

Both the glued rectangular frame method and the roller frame method were traditional ways of stretching fabrics onto the embroidery frame in the historical periods of China, Korea, and Japan.

Stitchery

Even though embroidery is a decorative art, the Oriental approach to composition was painterly: that is, it strove for artistic realism within the two-dimensional limitations of the medium. Artistic realism, however, is not the same thing as photographic realism: The Oriental artist, whether in embroidery, painting, or any other art form, was never willing to sacrifice artistic effect to mere naturalism, and, as far as he or she was concerned, stylization fitted very nicely into this plan. Very often the effect achieved was evocatively beautiful, the truly naturalistic, yet fully artistic expression of a scene, subject, mood, or idea. This magnificent "painting with the needle" has never been quite paralleled in the history of the textile arts; it is the achievement for which Oriental embroidery is justly famous.

The painterly realism of Oriental embroiderers was not obtained through imitating painting, however, but quite the reverse: Embroidery was the forerunner of painting in early China. It was achieved through the artistic adaptation of the limitations of needlework to pictorial method. Stylization was a visual language developed to gain both natural effects and artistic expressiveness in textile design. Through modeling form, free use of artistic and traditional conventions, and ingenious arrangement of negative space, what had been textile limitations (flatness, lack of depth, linearity) were skillfully turned to advantage, although the superb craftsmanship, artistry, and carefully planned designing are hidden in the composition. (For a further exposition of design see Chapter 8.)

The painter can blend, mix, or soften colors; he or she can use the brush to express space or form or to build delicate color nuances and atmospheric relationships. The embroiderer can also do this,

using gradated color stitchery as his or her brush and the spatial shapes of design to express depth. Both were important in achieving effects as remarkable in their own way as painting. The beautiful embroidery compositions of the historical Orient seem fresh and modern today, although they were executed thousands of years ago, an ample proof of their timeless artistry. The quality of sculpture was also achieved by the embroiderer: Raised or stumped needlework added fascinating textures and created a sense of bas-relief, and such a rich, sculpturesque surface added immeasurably to the power and impressiveness of the finished oeuvre. Oriental embroidery, then, aimed for effects of painting and sculpture, and sought to disguise and minimize the techniques of needlework.

Various kinds of stitches were used in the process at varying times, but the reader may be surprised to learn that although fewer stitches are used than in the West, they are exactly the same stitches with which he or she may be familiar. Strangely enough, stitchery has been notably universal, almost since prehistoric times. The long and short and the satin stitch were the most important stitches in the Oriental master's repertoire. They effectively achieved the subtle, painterly qualities so much prized by Eastern needleworkers, and maintained a smooth surface through which texture and variety of tone could be more easily expressed. Long and short stitch especially lent itself to the soft gradation and blending of tones, as for example in flower renditions, where four or five different shades of a color were often used. The famous seed stitch of China and the couched loop stitch were used for soft textures, such as furs, and in small spaces, while the buttonhole, chain, and basketweave expressed rougher surfaces, such as those found on trees, rocks, still life in general, and sometimes animals. The outline (stem) stitch was used with great frequency in line work, in underdrawing, and in accenting, where it added considerably to the bas-relief effect.

Other stitches were used more specifically as the need arose. Holding (couching) stitches were necessary for securing very long laid stitches and metal thread work by keeping them down firmly, and they also improved the textural effects and increased general fabric strength. The familiar buttonhole stitch was used in China for strengthening cut edges or for edging in general. (See Fig. 2-8, page 32.) Both chain and split stitch are often seen in Oriental work, especially on curving lines or curvilinear scrolls. Any rough surface could be well expressed through the basketweave stitch and the hatch stitch, as well as with rough-twisted yarn, using combined long and short and satin stitch. Half-cross stitch came into play where short-length stitches were called for, as on gauze fabrics.

Needles

Both the needle and the yarns selected had to be appropriate to the fabric and the design. Oriental embroiderers used a variety of short, very fine, pin-like embroidery needles in a number of sizes, the average being about one inch long. The eye ends were flattened and had round eyes. The examples shown in Figure 1-17 have eyes that are rounder and blunt ends that are wider than Western needles. Early needles in China were made of bone and ivory, then copper, bronze, and finally steel, but ivory needles were still found in use there as late as the Ch'ing dynasty. Knotting of the thread end was never done in any Oriental technique, for knots created unsightly bulges in the surface after the composition had received its backing. For anchoring the thread without a knot, a top anchor knot was executed as follows: One inch of thread was held on the surface of the fabric with the thumb, as the needle entered and emerged several times in a fixed point, either above or below the spot where stitchery was intended to begin. The original one inch of thread was then clipped off. With the thread now firmly anchored, stitchery was ready to begin.

Fig. 1-17. Oriental embroidery tools. Upper left to right: Pin-cushion, embroidery thimbles, needle packages. Lower left to right: fabric scissors, yarn cutter, thread scissors, embroidery needles. Collection of the author.

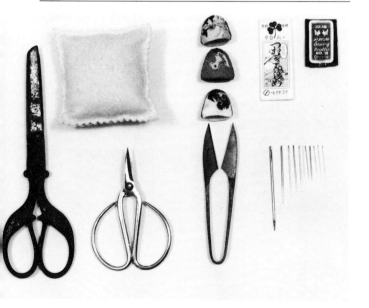

Example 1: Stem Stitch (Outline Stitch)
(Fig. 1-19)

The top anchor knot was first executed to anchor the thread.

A. The needle emerges at 1, reenters the fabric at 2, and exits again at 3, precisely in the center of 1 and 2. The needle is drawn up, keeping the thread to the right of the needle.

B. The needle reenters the fabric at 1, emerges at 2 (in the same hole made by entering at A2), and is drawn up, keeping the thread at all times to the right of the needle.

The stitch runs continuously by repeating step B. For concave lines it was customary to keep the thread to the left of the needle. Whichever method was used, the thread had to stay on the same side once the line was begun.

Fig. 1-18. Oriental embroidery yarns. Left to right: 1–4, dyed untwisted silk yarns; 5–8, half-twisted dyed silk yarns; metal threads; spools for metal thread. Collection of the author.

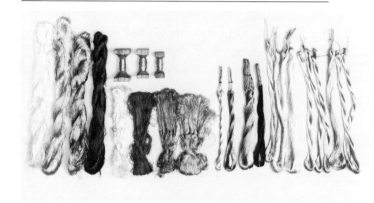

Fig. 1-19. Example 1: stem stitch.

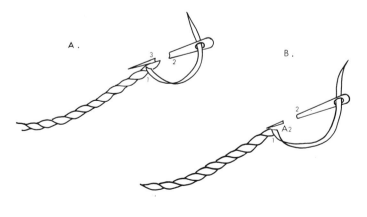

Example 2: Long and Short Stitch (Fig. 1-20)

A beautiful and useful stitch, the long and short was usually employed for shading or gradations of color. If it was worked correctly, none of the individual stitches would show, and it was thus ideal for the painterly blending of tones. Long and short is a variation of the satin stitch, which follows. The first row consists of alternate long and short stitches (see Figs. 1-20 and 1-21), while subsequent rows have stitches all of the same length. Shading is achieved through a gradual changing of the yarn in color value, working from either dark to light, or light to dark, until there is a soft radiation of color. An unbroken surface and stitches that were indistinguishable from each other were the ideal that was sought in this stitch. The examples to follow are from the Ch'ing peony design found in the lower center of Figure 7-1 (page 128), near the pheasant's tail, and the diagrams show exactly how that particular design was stitched.

A. After the top anchor knot, an outline of stem stitch was executed over the outside line of the petal (see Fig. 1-20), to be covered by the following long and short stitchery, its presence serving the dual purpose of relief, and adding a clean, separative outline. Using the darkest shade of color, the needle emerges at 1, and reenters the fabric at 2, over the outline stitch. With the shorter stitch kept about three-quarters of the length of the longer, a line of long and short stitches is created. It is important to maintain the same length in both the long and the short stitch.

B. For the next row, a medium shade of color was used. The needle emerges about three-quarters of the way in from the first row, as in B1, and reenters the fabric again at B2, overlapping the lower stitched rows by one-quarter of its length. The stitches of this row, and all subsequent rows, are of the same length. Although the first row (A) was long and short, each succeeding row is of the same length; in this way they interlock with the preceding row. Instead of working blind from the bottom, the smoothest effect was obtained by splitting one-quarter of the stitch length back into the previous stitch from the top.

C. In the following row, a still lighter shade of yarn was used. This third line was worked in the same way, and step B was repeated. It is essential that the needle split one-quarter back into the previous stitch from the top. It is also important that each row be long enough, and the stitches all of the same length, compensating for the one-quarter of the stitch that was lost in the previous row.

Fig. 1-20. Example 2: Long and short stitch.

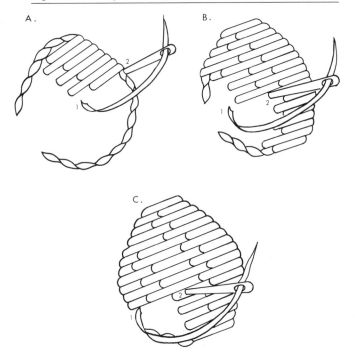

Fig. 1-21. Example 2: Peony design showing satin stitch, long and short stitch, stitchery direction. Detail drawing from Fig. 7-1, page 128.

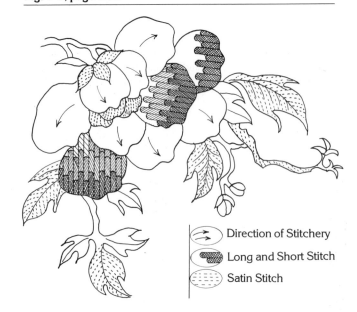

Direction of Stitchery

Long and Short Stitch

Satin Stitch

Example 3: Satin Stitch (Fig. 1-22)

The *t'ao chen* ("enveloping stitch"), as it was called in China, was never done with long stitches unless it was planned to couch the finished work with some type of holding stitch. If short stitches were not used, the work would not remain flat and secure. Since the stitch was intended for flat surfaces and a smooth effect, any kind of unevenness was not desirable. Usually satin stitch was done in one color, but multicolor gradations can be found which give much the same effect as the long and short. Satin stitch makes a broad line that can vary in width, but can be quite difficult to work properly, for although it is easy to do, the challenge lies in keeping the stitches meticulous and perfectly even, so that the smooth, satinlike appearance is maintained throughout.

Satin stitch was done simply by laying the threads side by side in an even manner to cover an area with color. Where textural variations were desired, satin stitch might still be used, but with a rough-twisted yarn. The texture of the thread here played the major part, rather than the simple evenness of the stitch.

The following examples show how a typical wave design, selected from the lower border area of the Chinese imperial court jacket in Figure 6-24, page 123, was executed in satin stitch, concentrating on the gradated rows of the stylized water.

A. After the top anchor knot is made, the needle enters at 1, over the underdrawing line, and emerges at 2, about a half inch outside the contour, then reenters at 3. (See Fig. 1-22.)

B. All three steps are continuously repeated, emerging on one side and entering on the other, to create a uniform row of stitchery. Stitches are either diagonal or straight, but must all be very flat, even, and next to each other.

During the great dynastic ages of China and Korea, embroidery, in all the high art with which it evolved, served to grace the luxuriant costumes, palaces, and homes of the emperor, the nobility, the rich, and the powerful. In Japan also, although there the art developed later, the elegantly embroidered kimonos and kosodes of the mighty shoguns were symbols of their affluence and power, by which militaristic clans sought to achieve political and territorial gains. But alongside all of this splendor and pomp, the magnificent work of thousands of professional embroidery studios, ran a current of embroidery of more humble origins, the work done in the homes of the people for their own enjoyment and for the multitude of uses the family could find for decoration of the home, costumes, holiday occasions, religious festivals, birthdays, and weddings. Much of this folk embroidery is charmingly beautiful, often touched with a naive grace, yet amazing in its artistic accomplishment, considering the lack of training of its creators. In the next chapter we will explore some of the purposes and techniques that millions of Oriental housewives and young ladies used in their home embroidery in the Old World of the East.

Fig. 1-22. Example 3. Water wave detail drawing from Chinese court jacket design (Fig. 6-24), showing gradation and direction of satin stitch.

2/ HOME ACCESSORIES

HISTORY AND AESTHETICS

China, the original center of Oriental embroidery, was continually the scene of the abundant production of lavishly embroidered fabrics of every variety and purpose. Inseparable from the cultural and artistic structure of Chinese society, this output far exceeded that of Korea and Japan, at least until the fourteenth century. In the home, the latter countries nevertheless retained unique features that were indigenous and traditional albeit less prolific than China, their domestic decoration being somewhat more restrained and simple. Chinese art has always been characterized by its floridity, and this tremendous profusion of decoration extended to every aspect of its society.

Nowhere was this more evident than in the Chinese home. It would not be an exaggeration to say that the Chinese housewife embroidered practically everything that was made of silk, and in the average upper- and middle-class home there was a lot of silk, for in China it was cheap and readily available. Embroidery was highly esteemed in historical China, both as an art form and as a domestic talent, so a husband would take great pride in a wife who could display her skill in accomplished needlework. It was, indeed, considered one of the essentials of the homemaker: All Chinese girls and young ladies were taught to sew and embroider from their earliest girlhood, and most were expert long before they married.

But the Chinese wife did not do her embroidery in mere response to cultural mores. Chinese women are far too spirited for that. Nor was she as repressed as history has sometimes painted her. She was highly respected, even adored, and always placed on a pedestal by her husband. But although she was treasured and protected, this protection and respect often restricted her movements to a very sheltered life, one isolated in some respects from the community, for it was not considered seemly in Chinese custom for wives and girls of marriageable age to be seen much abroad. Chinese paintings of the thriving marketplaces and bustling cities seldom show women in the streets or windows, save for a few prostitutes or concubines. But the Chinese lady is shown in all her glory in the garden, the court, the cool salons of her home. (See Fig. 1-14, page 17). She was, in addition, intelligent and creative, and for these reasons her embroidery was not only a pastime and a decorative household necessity, but a highly creative outlet as well. She pursued it for the rich satisfactions it gave her, and for the joy of creative work. Although not liberated in the modern sense, the Chinese homemaker led a life of very high ethical and artistic purpose, and was probably very serene and happy in her domestic life, as much of her gay embroidery reflects.

Family life in China was such a tightly knit community, and the place of the first wife and mother (concubinage was permitted) was so honored and busy, that it is unlikely she would have felt the lack of any other social life. It was part of Chinese custom that when a son married, he and his wife, and all of their subsequent children, would live with his parents in his father's house, which was duly enlarged to accommodate the newlyweds and their prospective family. Unmarried daughters, in turn, would go to live with their husband's families when they married. It was a daughter's duty to care for, and become as a daughter to, her new mother-in-law, bringing with her a dowry of embroidered gifts for her new family. With six or ten sons or daughters (sometimes ten or twenty) in each family, it is evident how the Chinese home estate soon became something like a small village! This was, in fact, one of the ways that Chinese communities originally sprang up, and often the villages bear the name of an original family nucleus, such as Liu or Chang, which created them at the outset. Since the way of life was mainly agricultural, these large family units served the very real purpose of help on the land, the management of family businesses, or the administration of large baronies.

From this complex domestic system, it is clear how the wife and mother, as well as the daughters, had a great deal of embroidery and sewing to do. There was, first of all, the decoration of everyday clothing and accessories (Fig. C-1), as well as children's wear; costumes for special events such as weddings and other family ceremonies; festival, funeral, and New Year celebration costumes; religious accessories; and all of the many textile and artistic decorations for the home. While the informal male costume did not normally have as much embroidery, feminine needs were great because of

tradition, family pride, respect for one's ancestors, and a great love for beautiful things. Embroidered dresses, jackets, and skirts were constantly in fashion, as well as shawls and other accessories and the *p'ao* style robe (Fig. 2-1), which had a low collar, voluminous sleeves, and border embroidery at the cuffs and hems. Handbags, parasols, fans, slippers, and even shoes were embroidered with every manner of design. During the T'ang and Sung dynasties thickly embroidered capes, fans, shawls, and hats were part of the chic elegance of the upper classes, and the entire outer *p'ao* was often also covered with thick, luxurious florals and arabesques showing the influence of Persian or Indian design, for a lively trade was carried on with those countries at that time.

Chinese home architecture was usually constructed in a plan that was essentially the same for both peasant and wealthy landowner or nobility, differing only in size and the degree of wealth or decoration. The estates of the upper classes were elegant, manorial, and sometimes extended over many acres, while others were more modest, although the basic construction was always similar. In general, the family unit lived inside a walled compound, which enclosed a complex of buildings

Fig. 2-1. Woman's informal robe. Flower and butterfly motif in satin, seed, stem, and long and short stitches; wave borders and Buddhist figures in satin, stem, and seed stitches. Crown copyright, Victoria and Albert Museum, London.

28.

around an open courtyard, with the main residence in the center rear of the courtyard and a walled, secluded garden behind it. The materials and decorations used, and the number of buildings either within the compound or added onto it to accommodate expanding families, were indicative of the amount of wealth a particular family had.

Wall decorations within the main hall and other buildings might consist of hanging scrolls of painted or embroidered bird and flower compositions (Fig. 7-3, page 130), the ever-popular landscapes, or examples of poetry or philosophical maxims in embroidered calligraphy. Paintings were also embroidered, the work being done directly upon the painted silk surface. Passages of a painting or the entire painting might be embellished in this way.

Square or circular coverlets of embroidered silk could be found on the center tables and tea tables of the reception halls and parlors, their compositions ranging from simple bird and flower designs to the most elaborate examples of religious and good luck symbols embroidered into complex and colorful pictures in polychrome silk thread or the more lavish gold-wrapped thread, or both. Richly furnished divans, covered with shimmering embroidered brocades or damasks in a wide variety of intriguing, restrained colors, graced the parlor interiors, and similar embroidery decorations could be found covering the seats and backs of the parlor and dining room chairs.

The most luxuriant embroidery was usually reserved for the bedroom, where, over a six-foot-long raised and carved rosewood, ebony, mahogany, ivory, or lacquerwork bedstead, an ornamental valance revealed beautifully executed embroidery depicting mythical or family historical scenes. At the head of the bed hung an embroidered wall hanging, the bridal medallion, which pictured the marriage of the first wife and her husband. At each side of the medallion hung ornaments of the kind shown in Figure C-10, while a lavishly embroidered quilt covered the bed. The round pillow ends also bore embroidered decorations: intricate flower, bird, tree, or happiness designs. Embroidered mirror holders (Fig. C-10) were also typical bedroom accessories.

The Korean bedroom, by contrast, was less formal, yet embroidery decorations were still a prominent part of the traditional decor. Because of the unusual Korean furnace method (the *ondol* system—a series of stone heating flues beneath the floor), the floor was the coziest place in the Korean

Fig. 2-2. Double-sleeved woman's informal robe. Silk gauze with woven designs of magnolias, chrysanthemums, butterflies, orchids; gold-couched happiness characters on field of purple silk gauze with thunder-line/swastika *k'ossu* borders. China, Ch'ing dynasty, nineteenth century. Courtesy of the National History Museum, Taipei.

Fig. 2-3. Key holder. Upper section: attached decorative, stuffed pads embroidered with Buddhist, peach, peony, lotus designs in satin, long and short, and stem stitches. Lower section: stuffed vertical panels embroidered with designs of lotus, peony, peach, cherry blossoms in long and short, stem, and satin stitches. Paneled, pieced, and tasseled damask silk fabric in tones of red, green, beige. Height, 2 1/2 feet; width, 1 foot (70.6 × 30.5 cm.). Korea, Yi dynasty, nineteenth century. Courtesy of the Folk Village Museum, Seoul.

Fig. 2-4. Fan holders. Left to right: bluish-toned silk gauze entirely covered with counted half-cross stitch and with metallic thread on characters; maroon silk ground embroidered with lotus and leaf. Chin dynasty. Collection of the author.

Fig. 2-5. Korean girl's hat *(gu-lae)*. Polychrome embroidery of long-life and happiness designs in satin stitch with gold couching; pastel-toned damask silk piece work; cordage and braidwork on crown; coral beads with whipped tassels. Korea, Yi dynasty, nineteenth century. Collection of the author.

home on which to sleep, and so a ten-inch-thick mattress of cotton was laid directly upon the floor and snugly covered with sheets and a heavy cotton quilt. Centered on the quilt was a large silk panel, about seven feet square, which was embroidered with traditional peacocks, flowers, and longevity symbols or characters. Pillows were of the round type, and, as in China, the flat end pieces of the pillowcases were also traditional locations for charming and colorful embroidery. Pillows were usually individual, except for the long pillows shared by honeymooning couples; these had special designs for happiness, fertility, and wedded blessedness embroidered on the ends.

The Korean wife or bride was as adept with the needle as her Chinese counterpart, and she engaged in a phenomenal amount of real craftsmanship in the fiber arts. Especially in suburban or rural homes, a Korean wife might well cultivate and raise her own silkworms, painstakingly go through all the steps of sericulture to produce her own silk yarn, spin the yarn, dye it, weave it, twist it, and finally embroider with it—all with her own hands! Needlecraft was a very important part of home education in old

Korea also, where a wife or bride was expected to make clothes and accessories for everyone in the home and to decorate them with embroidery, as well as doing more special design work on such household items as purses and spoon cases (Fig. C-28), notion sets, needle cases, and even on thimbles! That the Korean homemaker took pride in her needlework creativity is exemplified by such beautiful work as appears on the Korean girl's embroidered hat *(gu-lae)* in Figures 2-5 and 6-5 (page 103). Gift coin bags, such as the example in Figure C-28, were also presented to the mother-in-law on her sixty-first birthday.

In addition to the *gu-lae,* intricate designs were also embroidered on other children's accessories, such as belts and vests. Little Korean girls carried embroidered coin bags and wore dainty *chogori* (bolero jackets) embroidered with silk flowers or longevity designs, as well as white cotton socks usually embroidered with flowers. A special costume for a son's first birthday party was a major creative undertaking. The simple, clean, and orderly interior of the Korean home usually had embroidered scrolls as wall hangings, as well as heavily

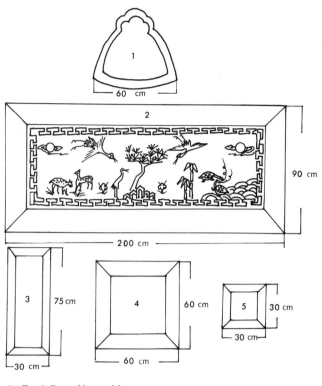

1. Back Rest (An-suk)
2. Reception Mat (Boryo)
3. Elbow Rest (Jan-Chim)
4. Guest Cushion (Bang-suk)
5. Small Elbow Rest (Sabang-Chim)

Fig. 2-6. Korean cushion and reception set (boryo) with Ten Longevities design.

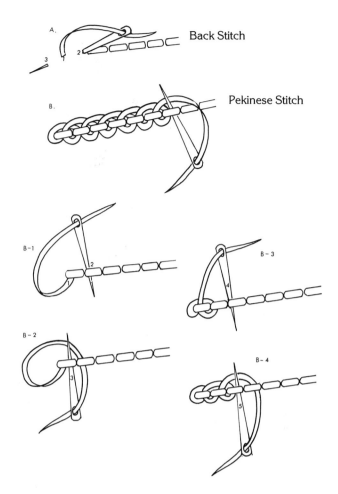

Fig. 2-7. Example 1: Pekinese stitch.

worked cushion designs. Special cushions (boryo) for the Korean floor also had lovely embroidery decoration on their end pieces. (See Fig. 2-6).

Embroidery done for the amusement of children was very common in China as well, much care being taken to make these objects as cute and charming as possible. Earmuffs, gaily embroidered with flowers and good luck symbols (Fig. 2-8), vests, and brightly embroidered pants suits for the girls were very typical, and are still worn in modern times, together with many other embroidered children's accessories and much carefully designed and adroitly executed work on games, toys, babywear, and special accessories for children's rooms.

Japanese home embroidery decoration was generally inclined to be somewhat more limited than Chinese or Korean work, since the Japanese home is traditionally kept very simple, spacious, and restrained. Floor cushions, covered with prints or woven with the inimitable Japanese gift for exquisitely tasteful design, typically had fans, butterflies, and special flowers, such as the cherry blossom and chrysanthemum, for motifs. Embroidered hanging scrolls were also carefully placed in key locations, while a special peg-type device for tilting framed embroidery pictures toward the floor, where everyone sat, was also tastefully embroidered. An original area of Japanese home embroidery was the extremely lovely work done on formal presentation cloths, or fukusa (see Figs. 2-10 and 2-11), which were used on ceremonial occasions to present gifts, and on the furoshiki, an all-purpose carrying cloth, which often served as a sort of shopping bag. Tie-dye work is found incidentally on such pieces also.

Fig. 2-8. Earmuffs. Designs of swastikas, flowers, Taoist and Buddhist symbols, characters, bats, butterflies, and thunder line in counted, satin, stem stitches; laidwork; edgings in satin, buttonhole stitches, and fur. China, Ch'ing dynasty, nineteenth century. Collection of the author.

Fig. 2-9. Belt purse. Design of women doing embroidery with *shou* characters, flowers, hanging bird cages, trees, domestic animals, in half-cross stitch on silk gauze. Edgings in varieties of weave stitch on tightly twisted silk with cardboard support. China, Ch'ing dynasty, eighteenth–nineteenth centuries. Collection of the author.

Fig. 2-10. Presentation cloth *(fukusa)*. *Washing the White Elephant.* Figure composition with elephant in interlocking satin stitch, laidwork on figures and costumes, stem stitch accents; silk on silk ground. Japan, Tokugawa period, eighteenth century. Crown copyright, Victoria and Albert Museum, London.

Fig. 2-11. Presentation cloth *(fukusa).* Vignette of cloth hangers, rooster, dragon-head drums in designs of clouds, scrolls, tortoise-shell hexagons, water waves in diagonal satin stitch, satin stitch, stem, long and short, and darning stitches, with accents in textured couched silk thread. Greens, white, blue, pinkish-red, gray, gold on navy blue damask silk. Japan, Tokugawa period, end of eighteenth century. Courtesy of the Museum of Fine Arts, Boston.

Fig. 2-12. Details of stitchery from presentation cloth, Fig. 2-11.

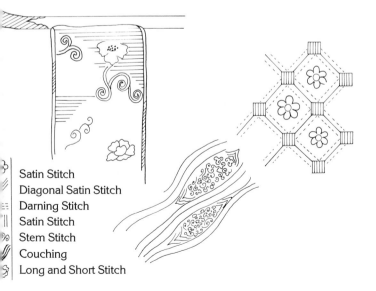

Satin Stitch
Diagonal Satin Stitch
Darning Stitch
Satin Stitch
Stem Stitch
Couching
Long and Short Stitch

The most important item in Japanese home embroidery, however, was the traditional sash worn with the kimono, the obi (Fig. 2-13), and Japanese wives and daughters, as well as professional embroiderers, lavished all of their most creative embroidery upon it, a tradition that began in the later eighteenth century (Tokugawa Period). The obi was six feet long, and about ten to twelve inches wide, its embroidery usually being done on an adjustable roller frame such as the example shown in Chapter 1 (page 18). Most obi embroidery was carried out on a silk ground of woven brocade or damask. Prints were also used as a ground fabric, and these were usually a twill weave with a very heavy weft. Obi designs were generally much simpler than Chinese or Korean accessories, expressing the placid Japanese outlook on life and their deep love of nature. Silk yarns were used in quiet pastel tones with

Fig. 2-13. Obi. Designs of Buddhist wheel, lozenges, peonies, willows, vines in gold-wrapped couching, satin and stem stitches on yellow velvet ground. Japan, Tokugawa period, nineteenth century. Crown copyright, Victoria and Albert Museum, London.

characteristic delicacy and restraint, expressing such varied themes as landscapes, trees, flowers, birds, clouds, butterflies, the waves of the sea, or the airy flight of dragonflies. While the Japanese obi is not as ornate or dramatic as some Chinese embroidery conceptions, what it loses in dynamics and grandeur is recovered in poetry and sheer lyrical loveliness, and it remains among the most artistic and beautiful of all Oriental designs. Mixed media, such as hand painting, tie-dye, metal thread, and gold leaf *(nuihaku)* techniques were also employed to great advantage in obi decoration. The wide obi was made for women, but an obi was also worn by men that was more austere and narrow, its decoration limited to simple woven geometric designs.

Among the most interesting works of ancient China and Korea were the embroidered rank badges of civil and imperial officials, popularly called mandarin squares (Fig. C-2). (Mandarin squares were never worn in Japan, since there was no mandarin class of civil service system as there was in China and Korea.) The mandarins were actually a favored scholar class, an intellectual elite who attained official positions or other places of honor and authority in the court or public life through a series of long and difficult competitive examinations, and through imperial appointment. The ranking system was designated by various colors and design symbols, and signified publicly by an embroidered square that the mandarin wore stitched upon the chest of the coat worn over his court robe. Worn by military officials as well, the rank badge motifs were executed in a variety of symbolic figures—bird designs for the civil system, and animal motifs for the military—and often they are striking little masterpieces of handsome color, carefully organized design, and skillful needlework. Many of these squares were done at home by the wives and daughters of the officials, while others were made to order by professional embroidery studios, many of which specialized in only one of the many designs. The wife of a civil official was entitled to all the benefits of his rank, as well as the right to wear his official insignia, which she proudly indulged (Fig. 2-14).

A similar project for the Chinese home embroiderer was the so-called birthday squares, colorful plaques about the size of the mandarin squares (and for which they are sometimes mistaken) which were given as birthday presents to friends and family. These squares were ordinarily done in lush floral designs, and can be distinguished from mandarin

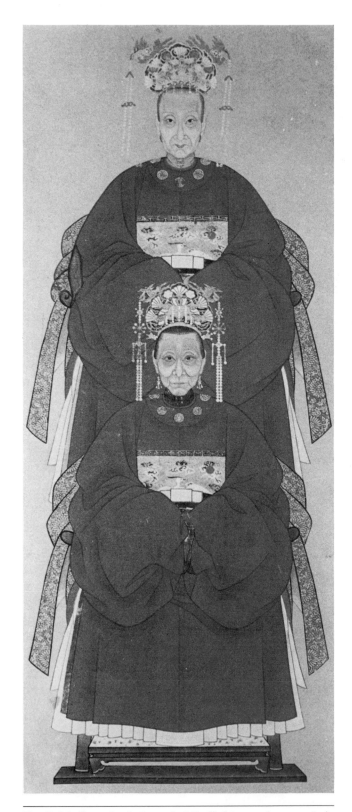

Fig. 2-14. Portrait of wives of civil officials wearing mandarin squares, sixth rank. Hanging scroll, color on silk. China, Ming dynasty (1368–1644). Collection of the author.

squares by the absence of bird, animal, or imperial symbols.

Another important opus for the Oriental home needleworker was the decoration of folding screens. Screens were made in six, twelve, or more folds, each fold or panel being decorated with embroidered landscapes or other subjects running continuously across the screen or each panel. Screens were one of the oldest objects of furniture, known to have been in use in China from at least Chou times and probably earlier. They were typical and highly practical in the Oriental home, serving the purpose of room dividers. Screens were decorated with a variety of materials: paint, gold leaf, semiprecious stones, and mother-of-pearl, as well as with embroidery and calligraphy, but embroidery was the most popular of these media. Even though they were very common in ancient China and Korea, very few examples of these distinctive works of art have survived to modern times, and extant pieces

are extremely rare and valuable. The screens are flammable and susceptible to both moisture and dryness, and many were probably destroyed by war or cut down and made into scrolls. The practice of burying them as accompaniments to the other world in the tombs of their owners also caused the loss of many. Both Chinese and Korean screen embroidery filled a rich tradition and comprises a special branch of Oriental needlework, which we shall consider in Chapter 7.

A wide range of smaller, miscellaneous household and costume accessories could be found in Chinese home embroidery also, in a startling gamut of varied styles, ingenious color combinations, remarkably professional stitchery, and seemingly infinite design concepts. Such objects as tablecloths, fan holders, and letter cases (Fig. 2-15), embroidered card and children's purses (Fig. 2-9), beautifully crafted slippers, skirt panels (Fig. 6-9, page 107), and embroidered earmuffs (Fig. 2-8), page

Fig. 2-15. Imperial letter carrier. Designs of *mang* dragons, thunder line, bats, trees, flowers, goats, rocks in satin, seed, long and short, stem, radiated, and continuous darning stitches; gold couching; gold-wire Pekinese stitch. Red and blue double-faced plain weave silk with gold-couched happi-

ness characters on reverse side. Pockets of red lined cardboard covered with beige, black, and yellow silk. China, Ch'ing dynasty, eighteenth–nineteenth century. Collection of the author.

Fig. 2-16. Tablecloth. Mythical beast, flower, scroll, and thunder-line designs in gold couched thread, with green and blue couching accents on plain weave red silk ground. China, Ch'ing dynasty, nineteenth century. Collection of the author.

Fig. 2-17. Mirror cover. Flower, fruit, bat, and Buddhist, secular, and Taoist figures in seed and satin stitches; some details in metal thread couching; galoon edgings. China, Ch'ing dynasty, nineteenth century. Collection of the author.

32) cover a panoply of artistic techniques that exemplify so well the tremendous creativity and expertise achieved in the embroidery arts of old China.

In addition to the traditional bird, tree, and flower motifs done by the Oriental wife, home embroidery designs were customarily replete with depictions of classic Taoist, Buddhist, and Confucian themes. The good luck and long life symbols are likewise much encountered: the *shou* character; the goldfish, heron, and phoenix; the tortoise, the bat, the peach, the peony. (For a discussion of design symbolism, see Appendix.) The pairing of birds, a familiar romantic conception, appears in many compositions as well. Although these designs were often rendered in conventions or stylized motifs, their basic pattern became a creative tool in the hands of the designer rather than a model for merely mechanical imitation. The refined arrangement of space and form is one of the finest features of Oriental embroidery design. The designs are essentially abstract patterns of line, color, shape; their mythical or religious content provides an added significance that is really quite aside from their artistic content, even though such significance was indissolubly blended into the artistic and social context. Oriental embroidery composition derives its character from the intuitive placement and patterning of harmoniously juxtaposed colors and shapes, combined with the universal qualities found in stylized drawing. (For a further explication of design philosophy and techniques, see Chapter 8.)

We now turn to some of the stitchery techniques of the Chinese home embroiderer, the work of the housewife or young daughter as she sat quietly in her garden or living room, doing her embroidery and enjoying the stillness of an afternoon long ago in the Ch'ing dynasty.

HOME ACCESSORY TECHNIQUES

The Chinese home embroiderer did an amazing amount of sophisticated, very free, intricate work with a very limited number of stitches. The stitches most commonly used were the long and short, the satin, the couching, and the famous seed stitch. The long and short and satin stitches are shown in

Chapter 1, Figures 1-20 and 1-22. In this chapter we will show the seed stitch, the couching metal thread stitch, and the chevron and brick stitches.

The seed stitch was rendered in China in so fine a manner that in some cases it can barely be seen from more than a foot away. There is really nothing like it anywhere in the world or at any point in the history of needlework. The closest approximation to the Chinese seed stitch in European work was the French knot, but it cannot compare with the fine perfection achieved in Chinese embroidery with minute yet basically simple execution. Part of this perfection was in the precise, patient laying and placing of each stitch, the exact spacing of stitches, the maintaining of an even and consistent tension on the thread, and the correct looping of the needle. The patience and eyestrain that were necessary to cover large areas of fabric with this tiny stitch were probably considerable, and continued years of use by lamplight may have indeed caused some blindness, especially in long hours of grueling shopwork in professional embroidery houses. Such eyestrain did not frighten the devoted Chinese housewife, however, and the loveliness of the results shows the benefits of her long hours of making beautiful things for her home.

Fig. 2-18. Cloud collar for a child's costume. Eight pieced silk lappets in light green and yellow, blue satin borders; with designs of pagodas and landscapes in Pekinese stitch; galoon accents. China, Ch'ing dynasty, nineteenth century. Collection of the author.

Example 2: Children's Hats, China, Ch'ing Dynasty (Fig. C-8, left center)

Made for a boy of elementary-school age, the swallowtail hat may well have been done by professional embroiderers for a child of the court nobility or the imperial family, since mountain and wave designs such as those on the cap's visor were usually imperial symbols. A colorful symphony of peony, butterfly, and spiriform floral figures, executed in seed stitch, swirl in a clockwise movement about the peak of the cap, the stylized leaf figures being done rather daringly in contrasting blue shades. The imperial symbols on the visor are in satin stitch.

In China, seed stitch was generally used to define details or act as a filler for small, precise color areas where satin stitch would be too obvious or inappropriate. its uniformity and peachlike softness were achieved by laying the stitches very evenly next to each other and by keeping the rows clearly visible and straight.

Seed Stitch (Fig. 2-19)

A. The needle enters the fabric from the bottom and comes up at 1. The thread is firmly grasped and looped three or four times around the needle, after which it enters the fabric again at 2, right next to 1. The needle is drawn through, the operator holding the thread very taut with her left hand.

B. The needle comes up at 1, about the width of a stitch away from the previous stitch, and the procedure is repeated until the first row is finished. The second and subsequent rows of stitches are done by alternating the stitches. This alternation effectively covers the tails left by the first row of stitchery and prevents wide gaps between the stitches.

Fig. 2-19. Example 2: seed stitch.

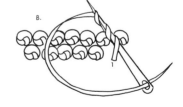

Example 3: Tablecloth (Mythical Beast Design), China, Ch'ing Dynasty (Fig. 2-16)

Chinese embroiderers invariably "couched" or anchored metal thread on a fabric, since it was difficult to stitch through the fabric without disastrous fraying of the gold or silver thread. Customarily, this kind of couching was done with red silk thread, for red tended to increase the visual intensity of the gold. This example is very unusual in that green and blue thread couching have been added as design elements. This was obviously done so that the green would harmonize effectively with the deep red background and the blues would tend to balance and cool the blazing intensity of so much red and gold. Mythical animal figures of this kind appeared on mandarin squares as military emblems, the animals symbolizing courage, so it is likely that this tablepiece may once have been in the household of a military official.

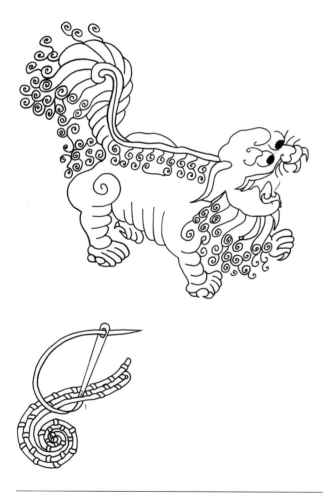

Fig. 2-20. Example 3: couching stitch.

Couching Stitch (Metal Thread Stitch) (Fig. 2-20)

A. The gold thread is first carefully laid along the concentric linear design shown in the illustration. Then, to couch it, the needle enters the fabric from the bottom at 1, after which the couching thread simply crosses over the gold thread and the needle reenters in the same place, at 1. The stitch is repeated again (2) at quarter-inch intervals. The gold thread to be couched is fed along the concentric line of the design as the holding stitches are simultaneously executed and repeated.

B. When an entire row of metal thread has been couched, the second row is firmly butted against the first row, and the couching process resumed, alternating the second row couching stitches halfway between the previously couched stitches of the previous row.

The practice of arranging couching stitches into design patterns as they lay on the couched material was not usually seen in most Oriental embroidery of the historical period, since simple and direct methods were preferred (and more effective), and many of the stitchery methods were dictated by prescribed customs and traditions.

Example 4: Mirror Decoration, China, Ch'ing Dynasty (Fig. C-10)

Mirror holders decorated in the manner shown in this example were typical accessories in ladies' apartments and dressing rooms and were also found as bedroom decorations. Mirrors were probably expensive, a luxury during the historical period, and decorative covers such as this one and Example 5 offered protection from dust and damage in addition to their handsome aesthetic qualities. An entirely flat piece, the embroidery here was executed in counted stitch on gauze silk, which was entirely covered by the needlework. If the amount of patience required for so much counted work seems staggering, it should be added that even much larger pieces, such as the summer dragon robe, were also done on gauze, which was covered completely with embroidery! The design of this mirror holder is a cleverly balanced, pastel-toned composition of traditional Chinese symbols—the shellfish, the peach, the bat, the cash, a copper coin. (For the meaning of design conventions, see the Appendix.) The tassels are in fresh pastel tones that harmonize delightfully with the tonalities of the holder, and they are finished in a braidwork example of the endless knot, the symbol of the Buddhist path to salvation. The design was embroidered entirely in chevron stitch on the background and brick stitch on the peach, shellfish, cash, leaf, and bat designs, while the outer contours of the various motifs have been outlined with gold-wrapped, couched thread.

Background (Peach Design) Chevron Stitch (Fig. 2-21)

The needle comes up at 1, five mesh strands are counted, and the needle reenters over the mesh at 2, skips one mesh up, and comes up at 3, again counts five mesh strands over and reenters at 4. This sequence is repeated until the point of the chevron is reached, at 14. For the second row, the needle drops down five meshes from stitch 1, comes up at 15, counts five meshes over, and reenters at 16, in the same box as stitch 1. It again skips one mesh up and comes up at 17, then reenters at 18, the same box as stitch 3. This procedure is repeated as necessary.

Brick Stitch (Shellfish Design) (Fig. 2-22)

First row: The needle comes up at 1. Six meshes are counted over, and the needle reenters at 2, leaves one box for the second row, and comes up at 3. Six meshes are counted and the needle reenters at 4, skips one box, and comes up at 5, reenters at 6, and repeats, up to 12.

Second row: The needle comes up at 13, counts six meshes, and reenters at 14, skips one box for the third row, and emerges at 15, again counts six meshes over and reenters the fabric at 16, skips one box and comes up at 17, reenters at 18, and so on. This sequence is repeated until the row is finished.

Third row: The needle comes up at 23, counts six meshes and reenters at 24 (in the same box as stitch 1), skips one box and emerges at 25, counts six meshes over, and reenters at 26 (the same box as stitch 5), skips one box for the next row and comes up again at 27, reenters the fabric again at 28, in the same box as stitch 7, and so on. This procedure is repeated as necessary.

In the example, the color gradations (lighter and darker beiges in the shellfish, and lighter and darker violets in the peaches) were done simply by changing the yarn color at the designer's discretion to create variety of color and form.

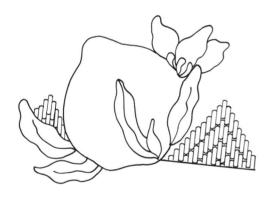

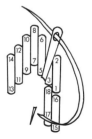

Fig. 2-21. Example 4: chevron stitch.

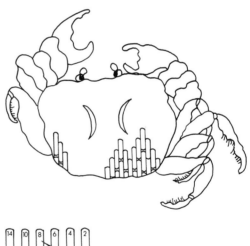

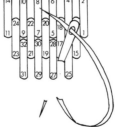

Fig. 2-22. Example 4: brick stitch.

Example 5: Mirror Cover, China, Ch'ing Dynasty (Fig. 2-17, page 36)

The main field of this unpretentious, elegant little cover is a formal motif consisting of a central lotus design in a vase, around which revolve the Taoist *pa pao,* or Eight Precious Things. From its predominant Taoist iconography, it is clear that the piece belonged to a family in which that religion was important, the only exception to the Taoist symbolism being in the central panel of the upper decorative flap, where the cash, the secular symbol of wealth, is centered above a bowl of peaches. The peach was a Taoist symbol of long life; therefore, a bowl of peaches means "many long lives."

The main design is executed entirely in combinations of blue and white satin stitch on a red plain weave silk ground, with a slender tassel motif (repeated at key points for design harmony) in couched gold thread. The upper decorative flap consists of three panels of seed-stitched figures on a black silk ground, showing flowering lotus, Taoist gourds and flute, and bats (the symbol of happiness) flanking the central cash figure. The main field has been edged with prewoven tapes in a decorative floral pattern and the entire piece neatly bordered with black satin, using a hidden stitch. The red holder into which the mirror was inserted can be seen at both sides of the upper panels.

In the next chapter we encounter what is perhaps the greatest masterpiece of historical Chinese embroidery, and certainly the most dramatic and famous of all Oriental textiles: the imperial dragon robe.

3/ THE CHINESE DRAGON ROBE

HISTORY AND AESTHETICS

Self-adornment and decoration are natural human activities and, in one form or another, are characteristic of both primitive and civilized societies. The practice of decorating costume is probably as old as the wearing of any kind of garment; certainly it is as old as embroidery, which came into being, strictly speaking, from the first time a bit of colored thread was used in decoration. This practice of self-decoration was part of the entire cultural environment of Ice Age and Mesolithic peoples as it was found in the original culture seats of northern Europe, Africa, and Asia.

The north Asian prehistoric tradition of self-adornment, shamanist symbolism, and magical rituals connected with the hunt, expressed in the proto-embroidery and embroidery decoration of costume, was carried, over many millennia, by the nomadic Mesolithic steppe and taiga peoples into China, where it became incorporated into the Neolithic development that resulted from their settlement there. Thus the stage was set for a tradition that evolved into the historical period and became the Chinese custom of costume construction and decoration in silk, with all manner of designs in silk embroidery, in an artistic mode, taking the place of more primitive forms of nature worship and hunting-ritual decoration. Personal adornment on the costume became the means of social and economic identification; the ranking of status, prestige, and wealth; the medium for expressing social unity and good will and for warding off misfortune. But, far more than these, it was the solidified expression of various religious, cosmic, and aesthetic philosophies, which, by the sixth century B.C., had become the most important foundations of Chinese society and the basis of much of their civilization. It was in this way that a custom that had its probable origin in tribal identity and ritual retained its ritual nature and became universal in Chinese society (and eventually in the entire Orient), through the complex artistic and social development of a most primitive form of expression.

The high art into which costume embroidery evolved found its greatest expression in the pinnacle of Chinese society: the imperial court. But the Chou dynasty (1027–249 B.C.) a tradition of the finest and most luxurious court costumes, with richly embroidered decorations appropriate to his royal station, was reserved for the emperor, his family, and his court entourage, as we can see in a painting of Emperor Wu Ti of the Chou in all his regalia (Fig. 3-1). The dragon design, which was later to become the dominant feature of the imperial robes, does not yet appear on the main field: The Emperor's collar and sleeve border decorations are in scroll-type leaf forms. Significantly, however, the dragon design can already be detected on his belt decoration. The dragon was probably an early imperial symbol, and the type represented here is very reminiscent of dragon designs on middle Shang chariot fittings. Early Korean tomb paintings show this type of slender dragon as well.

Already in use was the soft classic Chinese *p'ao* robe (Fig. 2-1, page 28), with its twelve meters of silk cloth, full, hanging sleeves, flat collar, and wrap-around closure, the basic cut of the classic dragon robe that was to come. That the dragon symbol continued in imperial use during the Han dynasty (206 B.C.–A.D. 220) we know from the emblems in the tomb of Lady Cheng, who was in fact a member of the nobility.

Fig. 3-2. Reconstructed ceremonial pheasant and dragon robe with portrait (below) of Empress Hui Yi of the Sung dynasty. China, Sui through Sung dynasties, third—eleventh century. From *The Research and Examination of Chinese Women's Gowns in Successive Dynasties* by Y. C. Wang, Chinese Chi Pao Research Assn., Taipei.

Fig. 3-1. *Portrait of Emperor Wu Ti of the Late Chou Dynasty* (detail). Attributed to Yen Li-Pen. China, Northern Chou dynasty, sixth century B.C. Courtesy of the Museum of Fine Arts, Boston.

Embroidered pheasant designs were an early pre-Han decoration on female court robes. By the Sui dynasty (A.D. 581–618), the pheasant design began to appear in combination with a now bolder dragon figure decorating the collar, sleeve bands, and lower border of female imperial robes, a tradition enduring into the Sung, as shown in the reconstructed example and portrait of Empress Hui Yi, a monarch of the Sung dynasty (A.D. 960–1279) (Fig. 3-2). No doubt such examples had parallels in a more ornate sacrificial emperor's robe and/or set of aprons that were referred to often in the dynastic literature and that may have had origins (along with the Twelve Symbols of Authority) in early Shang human sacrifices.

The dragon design itself also underwent a subtle evolution in China and Korea, beginning with a slender, writhing type that was typical of the early Shang in China and the Three Kingdoms Period

(57 B.C.–A.D. 668) in Korea through Han times, after which it became more gradually stabilized into the conventional facing, profile, and full-bodied form of medieval and later China and Korea (Fig. 3-17).

Once believed to have appeared dramatically for the first time in the T'ang, the dragon robe is now known to have had a long history of forerunners, and a steady development as an imperial symbol, many centuries before the first classic forms began to appear in the T'ang dynasty (A.D. 618–906). The first dragon robes were not as ornate as earlier examples of imperial costume embroidery had been (such as that of Wu Ti), nor did they presage any of the tremendous pomp and elegance that were to celebrate the Ming and Ch'ing dynasties. Compared with Han and Ch'in imperial robes, the early dragon robe was rather simple, with four large, circular, woven or embroidered gold dragon medallions on each shoulder, center chest, and back of the garment. A six-medallion type in polychrome embroidery was also worn during the T'ang (Fig. 3-4). The classic five-clawed dragon also appeared during the T'ang dynasty, as a ceramic roof tile of the period clearly shows. Up to and including part of the T'ang, a three-clawed dragon had been in use, but it was replaced by the five-clawed variety sometime during that period.

Empress Wu of the T'ang dynasty, a monarch of legendary beauty and courage, is credited with the earliest official use of these robes. About A.D. 694 a royal scholar, Tang Hui-yao, entered a notation in the court annals that the empress had awarded embroidered dragon robes to various high court officials who found favor with her, and the imperial tradition apparently was confirmed from this time onward. However, centuries of further evolution, foreign invasion, and artistic development were to affect the dragon robe before its final mature style, the luxuriant *ch'i-fu* of the Ch'ing dynasty, finally appeared (Fig. 3-13).

Once established, the imperial dragon robe became a firmly fixed tradition in Chinese court custom. Modified dragon robes of various types and styles continued to appear throughout the T'ang, Sung, and Yuan (A.D. 1280–1368) dynasties, as we know from the literature of those times, but unfortunately none of these resplendent pieces have survived. The earliest extant dragon robe dates from the Ming dynasty (A.D. 1368–1644) and is the only example from that entire period. It was the custom to bury emperors in their finest dragon robes, and, moreover, scientific methods of preserving textiles

Fig. 3-3. *Kublai Khan Hunting* by Lin Kuan-Tao. Hanging scroll, color on silk. China, Yuan dynasty, thirteenth century. Courtesy of the National Palace Museum, Taipei.

Fig. 3-4. *Portrait of Emperor T'ai-tsung of the T'ang Dynasty* (reigned A.D. 627–649). Hanging scroll, color on silk, China, T'ang dynasty, eighth–ninth century. Courtesy of the National Palace Museum, Taipei.

were unknown in ancient times. However, several Ming paintings provide us with a fairly clear picture of the Ming styles. The glorious T'ang silks, the rich treasures of the Sung court, the fabled opulence of the Yuan palaces, all are lost to us forever except in scattered examples and the record left by the brush drawings and paintings that have survived.

While several portraits of the Sung emperors show rather conservative robes without dragon designs, in plain white, yellow, or red silk, these were probably informal, casual court garments, for the dragon and pheasant symbols on the robe of Empress Hui Yi of that period (Fig. 3-2) and the very ornate costume embroidery on certain Buddhist guardian figures give evidence that the tradition was still very much in progress. In addition, the Sung Dynastic History mentions an emperor's court robe of deep-crimson brocade, with broad stripes of red and gold, that was embroidered with dragon and cloud designs. The Sung was the period of Chinese history when the textile industry boomed to its highest point. There were giant silk mills at Loyang, Kaifeng, and elsewhere, and emperors such as Hui-tsung and Kao-tsung took a great interest in the embroiderer's art, the latter instituting a Bureau of Fine Textiles in the Southern Sung capital of Hangchow in A.D. 1129. The Sung Dynastic History also relates that "the Bureau of Refined Embroideries was in charge of weaving and embroidery for use on carriages and as regalia and for use in sacrifices made by honored guests. Over three hundred embroiderers were brought together in the Bureau." Although Sung paintings reveal that a certain conservatism in costume embroidery confined secular ornamentation to belts, underrobes, and collar bands, there is no reason to believe that imperial finery would have been less ornate, while the presence of the dragon robe both before the dynasty, in the T'ang, and after it, in the Yuan, confirms the continuity of the tradition, and the robe of Empress Hui Yi is certainly evidence of this.

The barbarian Mongol hordes that overran and conquered China in the thirteenth century to become the Yuan dynasty were horse-riding nomads whose leader, Kublai Khan (Fig. 3-3), wished to capture China and its rich culture without destroying it, so they were consequently obliged to adapt to Chinese customs and civilization, a fact that eventually precipitated their own degeneration and overthrow. As a result, however, the dragon robe was sustained as an imperial symbol and was worn by the Mongol emperors. Marco Polo, who visited the court of Kublai Khan in the thirteenth century, related in his *Travels* his awe-struck wonder at the incredible beauty and luxury of the imperial palace. The fierce Mongol emperor must have received him in all the splendor of his court, seated upon the dragon throne and bedecked in a dragon robe of the finest silk, for a drawing from Ming encyclopedic sources shows him wearing a robe similar in style to that of Tang T'ai-t'sung in Figure 3-4, with large gold dragon medallions on each shoulder; his hunting costume in Figure 3-3 has similar medallions. The same Ming source shows that Kublai Khan also once issued a proclamation against the embroidery of silk robes with dragon, sun, moon, or tiger designs, all imperial symbols of the time, the edict made in order to check a growing tendency of the Chinese populace toward wearing royal emblems. But the Mongol invaders had little lasting influence upon Chinese culture and imparted little to it. The Yuan dynasty collapsed after only eighty-eight years, and the artistic, conservative Ming resumed Chinese culture as though the land had never been conquered.

The reconstruction of China fell to the Ming dynasty (A.D. 1368–1644), and it is from this time that a regulated symbolism, with increasingly codified design conventions, became part of the dragon robe. For example, the four-dragon and six-dragon medallion of the T'ang and Yuan were carried into the early Ming, for Emperor T'ai-tsu is shown in his portrait (Fig. 3-5) wearing the latter, but by 1405 imperial decrees had declared that the informal robes of the emperor should be yellow in color, with four woven dragon medallions in gold on both shoulders, chest, and back. The same man-

Fig. 3-5. *Portrait of Emperor T'ai-tsu of the Ming Dynasty* (reigned 1368–1398). Hanging scroll, color on silk. China, Ming dynasty, fourteenth century. Courtesy of the National Palace Museum, Taipei.

date proclaimed that first- and second-degree princes and their sons were to wear red robes with four dragon medallions in gold.

The reign of Emperor Hsuan-te, from 1426 to 1435, brought about the first marked changes from the four- and six-medallion robe, most notably in the institution of much larger, more impressive medallions on the latter (Fig. 3-6). After this time, a radical departure heralded the classic forms, that is, the inclusion on the main field of the robe the Twelve Symbols of Authority (see Appendix: Design Symbolism) and the use of twelve large embroidered dragon medallions in vivid colors. Hsuan-te and the later Ming emperors all wore the Twelve Symbols, which were extremely ancient in origin, having been used on sacrificial robes probably since Shang times. They now appeared on the dragon robe for the first time and were apparently the final step in the development of the Ming imperial dragon robe, remaining in use following the second reign of Emperor Ying-tsung. His robes, and those of his successors, continued the tradition of the Twelve Symbols and the twelve dragon medallions.

The number twelve had mystical connotations in China, being thought to be complete in form and auspicious. Early examples of the twelve-emblem robe showed only eight medallions on the outer body, the remainder embroidered on an underrobe. Four dragon medallions decorated the main front field, shoulders, and back, the field dragons placed vertically above one another. Those of the underrobe were also arranged vertically, as could be seen through vents in the outer robe's sides. By the reign of Emperor Shih-tsung (1522–1566), all twelve medallions were embroidered on the outer robe, as in Figure 3-7, with the Twelve Symbols also prominent in quite large embroidered forms.

The Twelve Symbols in Ming usage were either woven or embroidered in specified places on the dragon robe. The sun and moon symbols were situated on the left and right shoulders, the constellation on the back above the mountain, the two pheasants on each sleeve border. The remaining figures, in much larger size and in circular motifs that differed considerably from the later Ch'ing styles, were in vertical rows on either side of the lower front dragon medallions: the sacrificial cups, water weed, grain, fire, ax, and *fu* symbols. This design style is shown in the portrait of Emperor Shih-tsung (Fig. 3-7). His robe is a clear prototype of an ancient sacrificial robe and apron, which had paint-

Fig. 3-6. *Portrait of Emperor Hsuan-tsung* (Hsuan-te) *of the Ming dynasty* (reigned 1426–1435). Hanging scroll, color on silk. China, Ming dynasty, fifteenth century. Courtesy of the National Palace Museum, Taipei.

Fig. 3-7. *Portrait of Emperor Shih-tsung of the Ming Dynasty* (reigned 1522–1566). Hanging scroll, color on silk. China, Ming dynasty, fifteenth century. Courtesy of the National Palace Museum, Taipei.

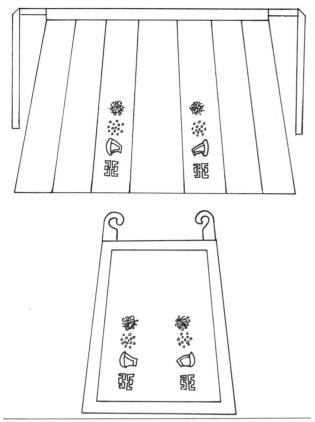

Fig. 3-8. Drawing of imperial sacrificial aprons showing embroidery designs. Korea, early Yi dynasty.

ed and embroidered dragons on both shoulders and the Twelve Symbols arranged vertically on the apron in exactly the same manner shown in this portrait. Dating from as early as the Warring States Period (481–221 B.C.), the apron was discarded sometime between then and the Ming, the Twelve Symbols appearing instead on the main field (Fig. 3-8).

The final years of the Ming were marred by internal disorder and corruption, and when the tottering regime finally fell in 1644, China again fell prey to a conqueror, the Manchus, who swept down from the north to seize the throne, establishing the Ch'ing dynasty (A.D. 1644–1912). The Manchus were barbarians by Chinese standards, having origins in Tungusic hunting and fishing tribes who had evolved into a feudal society of horse-riding nomads. By 1626, clever imitation of Chinese bureaucratic and military methods had enabled them to amass impressive military and political power north of the Great Wall, so that by 1644 they were in a favorable position to strike at the weakened Chinese government and seize the country. Despotic, cruel, and hated by the Chinese, the Manchus took extreme steps to impose their culture on China even as they were acculturated by it, a power struggle that was to end in the collapse of imperial China after the bloodiest civil war in history.

Fig. 3-9. Nine-symbol sacrificial robe showing cut and design patterns. Korea, early Yi dynasty.

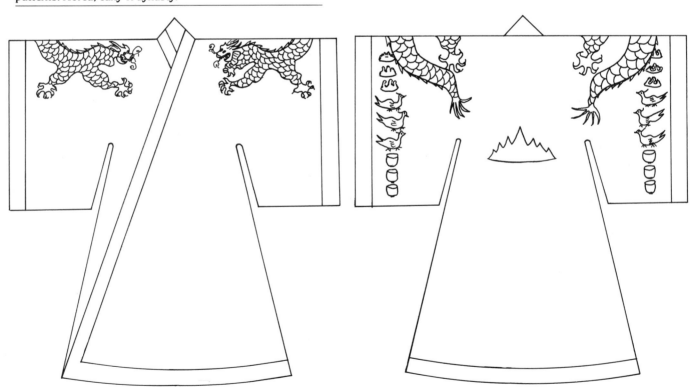

One of the first Manchu mandates was the imposition of style changes, based on Manchu court wear, on the dragon robe. Along with the mandatory wearing of the queue as a sign of Chinese enslavement, the Manchus insisted that their own national dress be worn by all persons in the service of the government. The first of these changes in the dragon robe was the *ch'ao-fu* style (Fig. 3-10), a strict replication of Manchu court costume. The male version consisted of two parts, an upper, riding jacket, and a lower set of overlapping aprons. The full, loosely hanging sleeves of the Chinese *p'ao* tradition were rejected in favor of the narrow Manchu sleeve, which was made in series of woven or embroidered ribs and which ended in the characteristic "horsehoof" cuff. The latter lay over the back of the hand almost to the fingertips and was so designed to protect the hands from the elements while riding. A decorative flap, the *jen*, was worn on the lower right side of the male costume, and this,

together with the typical ribbed sleeve, is useful in identifying the classic *ch'ao-fu.* The female court *ch'oa-fu* was also in two sections, having a long-sleeved, full-length coat with horsehoof cuffs, and a sleeveless vest of equal length worn over it (Fig. 3-12). Both types of *ch'ao-fu* were worn with detachable triangular collars, called *p'i-ling,* which were considered essential accessories and were always worn with it. (See also Chapter 6, Costume Accessories, Fig. 6-4, page 102).

The dragon designs embroidered or woven into the *ch'ao-fu* were consonant with Chinese styles of the time, for the Manchus had received them from China, while they were still a liege state of the latter, in the form of gifts from the Chinese emperors of yardage of embroidered dragon designs ready for tailoring (Fig. 3-23), or completed dragon robes, in return for Manchu tribute. By the early Ch'ing this type of five-clawed dragon *(lung)* was the facing, heavier-bodied form of the classic period, as was the four-clawed dragon *(mang),* identical to it except for its lesser claws. Both were used as part of the imperial ranking system, the five-clawed dragon being reserved for the emperor, the consort, and

Fig. 3-10. Imperial dragon robe *(ch'ao-fu).* Three-zoned design of dragons, Buddhist symbols, bats, clouds, waves, mountains in satin, stem stitches, gold couching; borders in *k'o-ssu* tapestry weave with tortoise-shell design. China, Ch'ing dynasty, Ch'ien-lung period (1736–1795). The Metropolitan Museum of Art, Pulitzer Bequest, 1935.

Fig. 3-11. Imperial dragon robe *(ch'ao-fu).* Yoke and zone design of dragons, bats, Eight Precious Things, and various sacrificial symbols with ribbed sleeves on yellow silk ground. China, Ch'ing dynasty. Crown copyright, Victoria and Albert Museum, London.

Fig. 3-12. Empress's dragon robe *(ch'ao-fu)*. Brocade of orange silk. China, Ch'ing dynasty. Courtesy of the Metropolitan Museum of Art, Pulitzer Bequest.

the immediate royal family and the four-clawed motif for all other lesser nobility and court officials who were entitled to wear the dragon robe.

The next step in the development of the dragon robe was the *ch'i-fu* (or *lung p'ao,* "dragon robe," as it was called in pre-Ching China) style (Fig. C-12). This evolved sometime between 1644 and 1759, most probably as a result of Chinese pressure upon the Manchus and the influence of Chinese culture. *Ch'i-fu* were produced in larger quantities than the *ch'ao-fu,* were more commonly worn by the imperial family and lesser nobles, and are generally considered the classic Ch'ing dragon robe, although *ch'ao-fu* continued to be worn well into the eighteenth century.

The *ch'i-fu* represented the Manchu adaptation to Chinese culture. Its full-length, bell-shaped tailoring, falling straight from a round collar, was based upon the cut of the Chinese traditional *p'ao* and marked a tacit bow to Chinese custom and a resumption of the classic heritage. As a concession to the Manchus, however, the *ch'ao-fu* sleeve and horsehoof cuff were generally retained, with some exceptions (Fig. 3-14), as a permanent feature on the *ch'i-fu.* Whether the compromising incorporation of the Chinese classic tradition with added Manchu features was a political device to enable the Manchus to rule more effectively, or whether the comparatively undeveloped Manchu culture was unable to withstand the force of Chinese civilization, seems a moot point, but from the record of China's history we must assume that her aloof predominance over invaders and her powers to withstand

Fig. 3-13. Imperial dragon robe *(ch'i-fu)*. Embroidered silk tabby with couched gold dragons. China, early Ch'ing dynasty (c. 1675). Crofts Collection, gift of the Robert Simpson Company, Royal Ontario Museum, Toronto.

Fig. 3-14. Imperial dragon robe. Design of five-clawed dragons *(lung)* in polychrome silk embroidery and couched gold thread. China, Ch'ing dynasty, Ch'ien-lung period (1736–1795). The Metropolitan Museum of Art, gift of Miss Marion Hague, 1943.

outside influence, in this case, amounted to a virtual moral victory for the Chinese. As John E. Vollmer points out in "In the Presence of the Dragon Throne":

> The use of costume to further political aims is very ancient in China; but few garments in its long history have managed to demonstrate these intentions as clearly as the *ch'i-fu*. *Ch'i-fu* decoration was consciously designed to symbolize the concept of universal order, upon which the principles of Chinese imperial statecraft rested. The basic decorative schema was transmitted from Ming period ornament. In the decoration found on the yoke and horizontal bands decorating the skirts of Ming court coats are the elements of Chinese cosmology. At first, as vassals of the Ming court, the Manchu had borrowed the outward forms of these symbols for their own garments; later, as rulers of the Central Kingdom, they embraced the spirit and substance of Chinese universal order.

The *ch'i-fu* differed from the *ch'ao-fu* in that the entire field of the robe was considered as a unified design (Fig. 3-13), and not divided into upper and lower zones. Although various evolutionary stages took place in the design structure, the basic motif consisted of eight field dragons in a formal balanced design, either with or without a larger, dominant dragon, and a ninth dragon placed out of sight on the inner flap of the front vent. This particular number of dragons had a double significance: The number eight was associated with both Buddhism and Taoism, while the number nine in ancient Taoist cosmology was considered the combinative form most symbolic of man. In addition to facing and profile dragons dominating the field, diagonal wave patterns *(li shui)* arose from the hem of the robe beneath curling roller waves, and above that arose the stylized forms of prism-like mountains. Cloud fillers and other good luck and longevity symbols circulated in the remaining field space. In 1759, imperial edicts codified the design conventions of the *ch'i-fu,* and the Twelve Symbols of Authority were added to various traditional locations on the field, similar to the Ming sacrificial robe (Fig. 3-7), but in much smaller, nonvertical motifs. The 1759 Sumptuary Laws also required the use of dark-colored, three-quarter-sleeve surcoats *(p'u-fu),* with chest rank badges, to be worn over the *ch'i-fu* for all public and semiformal imperial appearances. Such rank badges (mandarin squares) designated civil and military offices; the imperial

Fig. 3-15. Empress's dragon robe. Polychrome embroidery of Twelve Imperial Symbols on thunder-line silk damask ground; horsehoof cuffs. China, Ch'ing dynasty, middle nineteenth century. Courtesy of the Metropolitan Museum of Art, gift of Miss Annette Young, 1954, in memory of her brother Innis Young.

family and the nobility's rank badges consisted of four embroidered dragon medallions on the chest, back, and each shoulder of the *p'u-fu* (see Fig. 6-17, page 115).

Most of the design work on the *ch'i-fu* was executed in silk thread or metal thread embroidery or combinations of these. Color selection was extremely important, for the stitchery had to be harmonious with the ground color and couching stitches, and not clash. The lively Chinese color sense came into play here, using a system of complementary colors and color-value techniques discovered independently by them. In this method, which is now a time-honored artistic tool the world over, a color is chosen in terms of its value (its lightness or darkness), rather than by chroma, or intensity. In order to achieve maximum color effectiveness, artistic quality, drama, and color dynamics, a light color is placed against a darker color, or a dark is contrasted brilliantly against a lighter color. (See Figs. 3-16 and 3-18.) That this was a characteristic technique in Ch'ing dragon robe embroidery is clearly evident in most of the accompanying il-

Fig. 3-16. Imperial dragon robe *(ch'i-fu)*. Polychrome silk embroidery of dragons, clouds, chrysanthemums, endless knot, Buddhist canopy, goldfish, bats, mountains, waves on lemon-yellow satin ground. China, early Ch'ing dynasty. Courtesy of the Metropolitan Museum of Art, Pulitzer Bequest.

Fig. 3-17. Imperial dragon robe *(ch'i-fu)* (rear view). White satin brocade with dominant five-clawed dragon and conventional designs embroidered in colored silks and metal thread couching. China, Ch'ing dynasty. Courtesy of the Metropolitan Museum of Art, Pulitzer Bequest.

Fig. 3-18. Imperial court coat. Eight-medallion design embroidered with silk and metal thread on blue satin ground; accents in stem stitch. China, Ch'ing dynasty, early eighteenth century. The Metropolitan Museum of Art, Rogers Fund, 1943.

lustrations. A Chinese embroiderer, for example, would not place a dark-blue cloud motif on a dark-blue ground where it would be lost, weak, or ineffective, unless he or she intended to outline-stitch it with a lighter, more contrasting color.

Of the many kinds of yellow used on the *ch'i-fu,* the brightest were reserved for the emperor and his consort, where they were the ground color of the most formal robes. While there were also imperial robes of other colors—white, crimson, scintillating oranges, vibrant blues—these were usually worn by princes, princesses, and other members of the royal family or by high court officials. Nevertheless, some of these examples are among the most beautiful and striking of the dragon robes, largely because of the intense vibration of their color ranges, which were achieved through stringently controlled and regulated dyeing methods in the royal studios. With the Manchu compromise with Chinese tradition, the emperor was permitted the continued wearing of the yellow *ch'i-fu,* but later edicts stipulated that all ranks below were to wear "stone blue." This accounts for the many varieties of blue robes to be found in the middle and late Ch'ing, which can be observed in various paintings by the Italian painter Giuseppe Castiglione (who lived in China for a long period during the Ch'ien-lung epoch of the Ch'ing) showing many officials in blue robes and *p'u-fu* with mandarin squares.

The *ch'i-fu* was embroidered with many design conventions that were symbolic of civil and/or religious meaning. In addition to the writhing dragons in the symbolic, cloud-filled skies above the waves and mountains, there were various good luck and longevity symbols, such as the bat, the crane, and the swastika, as well as certain flowers, such as the peony and lotus. There were usually Buddhist symbols, such as the endless knot, and Taoist figures, such as the flower basket. Along with these, after 1759, the Twelve Symbols of Authority, derived from ancient sacrificial robes, were restored. Various conventions of Confucian origin, such as the secular Eight Precious Things, also appeared on the *ch'i-fu* at various times. The field of the *ch'i-fu* depicted the cosmic universal order: The waves were symbolic of the seas and waters of the earth, the mountains symbolized the world, and the dragons were the symbol of the Son of Heaven, the emperor, symbolically placed above, and ruler over all (Fig. C-13).

As noted earlier, the dragon was the supreme symbol of imperial authority, extremely ancient in Chinese history. An entirely mythical, spiritual figure, the dragon design probably originated in prehistory, but the earliest known motifs come from the Shang dynasty, the *k'uei* dragons. The *t'ao-t'ieh* masks of the Shang also closely resemble stylized dragons. Various theories have arisen concerning the origin of the dragon symbol. In "Dragons in Chinese Art," Hugo Munsterberg makes the interesting observation that its idea may have been drawn from some prehistoric dinosaur legend whose image was buried in the primordial collective mind or handed down from antediluvian myths. Professor Li Chi of the National Palace Museum in Taiwan thinks the figure was derived from the alligator, a species of which was native to prehistoric China. The short legs, the long snout, and the ferocity of the dragon symbol seem to make this connection quite credible also. Traditional Chinese mythology viewed the dragon as the symbol of heaven, the king of the elements and of nature. It

Fig. 3-19. Prince's dragon robe. Conventional designs in gold couching, stem and satin stitches; peony flowers in seed stitch. China, Ch'ing dynasty, middle nineteenth century. Length, 30 inches (76 cm.). The Metropolitan Museum of Art, Fletcher Fund, 1942.

also signified the god of water, the fertilizing bestower of rain. From an early period it became associated with the idea of divine imperial succession and eventually came to symbolize the emperor himself, as the Son of Heaven. In addition to the five-clawed *lung* and four-clawed *mang,* there was a winged dragon, which symbolized the skies; a horned dragon as the symbol of the river; and a hornless dragon for the symbol of the mountains. Such distinctions formed part of a vast mythology of auspicious symbols for the superstitious folk of the village peasantry, who lived in regions often devastated by terrible floods. But as an imperial symbol, the dragon evoked powerful associations of swift law, judgment, and authority, and this was one of its main psychological and political purposes on the robe. As a design feature, its flowing serpentine line added a strong rhythm and grace to the overall motif, and is actually its most striking and important artistic feature.

Mountain designs were prominent on the dragon robe, and they remind us that mountains have always held a sacred place in Chinese legendry, where they were regarded as the celestial home of spiritual beings. Lu Shan, near Kiukiang in Kiangsi Province, the site of many significant Buddhist sculptures, is foremost in such lore, with a complex mythology that goes back to the earliest dynasties. Emperor Huang Ti of the legendary Hsiao dynasty was said to be the first monarch to personify and deify such mountains, ordering that Lu Shan be declared a god in imperial history! T'ai Shu, in Shantung Province, another of the most ancient of the sacred peaks, was believed to hide in its clouds the celestial palaces of the fabled Jade Emperor and the mystic Queen Mother of the West, whose figures reappear frequently in Chinese embroideries.

Dragon robes were also worn in Korea as well as in Annam during the historical period. Korean culture and imperial customs closely paralleled those of China from an early date, at least from the Lo-Lang era (c. 8 B.C.). The Korean kings were frequent, welcome visitors at the Chinese court and were accorded the honor of the third imperial Chinese rank there. Korea was an unofficial protectorate of China until about the Yi dynasty (A.D. 1392–1910), and a tradition of presentation robes to Korean monarchs, as gifts of the Chinese emperors, dated from the year 1065, when a Liao dynasty emperor (Northern Sung period) awarded a sacrificial robe bearing nine of the Twelve Symbols to King Munjong (reigned 1046–1083) of the Koryo dynasty.

Robes with golden dragon patterns were the subject of Korean edicts of 1043, banning their use among the populace, so the dragon tradition was probably in long use in Korea before the first mention in the Korean annals of Ming presentations of a dragon medallion robe in 1444. In 1588, the Korean monarch of the time wrote a letter of gratitude for the gift of a four-clawed *mang* robe from the Wan-li emperor. After the reigning Korean king fled the Japanese (Momoyama) invasions of 1596 to Manchuria, a further entry in the annals makes ref-

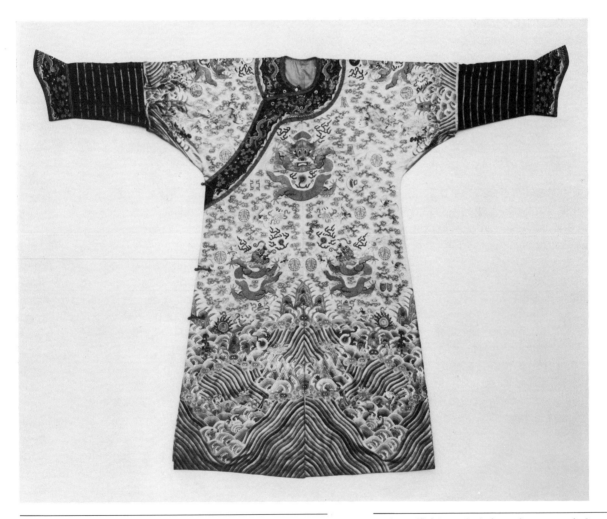

Fig. 3-20. Emperor's twelve-symbol dragon robe *(ch'i-fu)*. Double wave designs at hem and elbows in satin stitch; clouds, Eight Precious Things, dragons, bats, flaming pearls, and sacrificial symbols in satin, stem stitches, gold couching. China, Ch'ing dynasty, nineteenth century. The Metropolitan Museum of Art, Rogers Fund, 1945.

erence to a dragon robe he took with him to preserve it from the invaders.

In 1649 Korean documents referred to dragon robes made with square chest badges for use by imperial grandsons, and by 1751 the classic Korean dragon robe (gon-ryong-po) had emerged into the full light of history. Codified by Korean statutes of that time, the king's robe was of dark red satin with gold five-clawed dragons (lung) in circular medallions on the chest, back, and each shoulder (Fig. 3-5), in the Ming manner. The robes of princes were of black satin, also with four circular gold dragon medallions in the same locations on the robe, but these were of four-clawed dragons (mang). Imperial grandsons were given black satin robes with rectangular embroidered dragon badges in gold, located on the chest of the robe, and these bore three-clawed dragons. The consort and other female members of the court wore the same medallions or squares as their husbands on formal robes. The queen also wore the semiformal wansam with a dragon or phoenix square, and this robe became the eventual model for the traditional Korean bridal robe. (See Chapter 5.) The tang-ui, based on early T'ang styles, was another less formal Korean court robe, similar to the wan-sam. The Korean dragon robe continued in use until the late Yi dynasty. Because of a close similarity to the Korean imperial rank badge, the Korean dragon robe is sometimes mistaken for the latter, which was a single dragon medallion worn on the center chest of imperial Korean surcoats.

The last development of the Korean dragon robe came as late as 1863, when, according to the second volume of the Kook-cho-o-re-ui (Korean Dynastic Costume Records), the Korean king Kojong assumed the imperial yellow robe of China, with coiling dragons woven in gold on the chest, back, and shoulders, a symbolic severance of ties with China and Japan. At the same time, the heir apparent (taegun) was given an identical design, but on a red ground. With this occurrence, which can only be regarded as typical of the declining stages of tradition in imperial China and Korea, the wheel of time had come full circle, and the stage was set for the modern era.

As early as 1750, foreign interference in Chinese affairs, the growing monopolization of silk and tea lands by foreign business, the illegal introduction of opium into China by the British East India Company, a series of disastrous Opium Wars with England, and the growing decadence of the Manchu court had all contributed seriously to the imminent downfall of imperial China. Bankrupt and impoverished by Manchu corruption and foreign manipulation, she was now forced to import textiles instead of exporting them, and this led to the disintegration of the silk and embroidery industries and further financial collapse. By 1857, the Taiping Rebellion, a Chinese movement to oust the Manchus and restore the old culture, had begun, but the arming of the Manchus by foreign powers and British intervention in the war resulted in the defeat and slaughter of the Taiping by 1864, leaving the Manchus again in power. In the wake of this horrible war, and with the embroidery and textile industries now injured beyond repair, all that was left of the old traditions deteriorated even further, so that after 1875, with the exception of a few swan songs here and there, most embroidery became increasingly crude, exaggerated, and tasteless, a travesty of the old art. When the Manchus were finally overthrown by the Republic in 1911, the embroidery art of China, along with the dragon robe and the vast splendor of dynastic China, was lost forever.

The remarkable evolution of the dragon robe from prehistoric costume decoration into the collective symbol of Chinese imperial might at its peak, its use there as a political vehicle, as well as its expression of the cosmic philosophies and religions that kept China strong and unified, are no less remarkable when we consider the tremendous artistic development that accompanied it, contributed to it, and grew from its production. Always a great source of pride in China, craftsmanship and fine art both grew from the considerable pressure to production exerted upon its artists by the imperial nobility and the affluent classes, from the earliest dynasties onward. Supplying the needs of a growing civilization was, in fact, one of the catalysts that made Chinese art grow and become great. Some of the most important principles of design, of color, of dyeing, of the painter's art, were developed by Chinese embroiderers, as the ingenious and lively Chinese skills sought ever more refined and economic ways to produce beautiful objects of lasting, even eternal, artistic quality. In the following section we will study the construction of a hypothetical dragon robe and observe firsthand exactly how that vast ingenuity achieved its creative goals through disciplined procedures.

DRAGON ROBE TECHNIQUES

The Step-by-Step Creation of a Dragon Robe

The emperors of dynastic China lived in incredible opulence and luxury, and in order to supply the fine goods demanded by the court, a veritable army of craftsmen was kept busy providing furnishings and costumes for the palace. Among the busiest of these were the embroiderers, for, as one of the most important Chinese art forms with ages-old traditions, lavish embroidery was used to decorate the finest silk trappings of the court, especially the clothing, personal accessories, and domestic textiles of the royal family. Under the watchful eye of a master embroiderer and designer, a full-time embroidery studio, with teams of embroiderers sometimes numbering in the hundreds, practiced the art and craft that made them famous later in history. It was here, in the royal embroidery studios, that the great dragon robes were created, often taking years to complete and rigidly controlled and inspected, as the designers and stitchery experts struggled to outdo themselves and meet the orders of the court for even more magnificent robes.

The creation of a dragon robe was a carefully managed artistic process that proceeded in logical steps toward its goal of making a beautiful art object. That the object in this case had a secondary function as a garment in no way interfered with its artistic quality, for aesthetic purposes (deployed in decoration) were always uppermost in the minds of both the designers and the embroiderers. (This was equally true in Japanese and Korean costume embroidery.) As each step unfolds, it will be seen how this controlled craftwork led to a specific artistic expression that was far more artistic, and far transcended, its use as a mere royal garment. While an emperor's purpose for a robe may have been related to political motives or personal vanity, the embroiderers always aimed at fine art, and it is fine art and high craft that we see here in its growth from start to finish.

Step 1: The Pattern

A ground fabric and color were selected from yardage that was either plain weave, damask, twill satin, or gauze. Such yardage was available only in widths of about three feet, loom limitations in the historical period being unable to produce any wider fabric. This factor affected both the tailoring and the design of the dragon robe, as will be seen. The wearer's height, sleeve length, and chest were measured. A basic pattern for the robe's dimension was cut, consisting of three panels for the main body, and a separate piece for the sleeve section, cuffs, and collar. The pattern, shown in Figures 3-21 and 3-22, demonstrates the economy and ingenuity used in cutting and folding the main section of the robe to consist of two main field panels (right and left), and an additional upper left panel. The open, unfolded panels were used throughout the entire embroidery process.

Fig. 3-21. Basic cut pattern for a dragon robe (ch'i-fu).

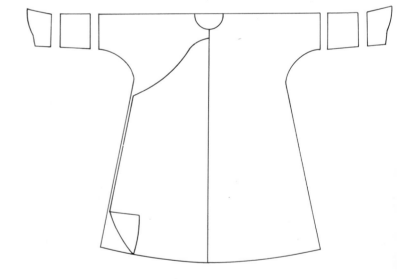

Step 2: Placing the Design

The majority of designs on the dragon robes were applied with precut templates or stencils, of which there was probably a vast library in the palace storerooms, consisting of thousands of designs in their conventional forms. The dragons were also executed with stencils, although some of these were possibly custom-made and never used again. The cut fabric panels were laid out on a long table, and the designs were stenciled onto the panels within the pattern outline, using a fine-pointed brush and inkstick, or dyes. The laying and arrangement of the field designs required great design skill and visualization, since the entire finished robe had to be conceived on the open, unjoined panels. To obtain designs in opposite pairs the stencil was simply turned over, moved to the opposite panel, and the tracing made in reverse. All of the smaller repeat elements, such as the cloud fillers, were executed by simply moving the stencils about judiciously on the field. On some of the custom-made robes, tracing paper may also have been used.

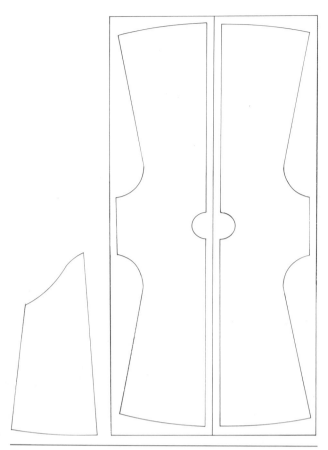

Fig. 3-22. Open yardage cut and ready for design application.

Fig. 3-23. Yardage for a dragon robe. Conventional designs with finished embroidery ready for tailoring. China, Ch'ing dynasty, Chia-ch'ing period (1796–1820). Crown copyright, Victoria and Albert Museum, London.

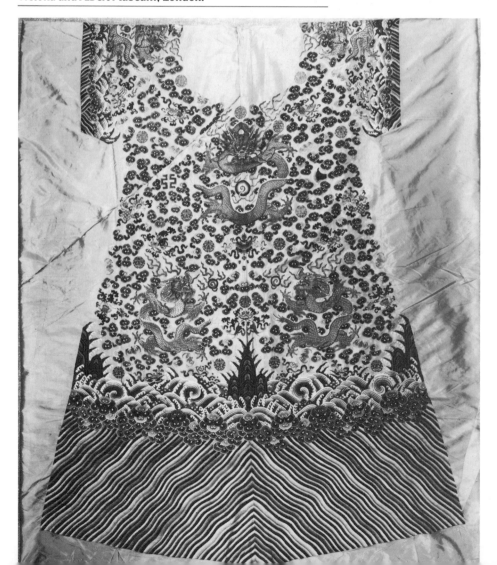

Step 3: Stretching the Fabric

Harmonious silk yarns for the stitchery were selected, the color was worked out on the master design (Fig. 3-24), and yarns were prepared to appropriate thicknesses. The fabric panels were then stretched onto separate rectangular frames and fixed there with a pasted-edge or stitched-border method, since a roller frame would have flattened or wrinkled the finished embroidery. Such stretching was done by hand, with many workers employed in the process, since each panel was about twelve feet long.

Fig. 3-24. Master design underdrawing on silk fabric for a twelve-symbol robe. Paint and ink. China, Ch'ing dynasty. Nelson Gallery–Atkins Museum, Kansas City, Missouri, Nelson Fund.

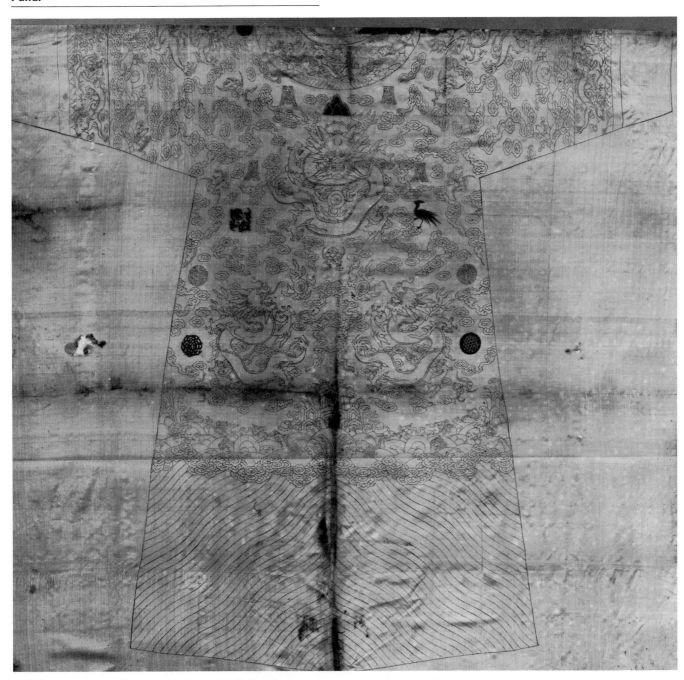

Step 4: Stitchery

With the future dragon robe now mounted on its various frames, a team of embroiderers took up their places on each frame, and stitchery was ready to begin.

As the stitchery progressed, rice paper friskets were probably used to mask unworked areas and to protect those already embroidered. Since the frame was wide (embroiderers had to reach over it constantly in their work), and the stitchery required much time, this protection was necessary.

Any raised work called for by the composition was done next to add a three-dimensional effect to certain areas, such as in the eyes and coils of the dragon. Stumping was applied with silk floss or vines (vegetable fiber), which was overstitched on the fabric with a darning stitch or couching until perfectly rounded and smooth.

The smaller compositional elements were probably embroidered in the order of their importance, the smaller motifs—such as the clouds, bats, peonies, fish, and other symbols—being worked first, and the major figures, such as the waves and mountains, being stitched last. The final and most important figures, the main dragon and flaming pearl designs, were done last of all, and these were worked over the center seam after joining. It was considered aesthetically desirable for the center dragon to be unbroken by the center seam, and for this reason, once all the other design elements were completely finished in their embroidery, the panels were removed from their frames for joining before the final dragon was added. (See Fig. 3-25.)

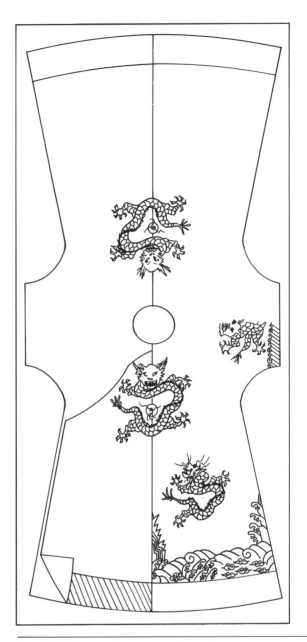

Fig. 3-25. Dragon design on stretched fabric.

Step 5: Joining

Subsequently, the panels were removed from their frames for joining. This was done with a hidden stitch, laying the panels edge to edge to create the center seam, and at this point matching of right and left halves of the embroidered design was necessary. The third, upper panel, rough-cut in a forty-five-degree angle at the top, was joined to the robe's right panel near the neck, along the chest, and at the armpit. (See Fig. 3-23.)

Step 6: Finishing the Dragon

Once the right, left, and upper panels were all joined, it was an easy matter to restretch the fabric in the area of the dragon only and to proceed with finishing it *over* the center seam. If stitchery was to be used on the dragon, it was usually in satin stitch, with a stem stitch outline to define and separate the dragon's scales and give them a relief effect.

If the dragon design was to be done in metal thread, it was laid in symmetrical loops that overlapped each other to form the scales, beginning from either the lowest coil, the tail, or the upper body, and then held down with a progressive couching stitch, usually in red thread, each scale being done separately. Most often only the scales of the dragon were done in metal thread, but there are examples in which the head has been executed in this way also. In the later dynasties sometimes oiled or gold paper-covered thread was used to simulate metal thread, because of the scarcity and high price of gold.

Step 7: Finishing the Sleeves and Collar

The frames that held the stretched fabric for the collar and cuffs were probably worked on simultaneously with the main design by another team of embroiderers. The procedure here was the same as on the main panels. The same stitchery was executed in the same places on the designs for the purpose of providing an overall harmony and continuity, and the cuff and collar designs were related to the field designs. The graceful spiriform shape that encircled the collar and covered the top of the vent was done in a standard width of about four inches, and was often further finished, after its embroidery, with brocade edgings on both sides. Similar brocade edging was used in finishing the cuff areas after embroidery.

A unique feature on the *ch'ao-fu* and most *ch'i-fu* was the sleeve adjustment panel, a length of unembroidered material between the elbow and wrist. This piece was essentially a joint, with both practical and aesthetic purposes. Its practical purpose was that the sleeve length could be sized and adjusted correctly through taking up or lengthening this piece. Also, thick embroidery in this region of the elbow would have proved uncomfortable and cumbersome. Its artistic purpose, brought about through its practical function, was that it added a broad, solid, unembroidered color area to the design, provided relief from embroidery, and a color contrast to the complex color and design array of the cuffs, shoulders, and field of the robe, a kind of painterly counterpoint. The color for the sleeve joint was naturally selected to harmonize with the rest of the robe.

Step 8: Final Tailoring, Backing, and Lining

In the traditional method of backing costumes, the frames were turned over for the backing process after the stitchery was completed. All hanging ends on the reverse side were sealed down with a soft rice glue; this solidified the embroidery work from the back. The backing was then subjected to a steaming until it was quite moist. This removed all dust and caused the stitchery to contract and gloss. After steaming, the robe was allowed to dry and, when completely dry, was removed from the frame. From this stage all that remained was adding the main dragons, final tailoring and finishing, such as joining the sleeves and cuffs, hemming, finishing, and edging the collar and cuffs, adding buttons or toggles (made of gold, ivory, jade, or semiprecious stones), and sewing the lining (usually of silk or ramie fabric) into the inside of the robe.

Summer Dragon Robes

Heavy silk or satin robes were too hot for summer use in China, so special summer robes were made for the imperial family. These were woven of very lightweight silk gauze that was quite transparent and airy. Usually they were worn with a light underrobe or a *tou-tou* (bib-brassiere)—a silk-embroidered, apron-shaped undergarment for men and women (see Fig. 3-27)—but sometimes nothing was worn beneath them, in a rather risqué manner. During the Han dynasty court ladies often wore sheer white gauze robes, nude beneath, so this practice was not unknown or found shocking. Comfort was, after all, uppermost in the wearers' minds, and on the palace grounds privacy was ensured.

The mesh of the gauze summer robe was similar in effect to that used in canvas petit-point and was even stitched in the same manner as modern petit-point, using a counted (darning, half-cross, or brick) stitch. This was really quite a historical coincidence, since true European canvas stitchery probably did not reach China until the middle of the eighteenth century, in the middle Ch'ing.

Circular, coiling designs are not easy to do in any kind of mesh, but the Chinese embroiderers were so skilled, and the silk gauze and thread they used were so fine, that the finished effect was more like embroidery on a solid weave than counted stitch. Typically, the diligent Chinese filled any holes left around the half-cross stitches with metal thread, which was couched around the edges of the dragon designs for covering and general strengthening of the fabric.

The Twelve-Symbol *ch'i-fu* shown in Figure C-13 is unusual in that the entire red silk gauze background has been covered with a counted darning stitch in gold-colored thread worked in diamond patterns. The use of gold-colored thread on the red ground contributed greatly to its stunning color intensity, a purpose that was definitely aimed at, since the use of red thread on the vivid yellow background resulted in a scintillating visual orange.

A dramatic and extremely vibrant color approach characterizes the *li shui* wave border also, whose narrowness—7 1/2 inches (19 cm.) high—places this robe in the early or middle Ch'ing. The wave lines have been executed 1/8 inch (3 mm.) apart, in green, red, blue, umber, and beige, each color being finished in five gradations of satin stitch. The mountains, clouds, and bats have been done in polychrome gradated satin stitch, which was later outlined in gold thread. The Twelve Symbols were embroidered with a combination of satin and long and short stitches, and outlined with stem stitch.

The dragon design was finished in couched gold thread, which was laid in a continuous movement that follows the direction of the scales from side to side without being cut, and which was then held down with red thread. The belly side of the dragon has an unusual treatment of pink gradated satin stitch, a dark brown stem stitch used with it making a clean outline and separation from the gold areas.

The collar border has been given the same technique as the ground, but a reverse color theme, with black darning stitch in diamond patterns on a red spiriform border.

A quick glance would not detect the complexity of the background stitchery on this robe, for it is so fine, smooth, and highly controlled that it seems part of the fabric. The clever harmonization of red thread with the yellow ground to achieve a stunning visual intensity is not nearly as astounding as the extreme virtuosity of the stitchery. The staggering amount of patience, labor, finesse, and artistry of the embroiderers is better appreciated when we realize that our stitchery diagram (Fig. 3-26) represents a half-inch square on the robe's background, and this square was divided into nine equal patterns, each of which contained nine rows of stitchery in areas only 3/16 inch (4 cm.) in width! The accented center of the squares is an important feature, and the shortened stitch lengths in this area serve the aesthetic goal of creating a unified, symmetrical design pattern in each of the tiny diamond shapes, and the practical purpose of strengthening and tightening the stitchery through avoiding overlong stitches from one side of the diamond to the other. The stitchery was executed as follows.

Darning Stitch (Fig. 3-26)

The needle comes up at 1, reenters the fabric at 2, emerges at 3, and proceeds as in the diagram to 13 to establish the center. It enters at 14, jumps one row, comes up at 15, reenters at 16, comes up at 17, enters the fabric again at 18, drops down one row and comes up at 19, and so on. This procedure is repeated until one diamond area is filled; then the same sequence is followed again in the next diamond area.

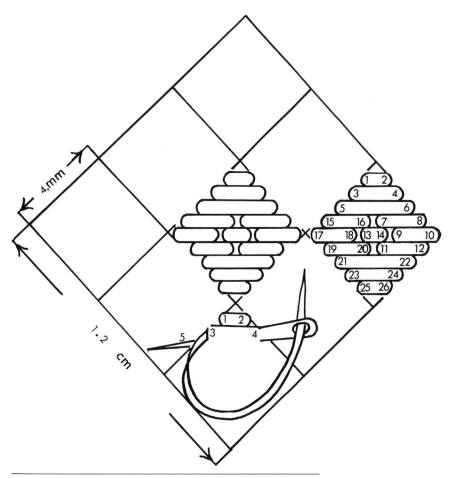

Fig. 3-26. Diaper lozenge of counted darning stitch from twelve-symbol robe (Fig. C-13).

The remarkable stitchery achievements on this robe, its beautiful color, and the length of time devoted to its completion are all examples of the kind of integrity of craftsmanship that led to the high art of the dragon robe.

Another outstanding example of distinguished dragon robe design, color, and stitchery is the famous "Hundred Cranes Robe" (Figs. C-14 and C-15) discovered in the Manchu tomb of Prince Kuo Ch'in Wang by Dr. Laurence Sickman in 1945.

Both formal and informal elements of design (see Chapter 8, "Techniques," page 157) were combined on this piece, the triangular structure of the three main dragon roundels dominating the middle field and the turbulent landscape and wave border below. The general conception of the robe is unique and highly original, departing significantly in its freedom from most conventional techniques of design and overall motif. The dragon roundels, for example, have been softened along their borders through the use of a tightly rendered cloud pattern which undulates along the circumference, rather than lying in sharp contrast to the ground. Many of the field cloud forms are connected, another original feature, even as they and the numerous flying cranes serve to create a sensitive, overall unity in the field. The lower wave border is certainly the most unique feature of this robe, with its very realistic tree and landscape areas nestled among and flanking the narrow wave border and roller waves about it, a radical departure from the conventional *li shui* concept of later robes. Although certain dragon robes and other costumes are occasionally seen with peony designs superimposed upon the wave border, as in Figures 3-19 and C-27, the use of a landscape in this area is extremely unusual and unconventional in dragon robe design.

In keeping with its originality, the artistic levels of the robe are sheerly magnificent. The distinguished drawing, designing, and imaginatively conceived realism, both in the sea and landscape and in the dragons above, prove this work to be one of the finest masterpieces of the classic dragon robe. Added to this are its exquisite, softly harmonious color tonalities and skillfully rendered stitchery techniques that serve the design's purpose to the maximum degree. The stitchery was greatly strengthened by the large areas of ground color, with its woven design of bats and clouds, and the work has been done in satin and stem stitches on the clouds and waves, with clusters of radiating darning stitch on the pine trees' needles, long and short and satin stitches on the cranes, and much gold couching on the dragons.

The extreme originality of this robe, obviously undertaken before the codified Sumptuary Laws of 1759 were enacted, the somewhat rounded crane forms, the similarity of the rocks to Ming styles, and the narrowness of the wave border in my opinion seem to indicate this robe came from an early period in the Ch'ing dynasty.

Our next excursion into the world of Oriental embroidery will be to experience the equally famous artistic counterpart of the dragon robe, the beautiful poetry of the Japanese kimono. Here we will see a world quite different from that of Chinese embroidery, one that had many of its roots and influences in China and Korea, but that grew into one of the greatest textile arts the world has ever seen, a special artistic expression that was uniquely and typically Japanese.

Fig. 3-27. *Tou-tou* (bib-brassiere). Polychrome silk embroidered chest cover piece. The garment design is divided into two sections that depict religious symbols: lotus, pheasant, phoenix, Mandarin duck, Manchurian crane, peony, and sacred fungus, in satin, long and short, Pekinese, and stem stitch. 18″ × 18″ (78 cm). Ch'ing dynasty, nineteenth century. Collection of the author.

4/ THE JAPANESE KIMONO

HISTORY AND AESTHETICS

Reminiscent of cherry blossoms, the fabled beauty of Nippon's ladies, and the tea ceremony, the kimono has virtually become the symbol of Japan, famous and admired the world over. Yet, like the dragon robe of China, it was a comparative newcomer in Japanese history, developing at about the same time as a national Japanese style in art, the early thirteenth century. Originally the kosode, as the most typical type of kimono is called, was a plain, undecorated garment that was worn beneath the heavy formal court robes of the Heian period (A.D. 794–1185). It came into prominence from these humble beginnings for simple reasons of comfort: It was lighter, permitted greater freedom of movement than the heavier robes, and was cooler during warm weather. In a gradual transition, the kosode began to appear as an outer garment, sometime during the Kamakura period (A.D. 1185–1333).

Before this era Japan was very much caught up in the cultural domain of China, not only in costumes and textile design, but in all of the arts, including architecture. Younger and more leisurely in its development than China, Japan owed a great debt to the long-range cultural influence and tutelage of the former, which was brought about both through the medium of visiting Korean craftsmen and through many cultural exchanges and ambassadorial trips to the Chinese mainland. During the first part of the Nara period, from A.D. 645 to 794, the T'ang emperor sent a treasury of embroidered robes, screens, scrolls, textiles, carpets, and other imperial gifts to Emperor Shomu (reigned 724–749). Their beauty and splendor created an avid Japanese enthusiasm for everything Chinese, and Shomu built for them the famous Shoso-in repository at Nara, housing some of the treasures there and some in the Horyu-ji monastery, where they still remain. This influence, comparatively early in Japanese history, was intense, prevailed for more than five hundred years, and is very apparent in all pre-Kamakura Japanese art.

Before the Nara lies the Asuka period (A.D. 552–645), the textiles of which are uncertainly known to us, which was also dominated by Chinese influence, and of which Buddhist sculptures reveal little evidence of embroidery decoration on costumes. Before the Asuka, the prehistoric Yayoi and Jomon periods are still shrouded in comparative obscurity. While much work remains to be done in Japanese early history and prehistory, and Japanese archeologists are very busy in this area, at the present time it is impossible to say whether a native embroidery art ever existed in Japan before the introduction of sericulture and silk embroidery from Korea during the third century A.D. (Kofun period, A.D. 200–552). The aboriginal Ainu, who still live in northern Japan, are known to have been among its original settlers, and they were probably descendants of the same Mesolithic peoples who migrated south and east from original culture centers in Asian Siberia. If this is so, then native Ainu proto-embroidery (metal ornaments, colorful stones, and other objects sewn to woven linen or elm-bark fiber robes), and appliqué in combination with embroidery, may reflect an original embroidery tradition that was native to prehistoric and pre-Chinese-influenced Japan. The Tenju-koku Mandala (Fig. 4-1), which dates from the Asuka period, is one of the earliest known embroidery works of Japanese origin.

Fig. 4-1. Detail from the Tenju-koku Mandala (Buddhist Paradise). Cloud, phoenix, lotus, tortoise, Buddhist monks in T'ang style designs in variations of satin and stem stitch with tightly twisted yarn. Oranges, greens, reds, maroons, beiges, ochers, whites on coarse charcoal gray hemp cloth ground. Underdrawing by Korean artists. Japan, Asuka period, sixth–seventh century. From *Japanese Embroidery* by Mutsuko Imai, Mainichi Newspapers, Tokyo. Courtesy of Chugu-ji Temple, Nara.

Fig. 4-2. Detail from *Mountain God Riding a Tiger*. Clouds, flowers, bats, waves, Secular Eight Precious Things, trees, rocks, costumed figures in overall embroidery of interlocking satin stitch, counted darning, stem and satin stitches, tiger and contours in gold couching; tightly twisted yarns on black damask silk ground. Korea, Yi dynasty, fourteenth–fifteenth century. From *Korean Embroidery* by Huh Dong Hwa, Sam-Sung Publications, Seoul. Collection of Huh Dong Hwa.

The *Nihon-shoki* (Chronicles of Japan) records faithfully that the visits of various Korean dignitaries and craftsmen brought sericulture to Japan. Silk presentations made to the female regent Jingu, about A.D. 284, were accompanied by silk embroidery hangings and other compositions, offered by the king of Silla (from the Korean Three Kingdoms period, 57 B.C.–A.D. 688, when Korea was divided into three separate states: Silla, Paekche, and Koguryo). In A.D. 284 and 286, the king of Paekche also presented a silk maiden (craftswoman) at the Japanese court, accompanied by an entourage of

120 other silk workers with him in his visit. The *Nihon-shoki* also gives the year A.D. 307 as the period when four silk maidens brought sericulture from Wu (China) to Japan. The Silla king of A.D. 330 is recorded as having presented 1,460 *tan* (35,040 yards) of silk at the court of Emperor Nintoku, while some fifteen years later the same emperor made a visit to Yamagi to view the growth of the mulberry trees. The early Japanese annal *Kojiki* (Record of Ancient Matters, compiled A.D. 712) mentioned an imperial visit to Yamanose to view the cultivation of silkworms that a Korean craftsman was growing,

stating that "they are strange bugs, sometimes crawling, at other times in cocoons, and [at] still other [times they] become flying birds." With the introduction of Buddhism into Japan from Korea in A.D. 552, it is apparent what potent forces both China and Korea were in the growth and development of early Japanese civilization, and this included Japan's first known contact with highly sophisticated textile arts.

So there were no real forerunners of the kimono, for before the Kamakura period there was a great eagerness to emulate Chinese civilization. Paintings from the Nara and Heian epochs show very clearly how the prevailing costume styles were literally prototypes of the same kind of *p'ao* robe common in T'ang and Sung China and Great Silla Korea, which these Japanese periods parallel. Although the basic style of the kimono was, in certain features, similar to the *p'ao,* when the eventual release from Chinese influence did come, and the under-kimono became the kosode, its design shape was what we now recognize as typically Japanese (Fig. 4-5). The progressive development of the kimono and its decoration can be said to be but one aspect of a gradual maturation and eventual transitional break with Chinese ties.

The kosode was not decoratively woven or embroidered when it first came into use as outer wear because of a strong Buddhist conservatism in the Kamakura, and it was not until the Muromachi period (1392–1573) that any decoration was done upon it. Even then, Buddhist ascetic tendencies still had the effect of limiting all such decoration. But in the fabulous Momoyama period (1573–1615) that followed, the kosode emerged in all its stunning glory, as the flowering of the Japanese textile arts celebrated the liberation and true birth of Japanese art, and created some of the most remarkably designed and beautifully executed examples the world has ever seen.

The kimono can be divided categorically into three main types. The most important artistically is the *kosode* (literally, "small sleeves"). Then there is the *furisode* (Fig. C-21), or long-sleeved kimono (literally, "swinging sleeves"), and the *yukata,* a more casual, usually unembroidered print robe designed for use at home and in the bath. Several other types of kimonos and jackets, such as the *karaginu* ("hunting robe") (Fig. 4-4), *choken* ("long silk"), and *happi* are seen only in the Noh or Kyogen theater, are prototypes of medieval court or nobility garments, and are basically derived from

Fig. 4-3. Detail from *Flowering Trees and Peacocks.* Reversible embroidery design of peacocks, flowering plants, trees in interlocking satin stitch, variations of stem and chain stitch on brocaded dark brown silk. Yellows, greens, blues.

Fig. 4-4. *Karaginu* hunting jacket. Designs of paulownia leaves and flowers on brocade silk gauze. Japan, Tokugawa period, eighteenth century. The Metropolitan Museum of Art, gift of Mrs. Howard Mansfield, 1950.

kosode or *furisode* styles. Although many lovely compositions can be found on the *furisode,* it did not reach its peak of popularity or artistic maturity until the Tokugawa (also called Edo) period, in the nineteenth century. The *furisode* has been more frequently seen and is better known in the West as the true kimono, but it is in the short-sleeved kosode that the heart of Japanese textile mastery is found, especially as represented by the important Momoyama epoch.

The main differences between the kosode and *furisode,* therefore, are in their historical situations, and in the length of the sleeve. The kosode has sleeves that are shorter and narrower than the *furisode;* the very long, hanging sleeves of the

furisode have a wider arm opening, and are nearly three times as long as the kosode sleeve. By the Tokugawa or Edo period (1615–1868), the kosode was worn only by married women, and this accounts for the prevalence of the *furisode* in the woodblock prints of the time (many of which reached Europe and had a decided influence on French Impressionist art), for these prints were usually of unmarried girls and geisha.

The tailoring of the kosode has a dynamic linearity that is distinctly Japanese. There is a broad, dramatic sweep to the shoulders because of the straight line directly across them from sleeve tip to sleeve tip, an important design feature that is confirmed by the flat, minimal collar that lies snugly on

Fig. 4-5. Noh theater kosode. Designs of wisteria leaves, flowers, and twining vines in stem and satin stitches. Greens, oranges, pinks, blues, yellows, purples, browns, and white on geometric silk ground. Japan, Tokugawa period (1789–1799). Courtesy of the Royal Ontario Museum, Toronto, gift of Mrs. Edgar J. Stone.

the lower neck and is part of a narrow chest panel reaching almost to the waist (Fig. C-18). From the back, the straight line across the shoulders forms a perfect T shape when open and also has very clean, straight lines that originate vertically and horizontally from the armpits. When the kosode is open, the back view has a butterfly shape, and the shortened upper chest and neck panel adds to this winglike effect. The ground material of the robe was usually made of woven, single-layered silk or satin, innerfaced with very fine cotton fabric. Women wore it wrapped to the left, men to the right, and, in Momoyama times, it was held in place by a narrow sash, the small obi, or *hoso-obi.* The wide obi of modern Japan did not come into use until the eighteenth century, during the Tokugawa. (For a discussion of obi embroidery, see Chapter 2).

The embroidery designing done on the kosode was both figurative and geometrical, and it was conceived as a single and complete decorative composition. The robes were literally works of art and were so admired by their owners that special display racks of ebony, polished bamboo, lacquerwork, or ivory were made to hang and exhibit the kosode in its open-arm position; the most prized robes of a family were shown in this way to admiring friends or visitors. Intended to be enjoyed from all sides, the kosode had a continuously unified design motif reaching around the sides from front to back and thus had four distinct viewpoints and a pleasing, harmonious visual impact, regardless of the direction from which it was seen. Designs were of startling originality and unending variety: There were never two alike, for each robe was a completely original, singular, custom-made production. When a patron ordered a kosode for himself, he had the satisfaction of knowing there was no other garment in the world like it. It was indisputably chic.

The Momoyama kosode designers were masters of bravura execution and daring artistic concept. They refused to be restricted by any limitation of form or tailoring, and the motifs either ignore the garment idea entirely and flow boldly across it (Fig. C-17) or incorporate the tailored form into the design, making the robe shape conform to the design, rather than vice versa, as was done on the dragon robe (Fig. 4-19). The effects achieved by such artistic boldness and daring are virtually breathtaking, and resulted in a tremendously modern, far less formal creation than that of the Chinese dragon robe. The thrilling originality and artistic liberation of the Momoyama kosode designers marked the be-

Fig. 4-6. Kosode. Multicolor embroidery of stem, long and short, satin stitches in pastel-toned silk yarns on gold *nuihaku* ground. Japan, Momoyama period. Courtesy of the Metropolitan Museum of Art, Pulitzer Bequest.

ginning of a new color and design consciousness that was to reach around the world and ensure the place of Japan in art history. But besides being the equivalent of a cultural and artistic renaissance, the Momoyama period gave birth to a textile industry so creative that it threatened to rival even the prolific artistry of China!

What brought about this vital upsurge of creativity, this efflorescence of mature Japanese art? Strangely enough, the stimuli were largely military and political. By the end of the sixteenth century, Japan was parceled into the control of feudal landlords and barons, the *daimyo,* who had considerable armies of samurai warriors to back up their claims to power. The most powerful of these warlords—Oda Nobunaga (1534–1582), Toyotomi Hideyoshi (1536–1598), and Tokugawa Ieyasu (1542–1616)—were later to become regents who successively unified the country and ruled it (in the guise of protecting it), in fact if not in appearance, while the emperor remained a mere figurehead. The intense rivalry of the *daimyo* in time became a power struggle that was more symbolic

Fig. 4-7. *Geisha* by Kuniyoshi. Hanging scroll, color on silk. Japan, Tokugawa period. Courtesy of the Museum of Fine Arts, Boston, Bigelow Collection.

than actual. A hectic competition for the trappings of wealth, prestige, and influence took the form of cultural and artistic sophistication, and of patronage of the arts. Extreme wealth, derived from conquests abroad and the discovery of gold deposits in medieval Japan, enabled the *daimyo* to spare no expense in the pursuit of prestige and the symbols of affluent power, and this was reflected typically by their elegance of costume and the lavish furnishing and decoration of their gigantic castles and manor baronies.

Flamboyant, extravagant, hedonistic, the vigorous Momoyama patronage of the arts supplied both the funds and the inspiration that were to completely transform the Japanese textile industry into a whirlwind of production and unprecedented creativity. Encouraged to be daring and dramatic, the textile designers, inspired by their new liberation and support, explored every technique known or possible in the fiber arts, every facet of media or materials that could be employed in the designing and embroidery of a robe or a fabric. Remarkable, innovative combinations of weaving, embroidery, appliqué, various forms of tie-dyeing and shaded dyeing, even hand painting of fabrics and the use of gold or silver foil grounds *(nuihaku),* all came into play, a dazzling display of virtuosity, in the conceptualization and creation of the kosode.

Many of the finest examples of kosode embroidery come from the highly decorated robes of the Noh theater (Fig. C-16). The Noh plays are a series of traditional, highly stylized, ritual dramas laden with tragically poignant, mysterious, mystical overtones. Generally they are based on moral themes taken from history, poetry, or legend. The splendor of the costumes, heightened by the effects of masks, mime, stylized ritual movement, and song, were designed to create a sense of unreality, to lead the audience into a shimmering dimension of spiritual beauty. The thickly encrusted brocades and embroideries of the robes created stiff, angular lines evocative of the purest kind of linear art, minimizing the forms of the actors' bodies beneath them and adding to the overall effects of a phantasmic aesthetic realm, the portrayals of visions, ghosts, and spirits. The decorated robes are so vital to the presentation of the plays that the Noh cannot be considered without their inclusion. Other Japanese drama, the comic Kyogen theater, for example, is more earthy and uses less stylized language and gesture, as well as more everyday, informal robes. In the Noh, the decorated kosode has the important purpose of adding to the experience of a beautiful supernatural world of the spirit.

In the beginning, Noh robes had been the gifts of the court, presentations of their own garments made by the shoguns to their favorite actors, who wore them in their roles. However, by the time of the Momoyama the creation of the robes had become the province of the professional embroidery designer, and the Noh kosode cannot be considered representative of the costumes worn by the shoguns of that period, since they are, for the most part, theatrically exaggerated. The Noh kosode became a special work of art, with the embroidery designers expending their most creative energy upon it. Even the nature of Noh gave their artistry a supreme outlet: extravagantly lavish, luxuriantly embroidered robes and fabric weaves that would have been inappropriate elsewhere found complete artistic freedom there. The designers took every advantage of that fact, pushing the limits of artistic imagery from extremes of the most dynamic, colorful design impact carried to its utmost potential, to contrasting whispers of exquisitely restrained, poetic, spiritual delicacy.

The embroidery needle was, once more, the artist's brush that painted the remarkable Noh motifs. Every known needlework resource was brought to bear to bring these resplendent costumes to life; the amount of skill, patience, and sheer artistic ingenuity that went into them is truly astonishing, and they will always remain among the great masterworks of Japan. Typically, as in most Oriental craftwork, they are usually unsigned, their makers anonymous. Some may have been the work of single individuals; others were probably a team effort, produced by many embroiderers working in concert in professional studios, sometimes requiring two or more years to complete a single robe.

Throughout the Noh kosode motifs there is a characteristic Japanese blending of the symbols of nature and man (Figs. 4-9, 4-10, and 4-16): fans and climbing clematis scrolls; chrysanthemums and thatched flower baskets; paulownia leaves and bamboo grass interlaced with stripes; gold foil grounds covered with snow-laden plaintain bushes; reeds and waterfowl combined with silver foil medallions. But floral or geometric designs are found alone on the robes also, the latter often seen on blue and white grounds with brown, red, blue, or yellow stripes, as well as many other color combinations. Typical mixed floral designs depict hydrangeas, maple leaves, and chrysanthemums floating

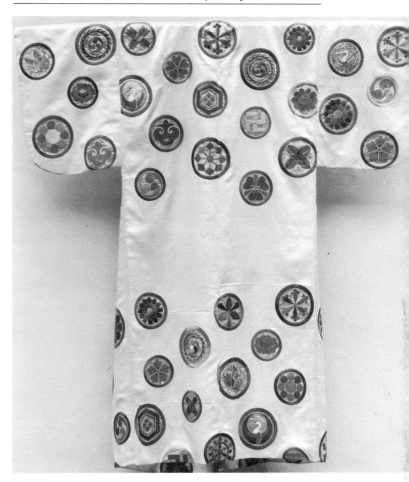

Fig. 4-8. Noh theater kosode. Design of large scattered crests in laidwork, stem and satin stitches; pastel-toned yarns in pinks, greens, yellows, blues, strawberry on white satin ground. Japan, Tokugawa period. Courtesy of the Metropolitan Museum of Art, Mrs. H. O. Havemeyer Bequest.

over fields of orange, white, or coffee brown, interrupted by gossamer, stylized clouds; butterflies and herons cling to willow and plum tree branches, startlingly patterned against radiant mists of gold leaf. Although stylized in drawing and design, these natural effects seem as fresh and lovely as nature itself, for they effectively express its essential spirit.

Many of the design motifs that appear on the kosode and *furisode* are of Chinese origin, but most have undergone a complex aesthetic development into Japanese style. Japanese figurative design work is far more stylized than the Chinese manner, the latter utilizing somewhat more realism and detail. Familiar Taoist motifs, the phoenix, crane, and heron, appear in kosode designs, but while the Buddhist lotus can be found in earlier Japanese sculpture, it never appears in any Japanese textile that is extant today. Probably its re-

Fig. 4-9. Kosode. Designs of fans, squares, wisteria leaves, and flowers in combinations of stem and satin stitches and *nuihaku*. Japan, Tokugawa period, eighteenth century. Courtesy of the Museum of Fine Arts, Boston, gift of William Sturgis Bigelow.

Fig. 4-10. Noh theater kosode. Thunder-line ground pattern with over-embroideries of paulownia leaves and vines in stem and satin stitches. Japan, Edo period, eighteenth century. Royal Ontario Museum, Toronto, gift of Mrs. Edgar J. Stone.

Fig. 4-11. Noh theater kosode. Design of water lines and flowers in *nuihaku* over-embroidered with harmonizing flower design in satin stitch. Japan, Tokugawa period, early nineteenth century. The Metropolitan Museum of Art, Pulitzer Fund, 1932.

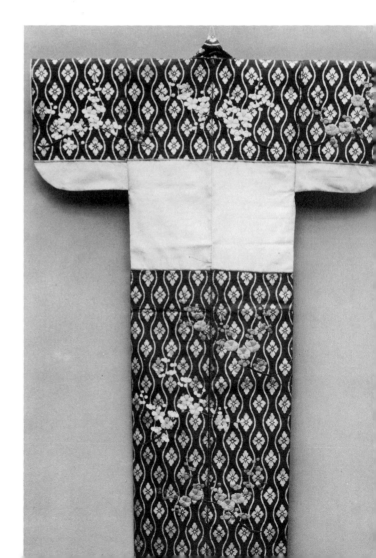

Fig. 4-12. Kosode. Designs of flowering plants, maple leaves, and water in gold *nuihaku*. Japan, Tokugawa period, late eighteenth century. The Metropolitan Museum of Art, Rogers Fund, 1958.

Fig. 4-13. Kosode. Designs of multicolor fans and snow crystals on ivory-colored silk ground. Japan, Tokugawa period, middle eighteenth century. Royal Ontario Museum, Toronto.

ligious significance was too revered in Japanese Buddhism for it to be thought appropriate on costume, although the figure was common on textiles and costumes of the Chinese, who were no less reverent. Civil and judicial symbols, such as appear on the dragon robe, are also less in evidence on the kosode, except for the heraldic crest designs. Such crests were designatory of the powerful family hierarchies and clans of medieval Japan, and of the samurai class (Fig. 4-15).

The Japanese love flowers and flower designs were very important in all of their figurative embroidery. Invariably they are expressed with the exquisite good taste and studied restraint that characterized their textile arts. Appreciated for their poetic and artistic value, flowers and flower designs were also important in Japanese domestic life, and much of their artistic significance was directly related to this importance in the home. Besides those mentioned earlier, the flowers found most often in textiles include the cherry, plum, bush clover, wisteria, peony, and chrysanthemum. The stylized peony, paulownia, and chrysanthemum were, of course, originally Chinese classic figures that had been adapted to Japanese expression.

Tree and bird designs were other favorite kosode and *furisode* embroidery motifs. Among the former, the most important were the pine, bamboo, yew, wisteria, red maple, and the popular flowering cherry and plum, which are very beautiful and most cherished in Japan (Fig. C-20). Certain symbolic combinations were traditional in some tree motifs. For example, the pine, bamboo, and plum, when used together, were called "The Three Friends," while the plum, bamboo, orchid, and chrysanthemum in combination were known as "The Four Gentlemen." Both of these sets were symbolic of virtuous character and were also considered lucky emblems. Tree designs were also often executed in close relationship with vining or twining flowering plants, such as the clematis. While bird motifs are not seen as frequently as in Chinese embroideries, nor as realistically depicted, the ancient Chinese influence nevertheless appears in their Japanese counterparts: the phoenix, crane, heron, mandarin duck, grouse, plover, falcon, and many others.

Supplementary figurative designs found in Japanese kosode embroidery with Chinese origins are the traditional stylized wave motif (Fig. 4-12), and the stylized cloud, as well as the dragon design, but even these were given a distinctly Japanese touch, their method of stylization being much more

Fig. 4-14. Ceremonial robe *(uchikake)* with padded hem. Design of clouds, banners, phoenixes, flowers, cranes, fans, dragons, waves, and various geometrical motifs in painted, dyed, and embroidered mixed techniques. Japan, Tokugawa period, late nineteenth century. The Metropolitan Museum of Art, Fletcher Fund, 1935.

Fig. 4-15. Wedding robe. Family crests, phoenixes, leaves, and flowers in long and short, stem, and satin stitches on black silk ground with red padded hem. Japan, Tokugawa period, nineteenth century. Length, 72 inches (183 cm.). The Metropolitan Museum of Art, gift of Mrs. John D. Rockefeller, Jr., 1937.

Fig. 4-16. Noh theater kosode. Design of swallows and bouquets on patterned silver *nuihaku* ground in long and short, stem, and satin stitches. Navy blues, cobalt, black, white, touches of pink. Japan, Tokugawa period, middle seventeenth century. Courtesy of the Museum of Fine Arts, Boston, gift of William Sturgis Bigelow.

patterned than Chinese techniques. The stylized wave, for example, only faintly evokes its Chinese parentage, while the dragon, which was not an imperial symbol in Japan, has a leaner look and is more often shown in profile.

Momoyama textile designers were also masters of geometric design. Even though some Chinese influence was inescapable, most kosode geometrics were highly original, achieving a breadth of concept and variety unheard of in the formal Chinese classic concept. However, designs of strictly Chinese influence were reflected in their Japanese counterparts, as in the *sayagata,* based on the swastika/thunder-line combination; the swastika itself; the checkerboard figure; the Buddhist wheel, called the "treasure wheel," or *rimbo;* various Chinese scroll figures, and the hemp leaf design. Many of the highly varied trellis motifs found in Japanese embroidery were also derived from Chinese figures of the same type.

Certain other geometrics in kosode embroidery were more originally Japanese. Examples of these are the patterned lozenges; the *kagome* (basket-work) pattern; the *komon* "small repeats"; *yamagata* mountain motifs; *kanze-mizu* ("flowing water") techniques, and the various tortoise-shell grids, especially of the *shokko* type. The *rai* (lightning) pattern seems to be an original version of a broken thunder line, as are such types as the *tatewaku* ("vertical seething") and *tomoe* (comma) motifs. The Japanese tortoise-shell grid has a very bold, dignified sumptuosity about it, largely because of the solidity of its connected, powerful hexagons. While lozenge designs were not a strictly Japanese invention, they were unique in the way they were used in Japan, a highly original method of patterning that suggested delicate purity. In historical Japan, such figures had feminine associations.

A special area of kimono embroidery was the unique family crest designs, which were printed in the fabric and often embroidered. A scattered style of large crests (shown in the Noh robe in Fig. 4-8) became popular in the Edo period, but most crests were small, not more than one inch in diameter, and were worn only on the upper chest, back, and both sleeves of ceremonial robes for special occasions, such as the *uchikake* wedding robe (Fig. 4-15). Very delicate stitchery was required for such small work, and most examples are in satin, couching, or stem stitches.

The decorative motifs found in crest designs number in the hundreds. Some, such as the chrysanthemum and pine, were more popular than others and have a complicated history. The sixteen-petal chrysanthemum, for example, had been used as early as the Heian period for clothing and furniture patterns. By the Kamakura, the chrysanthemum had become symbolic of honor and authority, and came into use by the imperial family as its crest. Various court nobles, feudal lords, and retainers of the shoguns also appropriated the chrysanthemum crest during the Edo period, but by 1869 its provision was finally reserved by decree for the imperial family, and it has remained an imperial symbol and crest ever since then.

The pine remains green throughout the year, hardily enduring the icy winds and snows of winter, and for such symbolic reasons it was a popular design in Japan, appearing on many fabrics, on furniture, and on many crests. The cones, branches, and needles of the pine were shown alone or together on the crests and in a three-tiered type like the one shown in our stitchery example (part 2, Fig. 4-23). While often expressed as a central motif, pines were also represented with other trees like the plum or bamboo, or with wildlife, such as the turtle and crane.

The turtle is also found alone on crest designs. It is a long-lived creature and therefore an enduring symbol of longevity, and enjoys a consistent history in Oriental mythology also. A Taoist legend relates that the eternal island, Feng Lai, the home of the immortals, rests on the back of a gigantic floating turtle. The sea turtles were thought to be messengers of the gods among the simple Japanese peasants, and many small fishing villages in Japan still wait for the arrival of the big turtles in their seasonal migrations to shore, where the people catch them, give them sake to drink, and let them return to the sea, they hope happier than before! Other popular and important motifs on crests were the wild geese *(kari-mon)* figures, the flowering iris, the lightning design, the orchid, and the *katabami-mon,* the lovely flower of the wood sorrel. Crest designs also demonstrated the curved-line techniques at which the Japanese were so adept, and some of these include the *ume* (plum blossom) and *sakura* (cherry blossom) motifs. The latter are extremely ancient figures, dating back to the tenth-century (Nara) epoch.

The military power that had been concentrated successively in the hands of Nobunaga, Hideyoshi,

and Tokugawa Ieyasu at last fell to Ieyasu upon the death of Hideyoshi in 1598. By 1603, Ieyasu had succeeded in reviving the ancient institution of shogunates, having himself been appointed shogun by the emperor and assuming tacit control of the country. He established a family dynasty and a strict feudal government at Edo (now Tokyo) that was to endure for the following three centuries, ushering in the epoch that marked the end of the Momoyama period and that took his name, the Tokugawa period (1615–1868). Established as shogun, Ieyasu monopolized the role of the court and enjoyed virtually unlimited power. The textile industry, however, was further strengthened rather than threatened by this transition, and the great traditions of the Momoyama embroidery designers were carried into the Tokugawa with an intensified support by the shogunate, a continuing interest in the Noh theater, and the rise of a prosperous and affluent merchant class, who demanded the best in kosode and *furisode* embroidery, print, and weaving styles (Fig. 4-17).

At this point, a long period of isolationism seized Japan as a reaction against Christian missionaries from Portugal and the later internal conflicts that beset China out of Manchu domination and Western imperialism. Aware of the external dangers to her own sovereignty, Japan was to cut off all contact with the world for 253 years, regarding the West with violent distrust. Sealed within its own culture, the Tokugawa period was nevertheless extremely fortunate economically, and, as a result, Japan's original and distinguished textile arts retained, for the most part, their magnificent quality. The Tokugawa designers successfully continued the unique aesthetic gains and artistic traditions established during the Momoyama, and the early phase is practically indistinguishable from the latter (Fig. 4-5).

The woodblock print became very popular in Tokugawa Japan. The great masters of Japanese painting—Sharaku, Korin, Utamaro, Hokusai, and others—lived and worked during this time, producing the dramatic innovations of color, design, and draftsmanship that were to have such impact on Western art when Japan finally opened her ports once again to the world. In addition to their woodblock prints and paintings, these same artists also turned their genius to textile designing, creating hundreds of original designs for *furisodes* and kosodes, which were instantly snapped up by eager collectors. These same woodblock prints provide us

Fig. 4-18. Kosode. Chrysanthemum and water wave design. Silk brocade and embroidery. Japan, Momoyama period, seventeenth century. The Metropolitan Museum of Art, gift of Howard Mansfield, 1936.

with a very comprehensive record of the costume and textile embroidery and design methods of the period. If we can imagine people actually wearing these marvelous, colorful robes in customary use in public or to social functions, some idea can be gained of the incredible richness, variety, and sophistication of the many-faceted, beauty-loving society of eighteenth- and nineteenth-century Japan.

By 1750 the designer's interest had shifted to the long-sleeved *furisode* (Fig. 4-14), although the wide obi had not yet come into use. The beauty of these designs and their embroidery decorations, depicted in and publicized by the woodblock prints, fired the popularity of the *furisode* to new levels, even though the classic kosode was still used in the Noh theater. Such prints were made and sold by the millions to the populace, and hand-painted catalogs containing samples of available one-of-a-kind designs sold by tailors and embroidery or textile studios were available for selection. In this way, the latest fashions of the geisha courtesans and the court came into circulation among the people, and they were in constant demand by an avid market,

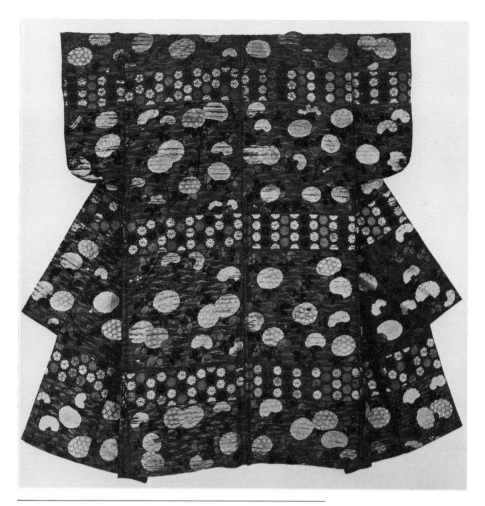

Fig. 4-19. Noh theater kosode. Hydrangeas and stylized clouds design in petal-patterned laidwork, stem stitch, and *nuihaku*. Japan, Momoyama period. From *Japanese Embroidery* by Mutsuko Imai, Mainichi Newspapers, Tokyo. Courtesy of Nagao Museum, Tokyo.

eager to be seen in the most chic styles. Women's dress had become such an important art form, because of the genius of the textile designers, that the watercolor painters studied them for design ideas and faithfully copied them in every detail in the woodblock prints. In other periods of Japanese history, such as the Fujiwara or the Momoyama, the purchase of such fine dress had been restricted to the aristocracy or the *daimyo* class, but now the rise of a very affluent merchantry and middle class enabled the general population to easily afford the same elegant costumes. Changes of fashion and new design creations came with dizzying speed, creating a panic among buyers to collect the latest renditions. As mentioned earlier, even the painters turned to the creation of *furisode* designs, competing openly with the textile designers and em-

broiderers, who were, as their work proves, themselves fine artists of the highest order.

A new freedom, expanding upon Momoyama art, came to typify most of Tokugawa textile art, in which unlimited variety of design, daring and vivid color, and the use of powerful visual patterns were foremost (Fig. C-17). When economic restrictions created a scarcity of the necessary raw materials, the designers relied on sheer decorative ingenuity, using embroidery more extensively than weaving designs, stencil-printing dyed fabrics, and incorporating stunning tie-dye and batik effects with these media. As the isolationist policies of the government caused greater restrictions on the importation of Chinese silks, the craftsmen turned to native materials. Relying more heavily on Japanese silk and less on Chinese brocades and damasks, they improved or revived old weaving techniques, such as the beautiful *karaori* brocade, making new and more beautiful creations with ever simpler means and materials.

The use of stencils for woodblock fabric prints greatly increased the manufacturing ease and speed of production of the Tokugawa textile industry without the loss of charm usually inherent in the hand-finished piece. One method of preserving such artistic integrity was the over-embroidery of printed fabrics with complementary designs that immeasurably enriched the surface and artistic quality of the robe. For this reason, the introduction of block printing on fabrics shortly after the turn of the eighteenth century greatly increased the quantities of fine textiles made available to the public, but without any significant loss of quality. While such developments were a form of mass production, they cannot be considered comparable to the destruction of craftsmanship by the use of machines in modern commercial methods, for the artistic integrity of the designers, and the general high level of public taste, prevented most effectively the decline of standards or a strictly commercial approach.

The Noh theater continued to receive the enthusiastic support of the shogun and the aristocracy during the Tokugawa period. Official performances in the special Noh theater of Nagoya Castle were given for the shogun, Ieyasu, and countless additional performances for his personal pleasure on the private stage of Nagoya, as well as in many secondary castles and manors elsewhere. The contents of Ieyasu's storeroom at Sunpu Castle, following his death in 1616, revealed an inventory of many of the properties and robes necessary for the production of extensive Noh dramas, including fifty-eight kosodes, thirteen obi, fourteen Noh masks, and over seventy other accessories and musical instruments. Later collections left by the Owari family clan included over six hundred robes, masks, musical instruments, and other props. The kosode fared less well as an artistic production during the later Tokugawa, however, because of an increasing reliance on brocades, a broadened dependence on *nuihaku* (gold leaf), less embroidery, and a reversion to traditional prototypes rather than original creation, becoming somewhat stereotyped and losing some of the vigor of the original Momoyama industry, a factor that probably contributed to its decline in popularity during the Tokugawa. Although the Tokugawa Noh kosode never experienced the decadent fate that befell the later Chinese

dragon robe, thanks to its consistently high artistic quality, the diminution of a certain vitality was perhaps inevitable.

With the arrival of Commodore Perry, the gun-toting, good-will ambassador of the West, Japan reluctantly agreed to open her gates to Western trade. By 1854 she had signed agreements with the United States and the other Western nations. In the meantime, internal dissension related to the fading feudal system and the pressure of the merchant class to abandon isolation, foreign urgings to trade, and the reinstitution of the emperor as the national leader and symbol of imperial Japan led to the decline and fall of the shogunate, and with it came the end of the Tokugawa regime in 1868.

The reassumption of the imperial throne by the emperor effectively marked the end of historical Japan and the attrition of her textile arts renaissance. By 1910 she had adapted to a military-industrial society and had assumed an imperialistic stance in world affairs. With the onset of machine production and the modern age, the rich history of Japanese embroidery came to an end with the closing days of the Tokugawa period.

The main distinctions between Chinese and Japanese costume embroidery, in their mature periods, lie in their national styles, which are as characteristic as individual handwriting. An omnipresent artistic and social symbolism is less evident in Japanese work than was found in China, although Japanese artistic conventions and shorthand stylizations were used to an equal degree, and

---

Fig. 4-20. Noh theater kosode. Peonies and leaves in laidwork with stem stitch; *nuihaku* trellis design on red satin ground. Japan, Edo period, eighteenth century. Royal Ontario Museum, Toronto, gift of Mrs. Edgar J. Stone.

even enlarged upon by them. Chinese design had more strictly formal and informal elements in a codified sense than was usual in Japanese embroidery design (see Chapter 8), while the Japanese tended to extremes of free expression and far more latitude of concept. In color, the Japanese usage leaned to soft pastel tones, whereas Chinese color was rich and opulent and Korean color was bright and vivid.

In the main, Chinese work can be typified by its power, symbol-laden content, and grandeur of imperial elegance, while Japanese robe embroidery is more delicate, restrained, lyrical, more purely poetic in an artistic sense. Both are certainly equal in quality; both achieved a mastery in the textile arts that is without any precedent in the history of art. But like the Chinese artist, the Japanese embroiderer sought to paint with the needle, and in painting the design a very special national style emerged, along with other differences of stitchery and technique, as well as some of the startling technical innovations of the Momoyama period, which we will now consider.

JAPANESE KIMONO TECHNIQUES

The distinctions between Chinese and Japanese embroidery styles become much more obvious as one more closely approaches and compares Japanese techniques, even though the embroiderers of both countries used the same stitches. An exception to this was the seed stitch, which had comparatively less use in Japan. More damasks and prints were used in the ground fabric of the kimono, and more of these grounds show through the embroidery. Whereas much untwisted yarn was used in China, and tightly twisted yarns in Korea, Japanese embroiderers used loosely twisted threads. Differences of cut and tailoring also emerge: the ch'i-fu hung straight and was a rather loose, flowing garment, whereas the kimono had a tighter waist and was worn with a belt or sash, the obi. The ceremonial furisode or uchikake also had a heavy padded hem that helped it to train on the floor, which the dragon robe did not. Korean costume embroiderers used metal thread only infrequently, but Japanese

craftsmen used it as often as the Chinese, as well as the gold-leaf nuihaku technique, of which a description follows. Finally, the kimono is not the equivalent of the dragon robe, nor was it a court robe exclusively, for it was worn by all kinds and classes of people. A dragon robe as such was never used in Japan, although dragons do occasionally appear in some kimono designs.

Example 1: *Nuihaku* (Gold-Leaf Appliqué)
(Fig. 4-21)

Some of the most dramatic effects on the kosode were achieved through the nuihaku gold-leaf technique, a Japanese innovation that rose to a peak of creativity during the Momoyama period.

To apply nuihaku, which was usually done on a satin ground of dark blue, dark brown, maroon, or purple as a stunning contrast, a stencil for the design was first cut in a heavyweight oiled paper equivalent to modern stencil paper, and a loose paste was squeegeed over and through this stencil, leaving the wet paste design imprinted on the fabric. The stencil was then removed, and gold or silver leaf, which came in thin sheets of various sizes as it does today, was pressed onto the wet paste areas, adhering to the fabric. After the paste was thoroughly dry, the area was burnished lightly, and the gold leaf fell away from any unpasted area. The effect of the gilded areas on the design, as they lay in contrast to the dark, scintillating complementary colors of the dyed silk ground, was extremely striking, not to mention the audacious brilliance achieved as the light shimmered over delicious gold, silver, and satin textures. The beauty of this original, tremendously rich technique can hardly be overstated. We can only imagine how magnificent the robes treated in this way were when seen in the sun of landscaped gardens or the dark interiors of feudal castles.

Strictly speaking, nuihaku was always used in combination with embroidery, being part of a range of gold-foil appliqué techniques called surihaku. Forerunners of both had appeared in Japan as far back as the Nara period (A.D. 618–906) and were probably influenced by the stamped-gold process that had come from China and Korea during the early Muromachi, and which was similar in technique. Today, *nuihaku* is still used on the robes of the modern Noh theater.

The *nuihaku* technique shown in Figure 4-21 was done in a drop-out process; that is, the ground, which was dark red satin, was entirely covered with gold foil in a negative print, by first applying frisket templates (A) in the shape of the bird and flower designs onto the fabric, and then covering whole ground (B) with rice paste. The friskets were then removed, the masked design areas would drop out as dry areas (C), and the gold foil was applied to the still wet paste, in this case, the entire robe. The design patterns were thus left in untouched satin ground, and when the gold leaf was completely dry, these areas were ready to receive their embroidery designs and subsequent stitchery (D).

Example 2: Peony Design, Noh Theater Kosode, Japan, Tokugawa Period
(Figs. C-19 and 4-22)

Although peonies were usually handled with satin or long and short stitch, this example shows a varied technique, done entirely in layer stitch with stem stitch accents. The layer stitch was simpler and easier to do than long and short, and the presence of broad areas of *nuihaku* on this particular robe may have contributed to its use, since much working over the gold leaf was risky.

Whereas long and short stitch follows the individual shape and contour of the leaves, and uses two or three shades of color gradation (sometimes with

Fig. 4-21. Example 1: *nuihaku* template technique and laid-work stitchery from Noh theater kosode (Fig. C-19).

Fig. 4-22. Example 2: peony design from Noh theater kosode (Fig. C-19), showing layer and stem stitches.

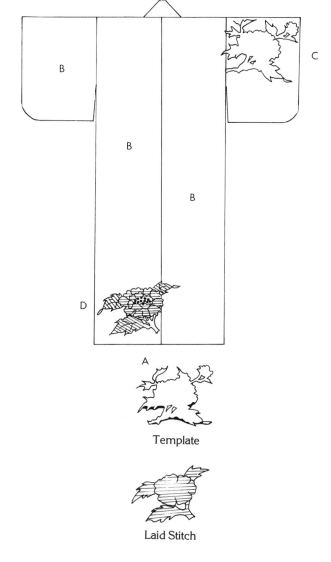

Template

Laid Stitch

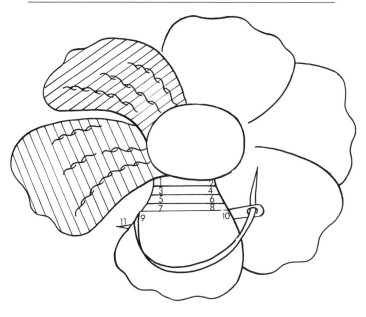

additional padding for a three-dimensional realism), the layer stitch technique covers an area solidly from side to side at right angles, without following the leaf shape. The overlaying of the stem stitch served a double purpose: It expressed the veins and textural direction of the leaf, and it held the layer stitch secure. In this way, artistic and technical purposes were accomplished at the same time.

Layer Stitch

A. The needle comes up at 1, enters the fabric at 2, emerges at 3, reenters again at 4, and reemerges at 5. This process is repeated until the particular design area (in this case, the petals) is entirely covered.

B. The stem stitch directional accents or veins are then done over the layer stitching in the manner shown in the drawing.

The scroll designs around the phoenixes (their tails) are in a layer stitch base that has been couched with a much lighter-weight thread at opposite angles to the layer stitch, each holding stitch staggered by halves across the surface in order to avoid overlong stitches. This created a somewhat patternized design on these figures.

An interesting design feature on this robe is the way the motifs have been crafted to overlap the arm seams, thus creating a total design harmony and continuity without interference by the garment shape.

Example 3: Pine Crest Design, Japan, Tokugawa Period (Fig. 4-23)

In this example, we again find the economical use of stitchery to accomplish both a technical and an artistic goal. The underlying layer stitch is held secure by the doubled strength of the metal thread holding stitch. The cross-diagonal gold thread stitchery in turn presents an intriguing color and design accent against the color of the layer-stitched yarn beneath it, and both are, in turn, harmonized and interrelated by the holding stitch color.

What was actually done here was that metal thread was couched onto the layer stitch with an appropriate color, red. Evenly spaced, lightweight

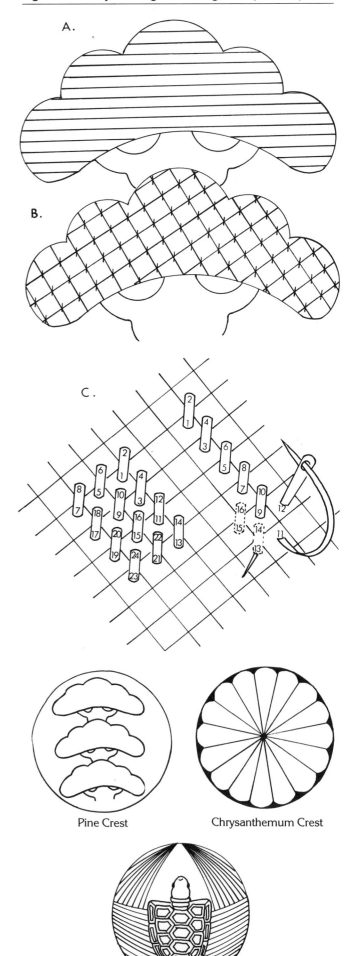

Fig. 4-23. Example 3: diagonal holding stitch (laidwork).

Pine Crest

Chrysanthemum Crest

Tortoise Crest

metal threads were laid diagonally on the fabric over the previously finished layer stitch. These metal threads were then overlaid with second diagonal lines that formed the diamond shapes shown in Figure 4-23B. At each crossing point of the diamond pattern two threads were gathered, either vertically or horizontally, and a holding stitch was made on the intersection of the diagonals in the following way.

Diagonal Holding Stitch with Gold Thread

The needle comes up at 1, enters at 2, comes up again at 3, and reenters the material at 4. This process is repeated at every intersection of each diagonal.

Each line was begun at the nearest X point to the last intersection finished, working either vertically or horizontally. This kind of metal thread holding stitch is very versatile, and it was in fact used on many types of design. (See Fig. 4-23B.)

Example 4: Incense Wrapper Design, Kosode, Japan, Momoyama Period
(Figs. C-16 and 4-24)

The incense wrappers in this design are the elongated shapes seen at the upper left and right shoulders, right sleeve, middle waist, and lower left corner. The incense wrappers are depicted in three segments in the design, which were all embroidered with untwisted yarns.

The lower third of each wrapper is done in satin and stem stitches in a variegated floral pattern, the tiny dark flowers adding variety and a delightful accent and contrast to the lighter-toned blossoms. The white border on the lower third is in diagonal satin stitch, while a dark stem stitch sharply accents the lower contours.

The middle thirds are the ground color of dark brown satin, which variously shows flower and water-line accents done with hand-painted silver. The ferns and leaves in this area were stitched directly onto the ground in satin stitch. (Note how effectively the open ground color contrasts with the stitchery on both sides of it, and the *nuihaku* next to it, a feast of shapes, colors, and textures, all set in close juxtaposition to one another.)

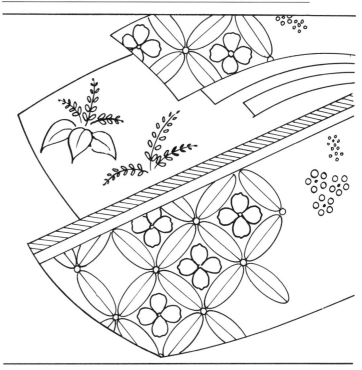

Fig. 4-24. Example 4: stitchery details of incense wrapper design (Fig. C-16).

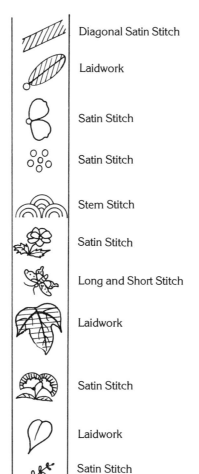

	Diagonal Satin Stitch
	Laidwork
	Satin Stitch
	Satin Stitch
	Stem Stitch
	Satin Stitch
	Long and Short Stitch
	Laidwork
	Satin Stitch
	Laidwork
	Satin Stitch

The upper third of the wrappers repeats the stitchery of the lower third, both the design and the textural repetition adding to the curling, three-dimensional, wrap-around effect.

The *nuihaku* on this robe was laid in the same technique demonstrated in Example 1, with the incense wrappers, the paulownia leaf masses, and some of the dark individual leaves being allowed to drop out. The leaves of white, blue, vermilion, and green were then executed in both satin and layer stitches for variety, and all of the leaf veins figured upon them in stem stitch. Here and there a leaf has been left as the dark satin ground, with the stem stitch veins being rendered in a contrasting, lighter color. The trellis designs seen on the left sleeve, the middle back, and the lower right panel were also dropped out of the *nuihaku* in fine lines ⅛ inch (4 mm.) in width, and heavier lines ½ inch (14 mm.) in

width. Satin stitch was then used on the thicker lines, and stem stitch on the finer lines and the vines that entwine among the trellis bars.

The carefully placed incense wrappers, the three dominant areas of *nuihaku* behind the trellises, and the bold, flowing masses of leaves that ramble gaily across the robe in a strong diagonal pattern, all contribute to the masterful distribution of space and mass, balance, and sense of growing nature and subtle beauty, to make this kosode one of the greatest of Momoyama masterpieces.

In the next chapter we enter a little-known but equally important and beautiful branch of Oriental costume embroidery, the rare world of Korean stitchery, to encounter the most important robe in the life of a Korean young lady, the bridal robe.

5/ THE KOREAN BRIDAL ROBE

HISTORY AND AESTHETICS

The Korean bride was truly a queen on her wedding day, for her bridal robe (Fig. C-22) was derived from the robes of Korean queens of the Great Silla dynasty (A.D. 668–935). The female Korean imperial court robe *(wan-sam)* was itself based on T'ang styles of dress that became popular among the Silla nobility of the same period, and became the model for the traditional Korean bridal robe (*hwal-ot,* or "flower robe"), which was traditionally used by brides of all classes and social levels in historical Korea.

The Korean Great Silla was an epoch when the mighty Chinese (T'ang) textile industry came into flower, operating vast textile mills and shipping its fine silks all over the known world. Korea, at the very crossroads of Asia, had always been among the first recipients of Chinese progress, and she had always been eager to learn and incorporate those benefits into her own culture. Through frequent visits and cultural exchanges with the Chinese mainland, the Korean kings and their legations brought back to Korea the best China had to offer in the arts, which the industrious Koreans quickly assimilated and, in some cases, improved upon, producing the exemplary crafts objects for which Korea is famous. In turn, much of their crafts expertise and silk technology were funneled into Japan, their neighbor to the East, where Koreans had been constant visitors from an early period in history.

It was during such a cultural exchange with China, in A.D. 647–654 (Queen Jin Duk era) that Kim Chun Chu, emissary of Korea, became entranced by the beauty of the women's robes worn in the T'ang court. He returned home with many gifts of the latest T'ang fashions and other textile acces-

Fig. 5-1. *Taoist Immortals As Attendants upon P'ei Tou.* Framed scroll, color on silk. This painting shows Chinese *p'ao* style robes in use in Korea. Korea, Yi dynasty, c. fourteenth–fifteenth century. Courtesy of the Museum of Fine Arts, Boston, Bequest of Charles B. Holt.

Fig. 5-2. Temple procession. Detail of wall painting from the Tomb of the Twin Pillars. Early Korean costume and textile design styles. Korea, Three Kingdoms period (Koguryo), fifth–sixth century. From *Ancient Arts of Korea,* Department of Cultural Affairs, Seoul. Photo courtesy of the Korean Department of Cultural Affairs.

Fig. 5-3. Imperial woman's court jacket *(tang-ui).*

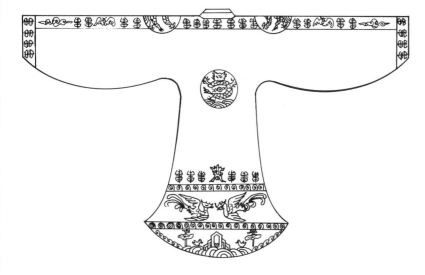

Fig. 5-4. Court jacket *(tang-ui)* worn over skirt *(chima).*

sories, including the *hwa-kwan (chock-du-ri).* These robes created an immediate sensation in the Korean court and were so popular that a Korean-style court dress based upon them quickly evolved and was to remain thereafter part of the traditional Korean court wardrobe. These were the *wan-sam* (literally, "round robe") and the informal court jacket, the *tang-ui,* both of which figured importantly in Korean costume history, the former becoming the inspiration for the traditional bridal robe, the latter the forerunner of the traditional *chima chogori,* a bolero *(chogori)* worn by Korean ladies over a long skirt *(chima)* (Fig. 5-5). Also, from this time on Korean imperial costume regulations permitted commoners to wear undergarments such as undertrousers, underskirts, and many embroidered accessories.

Fig. 5-5. *Chima chogori* with stamped border designs.

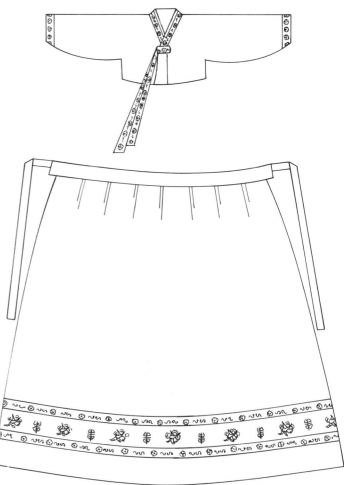

In the pre-Silla states of Korea, imperial ranking was protected by mandates forbidding the populace to wear imperial symbols, colors, or decorations, and this ban extended into the use of silk fabrics and embroidery. Such restrictions applied also to the nobility in some cases, and may have been one of the reasons why the simple white ramie garb of the common folk became a tradition in itself that still persists in Korea. Of all the Oriental countries, Korea has the most minimal costume embroidery, a possible throwback to the same restrictive traditions. The bridal robe is, of course, an exception to this.

For reasons that are still obscure, these imperial regulations relaxed somewhat during the early Great Silla dynasty, and it is from this period that the traditional embroidered bridal robe is believed to have evolved. Its close relationship to T'ang court styles seems to confirm this. An imperial decree may have permitted the robe of the queen to be used as the model for the commoner's bridal robe, but the exact manner of its development is unknown. That it was based upon female imperial robes was probably a clever political maneuver designed to placate the poor, to provide a medium of respect for the monarch, and to symbolize an ongoing harmony between the court and the people. Whatever the reasons, it was a popular gesture among the people, accepted willingly and established as a tradition. Known to have existed in its present form since at least the thirteenth century (Yi dynasty), the bridal robe is one of the most beautiful Korean creations.

On the wedding day, the careful dressing of the bride was a complicated procedure that required several hours of preparation, preceded by countless hours of embroidery, designing, and sewing. Over a pair of rather full, white silk undertrousers, called *sok-paji,* the bride wore three underskirts. The first was a slip of loose white silk. This was followed by a white hooped *chima* (skirt) worn high over the bosom. Next came a billowing blue silk *chima,* also worn high. After these skirts came the outer bridal *chima,* in brilliant red silk. Continuing the general layered look of the outfit, the bride next put on a bright yellow *chogori* (short bolero jacket) that had imperial symbols such as the phoenix, peonies, lotus, and stylized waves in stamped-gold designs at the cuff, collar, and vent borders. After the *chogori* came the luxuriant tailed robe of the bridal coat (Fig. C-22).

Over the red outer *chima,* which, like the

Fig. 5-6. Bridal robe *(hwal-ot)* (front view). Design of guardians, peonies, clouds, mountains, sacred fungus, in stem, long and short, and satin stitches on red satin ground; thunder-line borders in couched polychrome silk thread. Korea, Yi dynasty. Courtesy of the Folk Village Museum, Seoul.

chogori, had stamped gold designs of imperial symbols and waves rising about eight inches above the hem, the bride donned the ornate red robe that was the main feature of the costume. The bridal robe was cut in a vented jacket style, in exactly the same manner as the court *wan-sam,* with very full *p'ao* sleeves and two broad tails in front that lay against the *chima* at a point midway between knee and ankle. In back, a single broad, undivided tail fell to the same length. The formal outer *chima* beneath the robe trained to the rear on the floor. The robe was held in place by a long, embroidered sash that passed beneath the bosom and armpits and was tied at the center of the back in a large traditional bow, the tails of which lay over the wide rear tail of the robe. Usually made of red silk or satin, the robe was bountifully embroidered on the sleeves, cuffs, and tails with designs of ritual meaning.

An outstanding feature was the enormous *p'ao* sleeves, nearly three feet in diameter and cut in such a way that when held together they formed a striking embroidered picture—growing lotus flowers and their buds above stylized waves, a symbolic

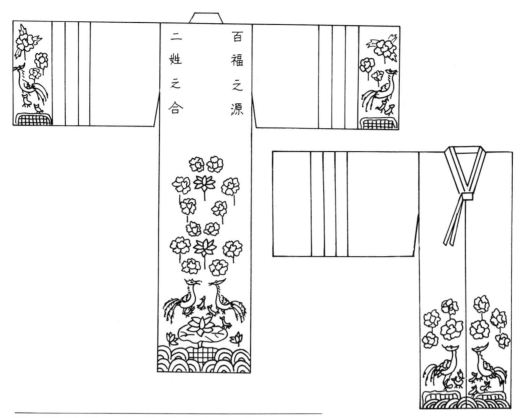

Fig. 5-7. Wedding robe *(hwal-ot)* showing front and back view design patterns and characters.

concept celebrating the miracle of life. Stitched in delicate pinks, greens, and soft blues on a white silk field, the sleeve picture extends from the edges of both cuffs to a width of from eight to twelve inches up each sleeve. When the sleeves were brought together, the composition became unified, and was more than two feet across its full width. This lovely, feminine effect was intensified by three vibrant color bands on each sleeve which flanked the central design on both sides and which symbolized good fortune for the bride. Where the color bands ended, embroidered flowers in bright pinks, yellows, greens, and purples covered the remaining, upper part of both sleeves and extended across the chest and rear shoulders, a dazzling display of brilliant color. Growing lotus flowers, peonies, and stylized waves were also stitched abundantly across the frontal and rear tails.

The bride's hair was braided into a bun in typical Korean style, and a dainty crown, the *chock-du-ri (hwa-kwan)* (Fig. 5-8), sat atop her head. The crown was ornately decorated in colored beadwork and was further embellished with gold and silver thread embroidery or stamped gold designs, with additional flower stitchery and pins of many sizes and shapes topped with jade, precious stones, or jewels.

Chinese techniques and Chinese classical influences are evident on the bridal robe, a witness to the popularity of Chinese art in ancient Korea. The stylized waves on the sleeve picture, for example, are reminiscent of those on the dragon robe and the mandarin square, while the placement of the lotus above the waves is typical of Buddhist observances. The peony, the Chinese symbol of summer and wealth, is designed and stitched in the Chinese style. The use of complex floral patterns on the upper sleeves of the robe follows Chinese decorative traditions, while the stylized wave designs of stamped gold on the *chima* and *chogori* are also recognizable as being in the Chinese manner. Finally, stamped gold process originated in China, invented there as early as the Chou dynasty.

Although Korea was not an eclectic culture in quite the same sense as Japan, a continual effort was made by the monarchy to effect a synthesis, or at least a reconciliation, of her art forms with those of imperial China. This emulation was partly politi-

Fig. 5-8. Bridal crown (*hwa kwan*). Geometric cut goldwork, silver, jade, seed pearls, coral, carnelian, and other semiprecious stones, seed pearl tassels, on black satin. Korea, Yi dynasty. Courtesy of the Institute of Folklore, Dan Kook University, Seoul.

cal: China represented a strong protective power for Korea; but it was also a matter of pride and self-respect: Chinese civilization was the ideal, the high point of culture in Old Asia, and while some of Korea's response to this intense influence may have been good-will gesturing, generally it was based upon a genuine admiration of Chinese art and culture. However, it should not be supposed that Korea either relinquished or was confused about her national identity, for this was clearly stable and secure. As a characteristic trait, Korean culture endured as strictly individual and autonomous down through the ages, despite many intrusions, invasions, and cultural influences from other countries.

Many purely Korean features are therefore also found on the bridal robe, two of the most prominent being the red, yellow, and blue sleeve band design and the vented jacket with tails. The bolero jacket *(chogori)*, worn with the bridal robe and the traditional lady's *chima chogori* outfit, is very originally Korean, for such jacket types are not worn anywhere in northern Asia. The lovely pictorial concept of the bridal sleeve design is also entirely Korean in origin, even though much of its symbolism came from China. I have been unable to find a pictorial sleeve design in this particular manner anywhere in Chinese or Japanese embroidery: It is unique to Korean art. The red, yellow, and blue band design has always been native to Korean culture and still appears on the Korean flag. It can also be found in many architectural ceiling designs dating from the Three Kingdoms period (57 B.C.–A.D. 668), from which time such color usages seem to date. Korean silk is especially fine and glossy, and has been thought to be the finest in Asia. Korean silk dyeing also deserves special mention, for the colors achieved on the bridal robe, the *chima chogori,* and other garments have a brilliant intensity, as well as a very lovely range of shades that are quite unlike any other in the Orient. In addition to their vividness and purity, Korean color combinations are also highly original in arrangement and contiguous placement with each other.

The groom's costume was also derived from a historical prototype, that of the imperial court official, denoted particularly by the mandarin square centered on the chest of his robe. The elegance of the groom's unembroidered, rich blue damask robe formed a perfect contrast to the vivid reds and yellows of the bride's costume. His outfit was completed by a distinguished hand-painted enamel belt and the black, traditional Korean court official's hat. (See Fig. 6-10.) The only embroidery on the groom's coat appears on the mandarin square that was placed on the chest and back, the ranking symbol being usually the Manchurian crane, insignia of a Korean official of the third rank.

Each of the Korean family ceremonies—funerals, puberty rites, memorial occasions—were attended by conventional symbolism and designated costume and color conventions, but the wedding (as in other parts of the world) had a special significance. In Korea, it was considered the bride's responsibility to present her husband with many sons, and much of the symbolism on the bridal robe is consequently related to fertility wishes for the new bride. There was also a general good will and protective affection proffered to the newlyweds by family and well-wishers, as well as an accompanying symbolism for happiness, good luck, and a long, abundant life together. All of these felicitations appear, in one form or another, in the embroidery symbolism of the bridal robe.

The two small figures flanking both sides of the collar on certain robes (Figs. 5-9 and 5-10) depict Buddhist guardian spirits. Executed in satin stitch,

Fig. 5-9. Bridal robe *(hwal-ot)*. Design of guardian figures with peach trees, characters, peonies, phoenixes, waves, and rocks in laidwork, stem, long and short, and satin stitches on red satin ground. Korea, Yi dynasty. Collection of Mr. and Mrs. Huh Dong Hwa, Seoul.

with stem stitch line work, the guardians are seen arising from the lotus, the Buddhist symbol of purity, to watch protectively over the newlyweds as they embark on the journey of life together. Mountains, the symbol of steadfastness and long life, are seen beneath the figures, while further down eight cloud motifs denote the celestial Buddhist realm. The peony and leaf designs on this robe are notably rich and abundant, those on the frontal tails and sleeves being rendered entirely in gradated satin stitch, with the mountains beneath them in radiating long and short stitch. The rectangular boxes that enclose the peonies on both the front view (Fig. 5-6) and the back (Fig. 5-12) are in couched metal thread versions of the Korean thunder line. The back view harmoniously reflects the frontal floral themes, with the insertion of a dominant pair of phoenixes *(feng-huang)*, the symbol of female nobility, presiding over the rear main panel, offset by growing water lilies in the lower third and some extremely vivid color stitchery and adroit designing in the rocks, waves, and sea of the lowest border motifs.

In Figures C-23 and C-24 we find a replica of an original Yi dynasty robe that was destroyed by fire in Chang-Dok Palace in Seoul in 1959. The accurate reconstruction work, supervised by Professor Joo Sun Suk of Dan Kook University, provides a fine in-

Fig. 5-10. Detail of bridal robe (Fig. 5-9). Guardian with peach tree and characters in laidwork, satin and stem stitches; couched silk contours; tightly twisted silk yarns on red satin ground. Korea, Yi dynasty. Collection of Mrs. and Mrs. Huh Dong Hwa, Seoul.

sight into an unusual and handsome historical example. The robe measures over 7 1/2 feet (234 cm.) from sleeve tip to sleeve tip, with an overall length of 5 feet (155 cm.). The sleeves are 33 inches (80.4 cm.) in diameter, and the width across the bust panel is 17 inches (40.3 cm.). The characters embroidered on the upper shoulders, loosely interpreted, mean "Happiness as Broad as the Sea—Life as Long as the Mountains." The pair of *feng-huang* phoenixes at the bottom front symbolizes nobility, but their cute little brood of eight babies (a symbolic Buddhist number) portends wishes of fertility for the new bride. The use of baby phoenixes is most unusual in Oriental embroidery, and one begins to suspect that here the typical wry Korean sense of humor is peeking through tradition.

The back view of the above garment (Fig. C-24) demonstrates an excellent example of Korean costume embroidery at its finest and shows what a splendid masterpiece this robe really is. Flowers, always a part of Oriental embroidery art, are important to the philosophy and aesthetic of Oriental life, but nowhere do we find them used with such overwhelming love and joyfulness, as if a hymn to life and nature were expressed by the sheer effulgence of color and vibrant design, which seems to literally surge upward, as nature itself does in the springtime. The composition has been worked on a

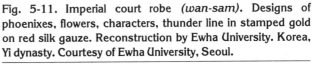

Fig. 5-11. Imperial court robe *(wan-sam)*. Designs of phoenixes, flowers, characters, thunder line in stamped gold on red silk gauze. Reconstruction by Ewha University. Korea, Yi dynasty. Courtesy of Ewha University, Seoul.

Fig. 5-12. Bridal robe (back view of Fig. 5-6). Designs of peonies, *feng-huang*, lotus, sacred fungus, waves, mountains in long and short, satin, stem stitches; thunder-line borders in couched polychrome silk threads. Korea, Yi dynasty. Courtesy of the Folk Village Museum, Seoul.

Fig. 5-13. Detail from bridal robe. Lotus, grouse, peony, phoenix, checkerboard, rocks, waves, in interlocking satin stitch, stem, and diagonal satin stitches; satin mounted on brocade silk. Korea, Yi dynasty. Crown copyright, Victoria and Albert Museum, London.

Fig. 5-14. Typical Korean embroidery techniques used on bridal robe. Phoenix, lotus, lotus leaves, sacred fungus, mountains, peach blossoms, flaming pearl designs. Korea, Yi dynasty. Collection of Mr. and Mrs. Huh Dong Hwa, Seoul.

damask satin ground, in long and short, satin, and diamond-trellis couching stitches. The regal white satin sleeve design repeats the frontal theme of the regal phoenix and her brood, while the mountains beneath her are in a delightful pastel checkerboard of satin stitch, the latter figure an unprecedented and original Korean design motif. The embroidered characters on the back view are a repetition of those on the front and have the same meaning.

On another robe (Fig. 5-9) we again encounter the guardian spirits on both sides of the collar, but here they resemble two frolicsome children, drawn and stitched with a naiveté that is utterly charming and a good general example of Korean folk embroidery. Each of the guardians holds a peach tree

Fig. 5-15. Example 1: lotus flower design stitchery techniques from Fig. 5-14.

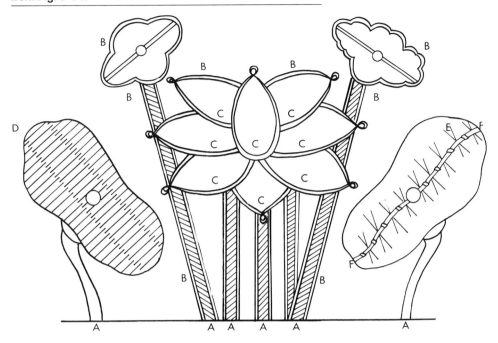

above his head (see Fig. 5-10). The peach was a fertility and long-life symbol; therefore, the peach tree symbolizes long lives and many children. The Korean characters that lie near the guardian spirits read "Two Names Joined as One." The characters on the left shoulder have the same meaning, but those on the right shoulder, loosely interpreted, read "Roots Grow Together—Many Happinesses." The design of this robe is considerably simpler than the previous example, although the main traditional elements—peonies, rocks, water, and pair of phoenixes—are represented. Consistent with the broad areas of open, unembroidered space is the absence of the sleeve picture in the front view. These combined features indicate the techniques of folk work or those of someone from the farm or rural areas of Korea.

The detail in Figure 5-16 shows the Korean lotus motif, the Buddhist symbol of purity, surrounded by flowering water lilies and golden and white Manchurian cranes. The lotus has been couched with a diamond-trellis pattern and sits on a lily pad of blue layer stitch. Beneath the lily pad, a stylized mountain, interrupted by circlets of swastikas and a half-circle of rising sun, is beautifully worked in a fresh, pastel-toned satin stitch. The circle lappet with swastika was a Chinese motif, but the use of a bro-

Fig. 5-16. Detail of bridal robe panel. Lotus, crane, leaves, sacred fungus, checkerboard rocks, rising sun, swastikas, waves, in layer stitch, satin, stem, and fly stitches; silk thread couchings on red silk ground. Korea, Yi dynasty. Collection of Mr. and Mrs. Huh Dong Hwa, Seoul.

ken color, pastel checkerboard design motif in this particular manner was unknown anywhere but in Korea. The swastika itself was a common Chinese symbol during the historical period, with obscure origins from prehistory that probably relate to early shamanism. (See Appendix.) Later it was converted into a Buddhist luck symbol and was also the shortened form of *wan,* meaning ten thousand, hence longevity. The pink, scroll-like growths on either side of the mountain design are the sacred fungus of Taoism (Chinese *ling-chih,* Korean *yong-ji-cho*), which was said to be the food of the Taoist immortals.

Metal thread embroidery was mostly reserved for the bridal robes of the wealthier classes in dynastic Korea, and these were often extremely luxuriant. Outline work was done in couched gold thread, while satin stitch and other special techniques were introduced on leaf and other designs. (See Figs. 5-14, 5-15.) It was a touching fact of life in old Korea that the amount of gold decoration on a bridal robe was often dependent on the wealth of a family, and many a village bride even had to await her turn to wear the communal bridal robe, which was shared among the unmarried women, the sleeve picture being carefully covered with white silk to protect it between weddings. Nevertheless, the simple farm girl still wore the robe of a queen.

The queen's *wan-sam* (see reconstructed example, Fig. 5-11), of which the *hwal-ot* bridal robe was the prototype, was a semiformal imperial robe that was bright red or deep red in color like the bridal robe. The cut was identical, with full *p'ao* style sleeves and vented jacket, the back tail being somewhat longer than the two frontal tails. A seven-foot sash was tied about the lower bust to a large bow at the center back, and the bridal robe follows this exactly also. The main distinctions between the *wan-sam* and the bridal robe were in the absence of embroidery of the sleeves, back, and tails of the former (stamped gold was used in these areas) and in the sleeve color bands, which in the *wan-sam* were red, yellow, and white only, without the blue band that appears on the bridal robe. The sleeve picture was also absent on the *wan-sam.* For informal or semiformal use, the *wan-sam* carried a rank badge on the chest and back with a woven or embroidered phoenix design, while at state or national ceremonial occasions the queen wore a *wan-sam* with five-clawed dragon medallions in gold on the chest, back, and both shoulders. Neither the rank badge nor the dragon medallion ever appeared on the bridal robe, since it was entirely a secular costume and not strictly for imperial use.

The Korean wedding ceremony was simple and codified according to time-honored ancient traditions. A bride and groom never met until the day of the wedding, for the marriage was arranged by go-betweens and/or the respective family members of the pair. Once arranged, the wedding day was eagerly awaited, and it was the occasion for festivities and much merrymaking after the formal vows were taken.

On the morning of the wedding, the groom approached the house of the bride and her family at the head of a long procession of family members, friends, and well-wishers, usually on horseback or carried in a sedan chair. Dismounting at the bride's home, the best man escorted the groom to the door, where they were met by the bride's father. At this point, the best man would present a carved wooden goose to the groom, who would enter the house, bow to the north, and kneel, awaiting the arrival of the bride's mother. The wooden goose was a festival symbol that, in the marriage ceremony, was an augury of fertility for the bride, the goose being one of the most fertile of creatures. The groom would present the wooden goose to the bride's mother, who would then retire to the bride's apartment and throw it through her open door. If the goose landed upright on the floor, it was an omen of a first-born son; if it lay on its side, of a daughter. These ritual proceedings marked the preliminary steps of the ceremony.

Next, the best man led the groom to the low ceremonial wedding table, where the groom faced east and was brought a vial of water, which he poured over his hands in symbolic purification. After this, the bride made her entrance, her face hidden in symbolic humility behind the voluminous sleeves of her beautiful robe, and took her place on the opposite side of the wedding table, where she stood facing the groom. The bride washed her hands also at this point, repeating the purificatory act. The groom then bowed ceremoniously to the bride, the latter returning the gesture with a curtsy. Both parties of the wedding then sat at the table opposite each other, the wedding party of family and friends remaining behind them. Glasses of ceremonial wine were given to both bride and groom, and they both drank twice, then exchanged cups and drank again. The wedding ceremony was now formally over.

The bride retired to her room, which was beautifully decorated with embroidered folding screens and embroidered *boryo* (floor cushions), where custom required that she sit, with downcast eyes, in a cross-legged, hands-folded position for the remainder of the day in demonstration of her patience and virtue.

After the wedding ceremony the groom also retired to a separate room, where he changed to more informal clothes: light, silver-gray trousers *(paji)*, a white *chogori* (jacket), and a navy blue vest *(cho-ki)*. He would then present himself to the bride's family and join in the general merrymaking of the wedding reception, usually for the rest of the day. Toward the early evening, the groom would go to the bride's chamber, where they would eat and drink wine together, after which he would ceremoniously remove her robe, for, once put on, the bride's robe could be removed by no one but her husband, and the marriage was considered symbolically consummated with its removal.

Korean culture is nearly as old as that of China, the peninsula being inhabited from as early as 4000 B.C. by Ural-Altaic nomads from the north and west who wandered down across her mountain ranges and craggy coastlines and settled there, first to establish prehistoric hunting and fishing communities, and later the simple pastoral life of agricultural towns and villages in the Neolithic. These peoples had originally been part of the pattern of Mesolithic tribes who inhabited the Gobi and southern Siberia as far back as the Ice Age. The Koreans, during their earlier nomadic period, had intermarried with Caucasian Finnic peoples, and also with Mongolian and various Tungusic peoples of southern Siberia and Manchuria, producing the unique Korean generic type and the Korean language, which is derived from Ural-Altaic dialects. A solid cultural nucleus, with fixed traditions and language, were thus established in Korea long before it met the impact of Chinese influence.

For these reasons, there was probably a native fiber arts and embroidery tradition there prior to the Chinese influence, which reached its peak during the Han, but little is known of it. Certainly the Koreans wove their traditional white garments from hemp or ramie, but whether these were decorated or not is still shrouded in the obscure Korean Neolithic. Many authorities believe Korea had been in touch with China as early as the Lung-shan Black Pottery phase of Chinese prehistory, and Chinese settlers are known to have been living on the peninsula by the Lo-Lang period (c. 8 B.C.). Korea had

been in contact with Japan since Neolithic times or earlier and was later instrumental in transmitting her own culture (and that of China) to Japan, introducing silk and Buddhism there in the fourth and sixth centuries A.D. With the first Korean contacts with China, we can almost certainly say an embroidery tradition was in progress, but whether any costume decoration was done before that time remains unknown at the present writing. As for the silk tradition, we know that it was in progress as early as 28 B.C. in Korea from edicts of King Dong Myung (reigned 37–19 B.C.) of the Koguryo kingdom, which stipulated that only the Korean nobility could wear silk costumes.

The earliest known evidence of Korean embroidery dates from the sixth-century wall paintings at Su-san-li in north Korea, in which a hip-length jacket and pleated skirt were worn, with simple embroidery designs on the collar, vent bands, and sleeve bands (Fig. 5-2). The pleated skirt seems to be originally Korean, as was the shorter jacket style, although the embroidery bands are reminiscent of Chinese styles of the Six Dynasties period, to which period this Koguryo (Three Kingdoms) example corresponds. Earlier tomb paintings from Korea show intense Han influence in *p'ao*-style robes, and these seem to be generally undecorated, even though we know that embroidery was a thoroughly established tradition by Han times. Probably Korean native costume and Chinese garments were both worn interchangeably in Korea following the first contacts with Chinese culture, and underwent a gradual merging all the way up to T'ang times (Fig. 5-1). By the beginning of the Great Silla, Korean tradition was firmly fixed, and any changes resulting after this period as a result of influences from abroad were filtered through Korean taste, tradition, and custom. The Korean mode of adapting the influence of the T'ang court in the case of the *wan-sam* and the *tang-ui* is a good example of such assimilation and synthesis. The bridal robe is also an example of purely Korean innovation comparatively distanced from Chinese influence.

The above commentary shows why the influx of Chinese culture and civilization into Korea during the Han dynasty (206 B.C.–A.D. 220) did not fully absorb and overwhelm the native Korean culture it found there, and how Korean art, culture, and its own special forms of embroidery and textile traditions persisted in a native national style. The Korean scholar's woven horsehair hat *(gat)* and white *yangban* costume (Fig. 5-17), the *chima chogori*, the *tang-ui, wan-sam,* and finally the *hwal-ot* bridal robe—all testify to the endurance and sophistication of a culture that was, if not equal in size to China, fully equal in quality and greatness of heart.

The several technical examples from the bridal robe which follow may serve to elaborate on some of the ways Korean embroiderers solved their creative problems in costume embroidery.

Fig. 5-17. *Yangban and Kisaeng beside a Lotus Pond* by Sin Yun-Bok (c. 1758–?). Album leaf, color and ink on paper. Female entertainers in *chima chogori* costumes and noblemen in *yangban* costumes in a traditional walled garden setting. Korea, Yi dynasty. Collection of Chon Hyong-Pil, Korea.

KOREAN BRIDAL ROBE TECHNIQUES

Example 1: Lotus Flower Design, Korea, Yi Dynasty (Fig. 5-15, page 91)

The lotus was the emblem of summer in ancient China, but the Buddhists regard it as a sacred flower, the symbol of the purity of the Buddha, and most of the venerated deities in Buddhist art and legend are shown either standing or seated upon a lotus throne. In Korea, the lotus was also an imperial symbol, and this, together with its Buddhist overtones, accounts for its presence on the bridal robe, demonstrating the imperial origins of the latter. The *feng-huang,* or double phoenix design (appearing in this detail on either side of the lotus), symbolize both nobility and the yin–yang principle—the male and female elements of Being, or the cosmic forces of creation and reproduction.

The stems beneath the lotus flowers are in two colors—yellows and greens gradated to a burnt sienna, using a diagonal satin stitch (A) for this purpose. When the satin stitch was completed, a quite heavy gold thread (B) was couched on both sides of the stems. Such couching served a double purpose: The gold added light-catching properties to the composition and finished any ragged edges left by the base stitchery. The same procedure was followed nearly everywhere on the robe's outlines. The lotus flowers, phoenixes' heads and bodies, and their colorful satin-stitched back feathers have all been edged with a somewhat lighter gold thread. (See Fig. 5-14.) The gold flaming pearls near the phoenixes' heads were couched directly onto the satin ground, without any understitching.

Parodoxically, the treatments of the lotus flowers show two different techniques: The red and white lower lotus's petals were done in a combination of flat satin and long and short stitches, but the dark greens of the center lotus's petals are in interlocking satin stitch (C), with a gradation from there upward, moving from dark green to light green and finally to white. (For a demonstration of interlocking satin stitch, see Chapter 7, "Scroll, Screen, and Banner Techniques," page 137.)

The lotus leaves that appear behind the body of each phoenix show an interesting couching method that is, again, both artistic and practical.

D. The entire surface of the leaf was covered completely from side to side with interlocking satin stitch in a medium green yarn.

E. The crisscross lines were done over the interlocking satin stitch in single darning stitches to create the effect of stylized veins in the leaf.

F. Gold thread was then couched in a straight center line *over* the crisscross lines to create the star effect in the finished leaf, and this couching anchors the previous interlocking satin and single darning stitches.

Example 2: Sunrise with Rainbow Design, Korea, Yi Dynasty (Fig. 5-18)

The clever, and really rather unique, stitchery on the rising sun design beneath the rainbow-colored rocks gives this bridal robe an added distinction, for a design and stitchery configuration of this type was rarely seen in most Oriental work. The style is nevertheless typically Korean, while the device of placing swastikas within circle lappets shows the ubiquitous Chinese influence. An extended form of seed stitch was combined with vertical darning stitches to create the sunrise radiating effect, through the following technique.

A. The arc of the sunrise is done in green thread on the red ground, using lightly spaced vertical darning stitches that radiate from the center.

B. The extended seed stitch joins into the green darning stitches with a yellow yarn, to create sunbeams. A tiny space separates the stitches, as follows.

The needle comes up at 1. The operator holds 1 1/2 inches of thread with the left hand and the thread is wrapped three times around the needle, drawing 1 inch of thread for the stem, as in 2. The needle then enters at 3, 3/16 inch from the previous stitch. This process was repeated as necessary, from the common center of the beams. All stems were 1 inch long, and the radiation was created by the 3/16-inch spaces between the stitches.

Fig. 5-18. Examples 2 and 3: extended seed stitch and fly stitch.

A.

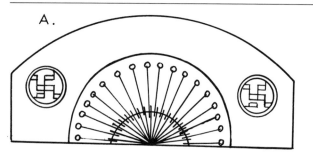

B.

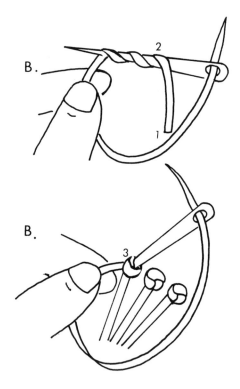

Example 3: White and Golden Crane Design, Korea, Yi Dynasty (Fig. 5-18)

The variegated dorsal feathers of the cranes are effectively expressed through skillful layer stitch, couching, and the use of fly stitch.

C. The entire oval area of the crane's backs is covered with layer stitch, then couched with a diamond trellis design in the same white thread. The dark, V-shaped feathers are centered in the diamonds with fly stitch, in the following technique.

D. The needle comes up at 1 and reenters at 2. The operator retains a slack of about ³/₄ inch with the left hand, and the needle comes up at 3 over the slack and is drawn through, stitching the slack down firmly, at 4. This procedure is then repeated as necessary.

For several chapters we have explored the colorful designs and needlework of imperial and ceremonial costumes, and some of the more elaborate textile art of the home, palace, and temple. In the next chapter we move to an equally interesting field of Oriental embroidery, the countless types of personal costume accessories and other informal secular and imperial wear, a subsidiary decorative tradition that existed for many centuries before the advent of the modern age.

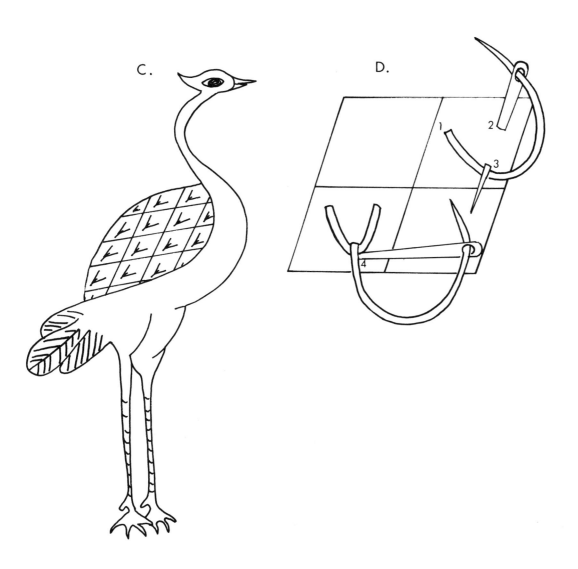

6/ COSTUME ACCESSORIES

HISTORY AND AESTHETICS

The informal wear of the Oriental countries during the historical period was replete with an impressive variety of interesting accessories that were considered part of the conventional costumes. Such accessories were commonly ornamented with embroidery, the fittest medium for the decoration of fabric, as a matter of style and self-expression, as well as of the precedents set by the most aristocratic families and the royalty. The love of color, art, and the beauty of fine fabrics found many ways of expressing itself in the ancient Orient, despite the fact that, as a sign of respect for the emperor, the use of the dragon and other imperial symbols by anyone but the imperial family was strictly forbidden by law, so strictly, in fact, that the transgressor could expect to pay with his head for wearing them.

The decoration of eye-catching costume accessories was especially typical in China, where fine embroidery work was greatly loved and highly esteemed, and the custom was popular in Korea also, where needlework costume embroidery on the costume itself was repressed by strict garment regulations, causing such decoration to appear mainly on accessories, perhaps as compensation. In Japan, the same custom was less popular. Japanese costume accessories and footwear were of different types than those ordinarily worn in Korea and China, and aside from the beautiful obi and the embroidered inner neckpiece *(eri),* which were worn with the kimono, and work done on certain small purses, the custom was limited. Although Chinese costume finery included what might be called the striving for status, and much of Korean needlework was a reflection of Chinese influence, in both coun-

tries the desire for beauty and the graceful embellishment of a cultured and refined way of life was uppermost. Consequently, even functional objects were decorated with embroidery if they had any silk on them, including an array of typical items such as ladies' shawls, fans, capes, jackets, vests, aprons, an endless assortment of the hats of both sexes, parasols, belts ,and belt tails, slippers, gloves, spoon-, eyeglass-, chopstick-, and fan cases, decorative *p'i-ling* collars, a wide assortment of many kinds of dainty, beautiful purses, as well as the most famous accessory of all, the mandarin square. The high quality of design and embroidery craftsmanship on so many of these fine artifacts reflected the highly sophisticated way of life and confirmed the importance of the embroiderer's art.

A typical, but often unnoticed, example was the embroidered shawl, which figured importantly in T'ang styles. In the painting detailed in Figure 6-1, each one of the ladies wears such a shawl, obviously a fashionable garment in China of that period. Tomb paintings found in Taiwan, dating from A.D. 696, also depict T'ang noblewomen wearing decorated shawls. Their appearance in numerous other paintings of the T'ang suggests a widespread popularity, at least among the more affluent classes.

A complex history attended the embroidered shawl in Korea. According to court records of A.D. 649, it was among other Chinese fashions at the official court reception of Queen Jin Duk (reigned 647–654). So strong was the lure of Chinese fashion that King Moon Mu made an imperial decree in A.D. 644 that all noblewomen's costumes had to be identical to those of China! The same embroidered

shawl is encountered in earlier traditions, however, before any T'ang influence, as the Korean "History of the Three Kingdoms" in *Han guk tongsa* relates, listing mandates against the wearing of silk shawls or gold and silver-thread costume decorations, which also suggests that the shawl as an accessory was limited to the use of the royal family. The same source provides tableaux of a hierarchy that included costume regulations in Korea: noblewomen of the fourth imperial rank were required to wear silk; the fifth rank, satin; and the sixth rank could wear neither any form of wool embroidery nor any gold or silver accessories, wool embroidery probably being a medium of the common people. A dotted embroidery pattern was typical on Korean shawls, as well as the figured floral, leaf, lozenge, and tortoise-shell hexagons seen on those of the T'ang ladies of rank (Fig. 6-1).

As indicated in Chapter 3, the corruption and decay of the Manchu court, the destructive effects of a raging civil war, and the intervention of unscrupulous Western business interests during the last fifty years of the Ch'ing dynasty succeeded in utterly destroying all of the embroidery and other crafts guilds of imperial China, the ruin of the textile industry, and the final downfall of the last of the imperial family. A sharp line must therefore be drawn

Fig. 6-3. Woman's informal jacket. Roundels and scattered designs of natural and geometric motifs in polychrome embroideries, galoon edgings, appliqué, on yellow silk damask ground of cloud designs. China, Ch'ing dynasty, late nineteenth century. The Metropolitan Museum of Art, by exchange, 1954.

between Ch'ing embroidery after 1875 and the high art of the dynasty before that time, although here and there a great piece emerges like the last strains of a dying melody.

Such an example is shown in Figure 6-3, a lyrical monument to an age that had already vanished, an age of poetry, art, music, and cultured living despite the Manchu accession to the throne, an age when the long, unbroken heritage of Chinese embroidery had been brought to fulfillment, when the sheltered serenity of age-old moon-garden courtyards, elegant country manors, and palatial estates still reflected the beauty and serenity of old China. Probably this jacket was worn by a young, unmarried woman for semiformal occasions such as wed-

dings, birthday celebrations, and national holidays. It is not an imperial garment, since it lacks dragon symbols, although the presence of many phoenix and pheasant motifs suggests a high rank in society, possibly a noble family, most assuredly a wealthy family.

The jacket's composition reveals the best elements of Chinese design brought to their highest points by the early and middle Ch'ing, and many of the finest features of Chinese aesthetics. There is, first of all, the characteristic emphasis on symmetry and balance, the five circular designs on the front and back carefully placed to render an exact distribution of mass poised in restful contrast to the circular roundels, which provide such distribution.

Fig. 6-4. Imperial *p'i-ling* collar. Designs of five-clawed dragons, clouds, bats, flaming pearl, waves, with thunder line/swastika border in *k'o-ssu* tapestry weave. China, Ch'ing dynasty, nineteenth century. Collection of the author.

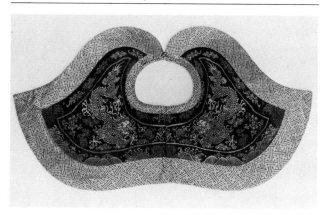

The impressive collar piece, with its series of prominent embroidered appliqué cloud lappets, creates a triangular thrust in both upward and downward direction, again, a form of balance, while its contrasting, diametrically opposed shapes offset and complement the main feature of the design, the circle roundels with their enclosed landscape embroideries. Chinese philosophy of art is implicit in such designs, as in all their art: The organic unity of the universe expressed by the infinity of the circle; the harmony and rightness of all living things as celebrated by nature, birds, trees, flowers; the work of man in the hub of this cosmos, expressed by the geometrical straight lines, the thunder line continuously repeated, the pagodas. Such pieces, showing landscapes, pagodas, houses, and bridges, were often, besides their implicit artistic and philosophical content, themes that told a popular legend or contemporary story, although in this case it is difficult to ascertain precisely what the legend was, for costume embroidery was never titled or signed.

The piece was managed almost entirely in satin stitch, augmented by the use of pre-embroidered appliqué work and prewoven tapes in complementary borders and edgings.

The twelve circular forms predominate, five on both front and back and one on each shoulder. The upper circles contain white doves and pagodas set in a landscape of trees and flowers. The central circles express pheasant, phoenix, and flower designs enclosed within a thunder line, while the lower roundels depict the long-life symbols, deer and cranes, amid auspicious flower and tree forms.

The exterior sleeve bands are in couched gold

thread that has darkened considerably, with deer, thunder line, and landscape motifs repeated on them. The interior sleeve borders are treated with embroidered appliqué, deer, thunder line, and patterned trellis designs. Color themes are repeated also in the seam and collar work, where the outer bands show embroidered satin stitch and inner strips of prewoven tape designs: pheasants, peacocks, and the Eight Precious Things. The vent and side borders are trimmed with floral tapes, and embroidered appliqué with birds, butterflies, a thunder line with floral accents, and diamond trellis designs.

The elaborate collar area was done with pre-embroidered appliqué and inlaid appliqué, some decorative prewoven galoon tapework, and a satin piping finish. The prewoven galoon tapes were laid in a carefully repeated theme, both around the collar, where three separate lines have been nicely spaced, and along the borders and seams. The precut appliqué sections of the internal collar border repeat some of the motifs found in the lower border areas. Gold braid, with embroidered flower designs, embellishes the inner collar area. The ground, in charming contrast, is in a bright yellow damask, with occasional bird, plant, and butterfly segments worked in satin stitch.

The quiet, poetic beauty of this jacket seems all the more poignant in that the balanced, tasteful design, the carefully placed prewoven tapes, and the lush opulence seem to echo the dying dynastic ages, even as they stop just short of the exaggeration and banality that characterized the Ch'ing decline.

Children's hats were a source of joy and pleasure for embroiderers in both China and Korea, and upon them all the care of a mother's love or a professional's expertise was lavished, along with a great deal of fine craftsmanship. While the idea of decoration was foremost, such hats were also practical, and were made, accordingly, of silk padded with cotton for winter and of raw silk and gauze for summer use. (Silk, incidentally, tends to hold body heat, and can be quite warm in cold weather). The Korean girl's winter hat *(gu-lae),* shown in Figure 6-5, and the Chinese children's hats, Figure C-8, were generally used by children between one and five years of age, and one cannot imagine anything cuter than a band of boys and girls wearing such headgear on their way to school or playing. The Korean boy's hat was less lavish than the girl's, made of navy blue gauze in plain or patterned weave, with

Fig. 6-5. Girl's hat (gu-lae). Polychrome embroidery in long and short, satin, and stem stitches; pink, yellow, and silver-couched cordage designs. Korea, Yi dynasty, Courtesy of Joo Sun Suk, Institute of Folklore, Dan Kook University, Seoul.

Back view

Top view

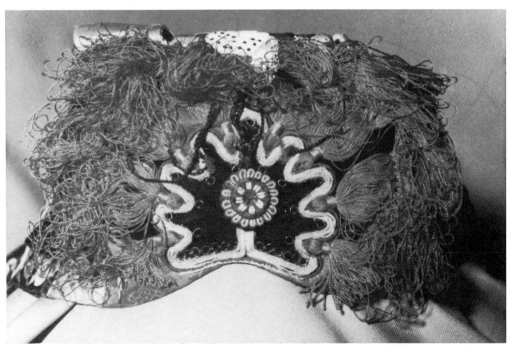

Fig. 6-6. Imperial woman's dragon robe: polychrome embroidered with Taoist and Buddhist symbols; in satin long and short and stem stitches on red satin ground. China, Ch'ing dynasty. Courtesy of the National History Museum, Taiwan.

two long tails that hung down the back, a stamped gold design bearing long-life and happiness characters upon the brow.

A Korean boy's first-year birthday costume, however, was much more ornate, with a long vest of blue floss silk tied with embroidered tails. Belt designs usually pertained to parents' good wishes for the child, and long-life symbols or the characters for wealth and happiness embroidered in satin, long and short, and stem stitches expressed such felicitations. Typically, each tail bore embroidered wishes for a good character and a virtuous life. "Swallow-tail" ends were characteristic, finished with a tiny tassel on each of the tail's three points.

Almost unknown in the Western world, the Korean imperial court apron *(fu-su)* is a splendid example of Korean accessory embroidery at its finest (Fig. C-26). Worn to indicate court rank before the appearance of the Korean mandarin square, the apron was an important ceremonial element in Korean court regalia. Made either of silk gauze or plain or damasklike weave, it was worn at the back over a red surcoat and secured by two of the four decorative belt tails. An ornamental enamelized belt was worn with it. Derived from a similar accessory worn in the Chinese court in Han and pre-Han times, the *fu-su* was first mentioned in the court costume chapter of the Imperial Costume Regulations *(Kook-cho-o-re-ui),* during the reign (1418–1450) of King Sejong, but it was probably in use much earlier.

A red background was common to most ranks,

although occasional color variations can be found. Rank was signified by the type of metal used in the two prominent rings near the waistband and by changes in the type of bird design depicted, as follows: First- and second-rank courtiers wore designs of flying cranes and clouds, with gold rings; the third rank had a perched-eagle design with silver rings; the fourth rank wore the Korean blue magpie, also with silver rings; the fifth and sixth ranks displayed the Korean magpie with brass rings, while the seventh, eighth, and ninth ranks showed the Siberian rail, also with brass rings.

MANDARIN SQUARE–TABLE OF RANKS

Civil

CHINA				KOREA	
Period Rank	Ming (1368–1644)	Ch'ing (1644–1912)	Yi (1446–1505)	Yi (1505–1865)	Yi (1865–1911)
1st	Crane*	Crane	Peacock	Crane	Double Crane
2nd	Golden Pheasant	Golden Pheasant	Goose	Golden Pheasant	Double Crane
3rd	Peacock*	Peacock	Silver Pheasant	Peacock	Double Crane
4th	Goose	Goose		Goose	Single Crane
5th	Silver Pheasant	Silver Pheasant		Silver Pheasant	Single Crane
6th	Egret*	Egret		Egret	Single Crane
7th	Mandarin Duck	Mandarin Duck		Mandarin Duck	Single Crane
8th	Oriole*	Quail**		Oriole	Single Crane
9th	Quail	Paradise Flycatcher**		Quail	Single Crane

*Worn interchangeably with rank beneath until 1527
**After 1652

Military

1st	Lion	Ch'i-lin**	Leopard	Lion	Double Leopard
2nd	Lion	Lion	Leopard	Lion	Double Leopard
3rd	Tiger*	Leopard***	Bear	Tiger*	Double Leopard
4th	Leopard	Tiger***		Leopard	Single Leopard
5th	Bear	Bear		Bear	Single Leopard
6th	Panther	Panther		Panther	Single Leopard
7th	Panther	Rhinoceros****		Panther	Single Leopard
8th	Rhinoceros	Rhinoceros		Rhinoceros	Single Leopard
9th	Sea Horse	Sea Horse		Sea Horse	Single Leopard

*Worn interchangeably with rank beneath until 1527
**After 1662
***After 1664
****After 1759

Fig. 6-7. Design pattern of Korean court apron *(fu-su)* showing stitchery.

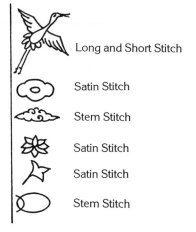

Long and Short Stitch

Satin Stitch

Stem Stitch

Satin Stitch

Satin Stitch

Stem Stitch

The ties of the apron were usually blue, but color themes of the other segments were also indicators of rank, the first, second, and third ranks wearing red, green, yellow, and purple themes; the fourth, fifth, and sixth ranks red, green, and yellow, and the seventh, eighth, and ninth ranks yellow and green only. (The number of colors increased or decreased according to the degree of the wearer.)

The *fu-su* (literally, "back apron") was the major accessory completing an elaborate ceremonial court costume *(kumkwan-chobok),* the wearing of which accompanied an elaborate ritual. Over a white underrobe *(chungdan)* and trousers *(paji),* the courtier donned a blue inner robe *(jung sam).* This was followed by a red underapron *(sang)* worn both front and back, tied over the blue robe. Then the red outer surcoat, the *chobok,* was put on, and over this the *fu-su* was tied and belted to hang at the back. The final touches on this handsome outfit were jade and bead pendants *(pae-ok),* which hung at the left waist, and the court hat *(kum-kwan)* with its elaborate goldwork.

The design structure of the *fu-su,* poetic, artistic, and imbued with an imposing formal dignity, was based on four main thematic points, rendered in the rich colors of the required conventions (see Figs. 6-5 and C-26): (1) the cloud pattern in the upper area above the rings; (2) the chain-link motif enclosing six swastikas; (3) the bird figures within floral, cloud, and vine squares—eight squares and eight birds, in the traditional iconography; and (4) the lower border pattern of spiriform vines and lotus blossoms. Much of its stately grandeur is achieved by the strong verticals at the sides and centers of the squares. This tendency is in turn offset by the loose, rather floral treatment of the cloud figures within the squares, and by the softly moving vine and flower forms in the lower border.

Figure C-26 shows an exceptionally fine example of *fu-su* stitchery, with generously used gold thread to finish accents. The divisions of the crane's feathers attained bas-relief effects from the same techniques demonstrated earlier on the bridal robe (see Chapter 5, "Korean Bridal Robe Techniques"), utilizing a thread padding. Over the carefully crafted padding work, a diagonal satin stitch was applied to each division, while the inner areas were worked in straight satin stitch. The neck was finished in long and short stitch.

The cloud designs in this example were embroidered in several values of satin stitch without any color gradation, the cloud sections divided into flat, unbroken color areas. The added gold-wrapped couching both unified the cloud figures and hid unsightly edges. No more than four colors appear on one cloud, and most have been padded beneath the satin stitch.

The chain designs were rendered in satin stitch, with contours accented by couched gold thread. The flowers on the lower border are in long and short (gradated) stitch, the leaves and vines in satin stitch.

Fortunately, quite a number of these excellent pieces have survived to modern times from the Yi dynasty and are presently in public and private collections in Seoul and elsewhere.

An astounding gamut of surprisingly beautiful purses are found among the accessories of China and Korea. These came in a variety of styles, shapes, and colors and were usually quite small and dainty in size, often with decorative drawstrings, braid, and tassel ornamentation, in soft pastel colors that were complementary to the main body of the bag. Marvelous craftsmanship is consistently displayed on these wonderful little artifacts, as for example the complex macramé drawstring work in Figure C-25.

Seven main shapes predominate in the purses' designs, a round-bottomed type (Fig. C-25), the hexagon (Fig. C-25), the heart shape, the cicada, the square belt purse (Fig. 6-20), a tiny eared purse (Fig. C-25), and the vertical butterfly shape (Fig. C-28).

Fig. 6-8. Embroidered shoes for bound feet. Design of orchid flowers and flowering plants in satin and stem stitches with shaped galoon edgings on white satin ground. China, Ch'ing dynasty, early twentieth century. Length, 4³/4 inches (12 cm.). Royal Ontario Museum, Toronto, gift of Mrs. C. M. Warren.

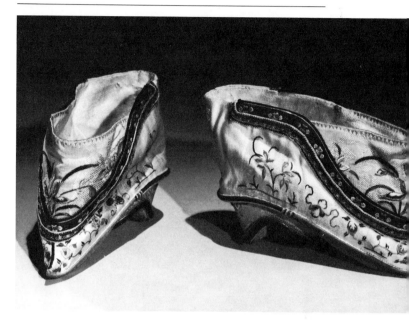

Fig. 6-9. Woman's pleated skirt. Scattered and paneled designs of peonies, orchids, butterflies, in long and short, stem, satin, and seed stitches; flower borders embroidered in satin stitch. Pinks, cobalt blue, light green, red, purple, yellow, in untwisted silk yarns on pink damask silk ground; linen waistband. China, Ch'ing dynasty, nineteenth century. Collection of the author.

Fig. 6-10. Ancestral portrait. Hanging scroll, color on silk. China, Ming dynasty. Royal Ontario Museum, Toronto, the George Crofts Collection.

Such handbags had a wide range of purposes, other than the carrying of money. The special shapes can often be identified for special uses, such as carriers of perfume bottles, medicine, lucky amulets, spoons, flint and tinder sets, signature seals, watches, fans, eyeglasses, and writing brush sets. The largest variety, the butterfly, are about eight inches high and seven inches wide at their broadest point, while the smaller, round examples are seldom more than four or five inches in diameter.

Traditionally, purses were special presents at specific family celebrations, such as the eightieth birthday party of grandparents in China and at the sixtieth anniversary of grandparents in Korea. Such gift purses were always very handsomely and heavily embroidered. They were also traditional children's New Year and birthday gifts in Korea, where tiny purses—2 1/2 by 3 inches (4.5 by 7.5 cm.)—were presented to the youngsters. These contained a popular snack, toasted beans wrapped in red paper, which were believed to protect children from smallpox.

The stitchery and gorgeous coloration of the smaller purses are particularly outstanding, while their daintiness adds to the charm of the object, intensifying its color and drawing maximum attention to its cute, chic qualities. Gauzes, embroidered in half-cross stitch (see Fig. 2-9, page 32), satins, damasks, and the brighter ranges of plain weave silk were treated with the extreme care and artistry of much larger and more important embroideries, as will be demonstrated in Example 1 of the technical section of this chapter. The amount of care and patient dedication given to these pieces shows how important and highly esteemed such accessories were, and how much charm they added to a lady's costume.

Typical purse designs, usually executed in satin stitch, follow the conventional paths of ritual and filial meaning: Lucky and long-life symbols, the propitious Shou character, peony, clematis, and other flowers and symbols characteristically embellish their surfaces. Certain geometrical motifs are also typical, such as the diagonal wave pattern *(li shui)*, the Buddhist Endless Knot, and the thunder line variation with swastika. Other figurative motifs include the goldfish, symbol of many sons, the lotus, symbol of purity, and the seeds of the lotus, which signify wealth.

The following poem expresses some of the understandable endearment these charming little keepsakes held for Oriental women of all ages.

SECRETS OF EMBROIDERY

This is the only one I haven't finished,
This small embroidered purse,
The purse my toiling hands
Have soiled so much,
Stopping and starting again and again
Is the reason
People say I haven't any sewing talent,
Working on the little purse so long.

Yet only I know the secret:
When my heart is heavy and full of pain,
My heavy, embroidered heart
Follows the golden thread that disappears
In tiny needle holes,
And from the little purse comes
A new, clear melody of my heart.

And still, in all this world, I have
Little treasure to put in that purse,
That small purse—except my troubles—
So I never want to finish it,
Only keep embroidering it.

Han Yong Un
Translation by Young Yang Chung

Fig. 6-11. Mandarin square for civil official, ninth rank. Design of paradise flycatcher in irregular-length satin stitch on body, diagonal satin stitch on feathers and tail, with couched, paper-wrapped accents on feather separations, cloud, and wave contours; waves, clouds, mountains in satin stitch; rocks in couched silk thread wrapped in downy fibers; entire background covered with couched metal thread in a light-catching design. China, early Ch'ing dynasty. The Metropolitan Museum of Art, Fletcher Fund, 1936.

Probably the most important costume accessory in historical China was the civil and military rank badge mentioned in Chapter 2, the mandarin square (see Fig. 6-11). Worn to indicate the specified ranks of military and civil officials, the mandarin square was a highly esteemed status symbol conferred only by the emperor. The nine degrees of rank were not hereditary but had to be achieved through education and rigorous examinations. These were open to anyone through meritorious advancement in local schools and promotion to the prestigious Han Lin, the Imperial Academy, where graduates were given official appointments to government posts beginning with the ninth rank, from which they could progress, through successive examinations and promotions, to the first rank.

As well known as the rank badges are in the West, it was a common misconception until fairly recent times that they originated in the earliest dynasties. Actually, they were comparative newcomers in Chinese history, having their beginning in the reign of Hung-wu of the early Ming dynasty (A.D. 1368–1644). By 1527, they were clearly prescribed in the Ming laws. There is some evidence that they were inspired by similar decorative plaques, not indicative of rank, which were worn by Mongol lords of the preceding Yuan dynasty. These were woven or embroidered rectangles or squares of flowers, or of bird and animal designs, worn on the front and back of nonofficial robes, as suggested by Chinese woodcuts of the period. The early Ming laws re-

quired that the dragon robes of the Sung and T'ang type be used for court and other ceremonial functions, but the ordinary dress robes of civil and military officials were to be of red silk or satin, with woven or embroidered rectangles on chest and back indicating the various civil and military ranks, with bird designs for the former and animals for the latter.

It is unknown why the specific bird and animal figures were chosen for each rank, although probably they are rooted in ancient Chinese mythology. The writings of Ch'in Hsun, a Ming statesman, intimate that the bird designs symbolized the literary refinement of the scholars, while the animal figures represented the courage of the military. Memorial

portraits (Figs. 2-14 and 6-10), extant from the Ming, show rank badges that were much larger and more of them rectangular than their later square Ch'ing counterparts, for they extended in an unbroken pattern from side seam to side seam on both the front and back of the robe. Ch'ing squares were somewhat smaller, and were centered on the chest and back. Most information on the Ming rank badges comes from these portraits, since Ming examples are comparatively rare. Extant pieces dating from the end of the dynasty are more often in tight k'o-ssu (tapestry) weave, which had a greater survival rate than the looser, more easily damaged embroideries. Wide divergency of styles and other variations in the insignias' embroidery may be ac-

counted for in part by the fact that they were done in various districts and widely spaced areas, whether in the capitals at Nanking and Peking, the large textile centers at Soochow and Yangchow, or in the towns and rural villages where some of the officials were given their magisterial posts, such custom embroidery always being done at the official's expense or by his family.

The system of colors and symbols established during the Ming for the nine ranks was generally maintained throughout the remainder of the historical period (except for some minor changes during the early Ch'ing dynasty) and can be seen in its entirety in the Table of Ranks on page 105.

Because of a close similarity among many of the figures, identifying the various bird and animal symbols has been the occasion for some consternation among modern scholars. Even the dynastic Chinese and Koreans were frequently confounded by these similarities, and the problem was further complicated by unscrupulous officials who would order embroidery designers to make their symbols as much as possible like the rank above theirs! This kind of sly maneuvering and the tendency of some officials to wear the rank above were among the reasons for the various costume laws, edicts, and mandates issued with such regularity by the emperors. Apparently the Koreans had the same problem, for according to the *Daechunfeitong* (Pictorial Costume Records), King Young Cho, in the tenth

year of his reign (1734), raised the strenuous question of why military men had been wearing the crane symbol, and reissued his edict that civil officials must wear only bird symbols and military men the animal figures.

An example of such confusion can be found in the Chinese first-rank military symbol *(ch'i-lin)* (Fig. 6-14), which is commonly called a unicorn. This figure is not a unicorn, but is in fact a stylized depiction of a prototypical giraffe. Evidence for this is provided, first, by the fact that the Koreans, who also used this motif on mandarin squares, called the figure *"kirin,"* yet have the same character for it as the Chinese. The word *kirin* in Korean means, literally, giraffe. The Chinese character, however, has understandably received conflicting and contradictory meanings, "unicorn" among them, for its semantic is more than a little ambiguous, imprecise, and archaic. Secondly, the *ch'i-lin,* or *kirin,* is commonly depicted on the rank badges with the two horns of a giraffe, rather than the single horn of the classic unicorn. The hoofed feet and bushy tail of the giraffe are indicated, and the long, mottled neck of the giraffe has been condensed into a stylized, striped form, shown beneath the head along the frontal portion of the chest in the illustra-

Fig. 6-15. Censor's badge *(h'sieh-chai)*. Sun, clouds, sacred fungus, waves, and mountains in stem and satin stitches with silk thread couched borders; White lion *(h'sieh-chai)* in stem, satin, and layer stitches with gold-couched eyes; on brown damask silk ground with cloud and Secular Eight Precious Things pattern. Korea, Yi dynasty, c. seventeenth century. From *Ancient Arts of Korea,* Department of Cultural Affairs. Courtesy of the Department of Cultural Affairs, Seoul.

tion. The reason for the shortened neck was apparently to make the figure fit into the square design shape of the rank badge, and still remain prominent; had a full, long neck appeared on the creature, the entire figure would have had to be considerably smaller in proportion, too small, in fact, for adequate representation. The origin of the motif can be found in an ancient Chinese myth that relates that the giraffe was the offspring of the dragon and the alligator; this mythological parentage would account for the scales of the *ch'i-lin.* Since the dragon was an imperial symbol, the *ch'i-lin* (giraffe) came to be included in the imperial iconography. All animals found on the mandarin square were essentially mythical; this was stressed by the stylized flame motifs which surround the *ch'i-lin* and other animal figures. In a typical blend of fact and fantasy, the giraffe assumed an added importance after it

Fig. 6-16. Empress's imperial rank badge. Design of *feng-huang* phoenixes, clouds, flaming pearl, mountains, waves, Secular Eight Precious Things, in satin stitch; *feng-huang*, flaming pearl, and all contours in couched gold-wrapped thread. Korea, Yi dynasty, nineteenth century. Collection of Joo Sun Suk. From *Ancient Arts of Korea*, Department of Cultural Affairs. Courtesy of the Department of Cultural Affairs, Seoul.

was believed to be a strange, unearthly creature of great purity; that is, it never ate meat, only the cleanest of herb and grass forage, made no sound, was thought to be very long-lived, and was believed to appear on earth only when a person of kingly or noble character was born. Given these mythological preconditions, it is not difficult to see how the symbol became incorporated into the imperial ranking system.

A similar misunderstanding surrounded the *pai-tse* (lion), often called the mythical beast, and the

censor's badge, the *hsieh-chai* (white lion), which were, and still are, frequently confused with each other and with the *ch'i-lin*. The *ch'i-lin* is identified by scales and hoofs; the *hsieh-chai* has a solid-colored body without scales, and without hoofs; the *pai-tse* has partial scales, but is also without hoofs. Thus the *ch'i-lin* can always be identified by its hoofs and complete body scales. The use of the *pai-tse* was abandoned in China after 1662 (Ch'ing dynasty), partly because of such confusions.

The Ch'ing civil and military rank badges mainly

followed the Ming laws of 1527 (with the exceptions above noted), and after 1759 the symbols remained stable until the end of the dynasty, not differing greatly from one epoch to the next, the only minor additional change being that court musicians were given the oriole symbol, which is, incidentally, one of the rarest of the rank badges.

Before 1759, imperial rank badges in the Ming and Ch'ing differed considerably from the mandarin square of the civil and military official. Badges of the emperor were five-clawed dragons (lung) in circu-

lar medallions on the chest, back, and shoulders of a yellow robe (Fig. 6-17), while those of his sons and grandsons appeared on red robes. Nobles not of the immediate royal family (dukes, earls, marquises, etc.) had various military animal figures, including the ch'i-lin and pai-tse, indicating their degree, woven in gold rectangular plaques on red robes. Beginning with the Ming, the empress wore phoenix badges embroidered in gold (Fig. 6-16), as did the emperor's concubines and the wife of the heir apparent to the throne. Wives and daughters of first- and second-degree princes, and the princesses, wore a less lavish phoenix badge with flower designs, and all other ladies of the court, other than the imperial family, wore the tartar pheasant design. During the reign of K'ang-hsi (1662), the *ch'i-lin* was given to the first-rank military, the use of the *pai-tse* was abandoned, and dukes, earls, marquises, and sons-in-law of first-degree princes were required to wear the four-clawed dragon *(mang)*. After 1759, the highest imperial degrees wore front-facing dragon medallions on the chest and back of surcoats *(p'u-fu)*, with profile dragons on the shoulders.

The insignia of the royal family were embroidered or woven in gold on the fabric before the robe was tailored, whereas other imperial officials and subsidiary nobles wore embroidered or woven plaques that were sewn as an addition to the robe, not being part of its ground fabric. The reason for this was to allow for the official's rank changes, whereas imperial ranks never changed. The latter wore their rank badges (circular dragon medallions) on outer vests *(ch'ang-fu)* or surcoats *(p'u-fu)* over their customary five-clawed dragon *ch'i-fu*, while lesser nobles and civil or military officials of the first three ranks wore square badges of rank on their *p'u-fu* only. The ceremonial robe of the mandarins, which was worn beneath the *p'u-fu* on court occasions, was decorated with four-clawed *mang* dragons for the first three ranks, and in all lower ranks the square rank badge was repeated in the center chest (where the main dragon was placed on the emperor's robe), with two lesser dragons, either *lung* or *mang,* placed on the lower left and right fields above a rising *li shui* wave pattern.

Korean mandarin squares (Fig. 6-15) first came into official use in 1454 (Yi dynasty), when court edicts were given that all civil and military officials must wear rank badges on the back and chest of round-collared robes. Korea was the first country outside of China to adopt the rank badge, and its origin there may have dated from the time a set of court robes was presented to the Korean king Gong Min (reigned 1351–1374) by Emperor Hung-wu in 1370, which would correspond to the first Ming usages. Clearly, the rank badge could not have been in use in Korea much earlier, although the native Korean court apron *(fu-su)* seems to denote a ranking system from an earlier period.

Between 1454 and 1865, Korean records on the ranking system are fragmentary, but some inferences can be drawn from various sources. Court

documents from 1446, in the twenty-eighth year of the reign of King Sejong (1418–1450), indicate that the earliest native Korean rank badges were in six degrees only—three civil and three military—and that these ranks did not correspond to the same ranks in China. The first civil rank Korean was a peacock; the second rank, a goose with clouds; the third rank, a silver pheasant. This would be consistent with the third imperial rank given to Korea in the Chinese court. (Compare these motifs, actually three degrees lower than their corresponding ranks in China; see the Table of Ranks, page 105.) The Korean first- and second-rank military wore the leopard; the third rank, the bear. By 1505, a court edict by King Youn San (reigned 1494–1506) had commanded the use of nine ranks of insignia, and it is probably safe to assume that these were the same nine ranks found in China. This notion is further reinforced by a large body of memorial portraits (see Fig. 6-18) showing Korean civil and military of-

Fig. 6-18. State portrait of Kim Seoug-Ju, minister of state. Hanging scroll, color on silk. The official is wearing a blue damask robe with a mandarin square, first rank civil. Korea, Yi dynasty, seventeenth century. From *Portraits of Historic Koreans* by Lee Kang-Chil, published by Tam-Gu-Dang, Seoul. Collection of Mr. Kim Jong-Gu, Korea.

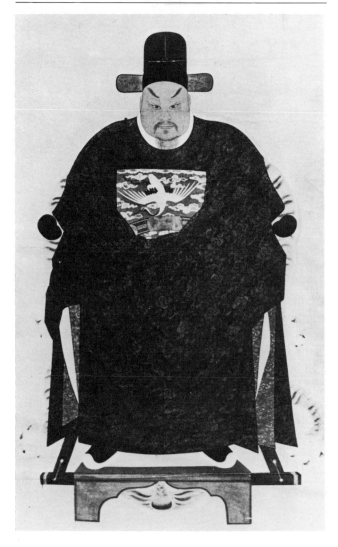

ficials wearing Chinese insignia badges throughout most of the feudal and later historical period. Although the native Korean motifs apparently remained in use, they were less favored and less frequently worn by Korean officials, who obviously preferred the more prestigious Chinese symbols.

In the same time period as above, the Korean imperial ranks were denoted by circular five-clawed dragon medallions, embroidered or woven in gold, which had appeared on the dragon robe (chest, back, and shoulders) of the royal family since 1444.

Apparently no additional rank badges were used by the Korean king or his sons, for no accessory court coats are known to exist at the present time, other than the dragon robe itself. The Korean imperial rank badge and the imperial dragon robe (gon-ryong-po) were, to all appearances, synonymous, and did not exist in two separate forms, as in China. The *kirin (ch'i-lin)* design was worn in a chest plaque by the *taegun* (heir apparent), the *pai-tse* by second-degree princes, and the *hsieh-chai* by the minister of justice. (The *hsieh-chai* is the rarest among extant Korean rank badges, the oldest dating from about the seventeenth century.)

Among the female Korean royalty, princesses and secondary consorts used the phoenix design up until the late Yi dynasty (1897) on their rank badges, but after that time their insignia became the four-clawed dragon *(mang)* that princes wore on formal court robes. As late as 1897, the Korean queen was still wearing the phoenix design on the semiformal *wan-sam* and *tang-ui.* By 1865, nobles and court officers were wearing rank badges also on their ordinary street robes. The *taegun* still wore the *kirin,* while princes had been given the *pai-tse,* a change from the three-clawed dragon medallion they had formerly worn on court robes.

The cultural disintegration and decline that wracked China in the middle nineteenth century also affected imperial Korea, and many liberties began to be taken in the various symbols as the monarchy declined and finally collapsed at the end of the Yi dynasty in 1910. For example, the father of King Go Jong (1863–1907) *(Taewan-gun),* had once also worn the *kirin* (along with the heir apparent), but since 1895 wore a sacred tortoise design on his rank badge, a radical departure, and the civil and military ranks were reduced to single or double cranes or leopards, respectively, in the nine ranks; that is, ranks one to three civil wore double cranes, all ranks below that wearing single cranes, and in the military, ranks one to three wore double leopards (see Fig. C-2), all ranks below wearing single leopards.

The following techniques on select examples demonstrate how meticulous the craftsmanship was on the majority of Oriental costume accessories, and how this high level of artistic integrity, preserved so strenuously on even the most minute details with remarkably skillful stitchery and designing, produced the aesthetic effects that make these objects so evocatively beautiful.

Fig. 6-20. Belt purses. Designs of characters, flowers, insects, in satin, stem, chevron, and brick stitches. Purple, pinks, greens, yellows, black on satin and/or gauze cardboard-padded silk grounds. China, Ch'ing dynasty, nineteenth century. Collection of the author.

COSTUME ACCESSORY TECHNIQUES

Example 1: Child's Belt Purse, China, Ch'ing Dynasty (Figs. 6-21 and 6-22)

The unbelievable uniformity of hand stitchery on this piece could easily lead to the erroneous conclusion that it was done by machine, so the purse was opened from the back in order to ascertain the precise stitchery techniques used, which are amazingly skillful.

A cardboard backing in the shape of the design provided the sculptured effect. All color areas are rendered flatly, without gradation, using untwisted yarn throughout, which added considerable sheen to the surface. A vertical laid satin stitch acted as the foundation for a weave stitch, which was worked into it to create the linear floral designs, as will be demonstrated shortly. The weave stitch, used in this way, appears in six different types of design on the purse: swastika, lozenge, endless knot, sawtooth, leaf chevron, and broken line.

The example has been done entirely in satin and weave stitches, with some incidental chain stitch. The backing was used very ingeniously for several purposes: It acted as a shield to prevent the weave stitch (done entirely in the satin stitch level) from penetrating through the fabric, and was also a firm, general backing for the desired three-dimensional surface. An additional outside backing was also applied, which served to seal up and hide the needlework. Usually such backing was done with rice paper, but because this object was to be a purse and needed additional stiffness to keep it square, a secondary cardboard backing both closed and firmed the piece. This was covered with a double-lined, blue-gray fabric, which has a hidden pocket in it, and was finished with decorative edging tape (galoon).

The very complex stitchery was executed as follows:

The weave stitch was done with layer stitch used as a warp thread which was literally woven into the weft of the underlying satin stitch. A very hard, fine, coated (probably waxed) thread was used to slip easily over the silk yarn without dragging.

A. To begin, the main design center points are counted and marked on the fabric. Then the needle

Fig. 6-21. Child's belt purse. Fruit, flowers, and butterfly designs in satin, stem, and weave stitches on red plain weave silk ground. Bright greens, yellows, navy blue, purple. China, Ch'ing dynasty, nineteenth century. Collection of the author.

comes up at 1, enters at 2, skips seven (warp) threads and comes up at 3, enters at 4, skips seven threads again, emerges at 5, and reenters the fabric at 6. This process is repeated as necessary across the line.

B. For the second row, the needle emerges at 7, goes down at 8, skips one warp thread and comes up at 9, reenters at 10, skips five warp threads, comes up at 11, reenters at 12, comes up at 13 and down at 14, skips five threads again to come up at 15, and reenters the fabric at 16. This sequence is repeated as necessary across the line.

C. In the third row, the needle comes up at 17, reenters at 18, skips three threads and emerges at 19, reenters at 20, skips three threads once more,

and comes up at 21. This procedure is repeated across the line.

D. In the fourth row, the needle comes up at 27, reenters at 28, skips five threads, comes up at 29 and reenters at 30, skips one thread, emerges at 31, and repeats across the line.

E. The fifth row is the same as the first row, and the needle comes up at 37, reenters the fabric at 38, skips seven threads and emerges at 39 to reenter again at 40. The procedure is repeated across the line.

This stitchery produced the single-line design, and the double sawtooth was achieved merely by following the first line.

Fig. 6-22. Example 1: weave stitch.

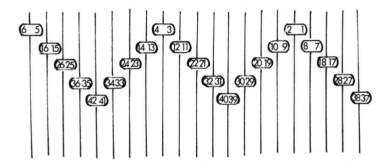

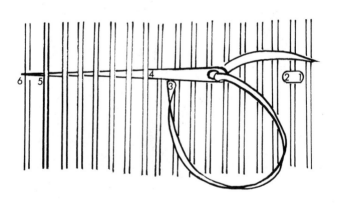

C-1. Women's informal robes for summer. Silk gauze with counted stitches in silk. Details in couched, wrapped gold thread. China, Ch'ing dynasty, eighteenth-nineteenth centuries. Gallery view from *Costumes from the Forbidden City*, exhibition by Alan Priest, Metropolitan Museum of Art, 1949. Courtesy of the Metropolitan Museum of Art.

C-2. Mandarin square for military official, first to third rank. Polychrome silk embroidery with stem, laidwork, and interlocking satin stitches. Korea, late Yi dynasty, late nineteenth century. Courtesy of the Folk Village Museum, Seoul.

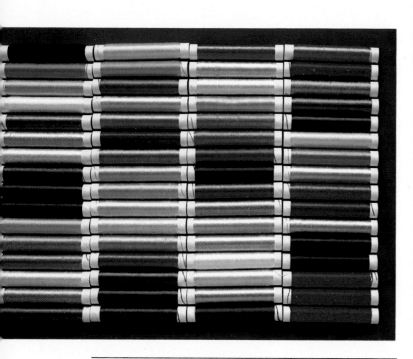

C-3. Dyed, untwisted silk yarns on spools. Collection of the author.

C-4. Peony blossom *(detail)*, with unfinished cotton padding and couching stitches for raised work. From *Maytime* (3 x 4 feet; 91.5 x 121.9 cm.), wall hanging by the author.

C-5. Peacock chest medallion for wife of civil official, third rank. Buddhist designs in polychrome silk embroidery of satin and stem stitches, with couched gold thread. China, Ch'ing dynasty, nineteenth century. Collection of the author.

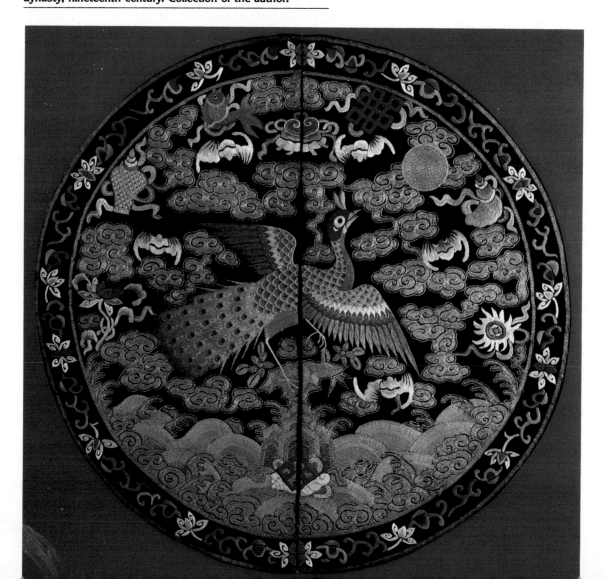

C-6. Wall hanging. Polychrome silk embroidery on satin fabric, with long and short, stem, and satin stitches. China, Ch'ing dynasty, nineteenth century. Collection of the author.

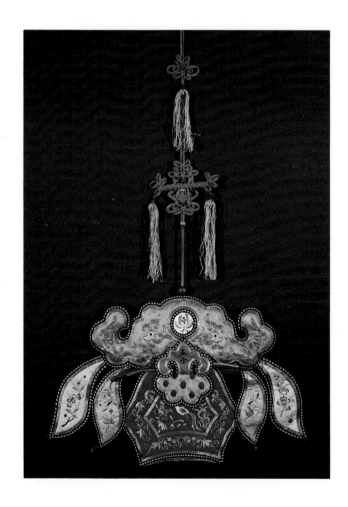

C-7. Matriarchal gift charm. Design of phoenixes, bats, flowers, Buddhist and Taoist symbols on padded silk fabric in shape of Buddhist canopy. Polychrome silk embroidery in satin and stem stitches, with couched gold borders and scrolls; some details outlined in couched gold; finished in galoon edgings. China, Ch'ing dynasty, seventeenth-nineteenth centuries. 9½ x 14 inches (24 x 35 cm.). Collection of the author.

C-8. Children's hats. Above, left to right: fruit basket and fruit in Pekinese stitch; couched metal thread dragon and flower designs; flower and butterfly designs in seed stitch with couched cordage contours, visor waves in satin stitch; tailed example— fish, lotus, and water wave designs in satin stitch with all contours in couched metal thread. Left, top to bottom: paper-padded fruit and flowers in satin stitch; chrysanthemum and orchid designs in satin stitch; Buddhist vase and peony designs in seed, satin, and stem stitches; flower and wave designs in stem and satin stitches; flower designs in stem and satin stitches on silk gauze fabric. Decorative galoon and black satin edgings. China, Ch'ing dynasty, nineteenth century. Collection of the author.

C-9. Detail of letter carrier. Peacock feather designs in continuous darning stitch; pine needles in radiated darning stitch; flowers and birds in long and short, stem, and satin stitches; rocks in irregular-length satin stitch. China, Ch'ing dynasty, nineteenth century. Collection of the author.

C-10. Mirror holder and decorative hanging. Left to right: design of shellfish, peaches, and bats in counted stitch with cash design in satin stitch on silk ground; lotus and Taoist tube and rods in counted and satin stitches on silk gauze ground. China, Ch'ing dynasty, nineteenth century. Collection of the author.

C-11. Imperial dragon robes. Left to right: polychrome embroidery in satin and split stitches and couched wrapped gold on brocade satin; dark blue satin embroidered with seed pearls, coral beads, silk yarns, and couched, wrapped gold on brocade satin; coffee-brown silk gauze with couched, wrapped gold and silver yarns, details in silk yarns. China, Ch'ing dynasty, late nineteenth century. Gallery view from *Costumes of the Forbidden City*, exhibition by Alan Priest, Metropolitan Museum of Art, 1949. Courtesy of the Metropolitan Museum of Art.

C-12. Dragon robe. Emperor's *ch'i-fu* embroidered with various sacrificial symbols in long and short and satin stitches; gold thread couching. China, Ch'ing dynasty, Tao-kuang period (1821-1851). George Crofts Collection, gift of the Robert Simpson Company. Courtesy of the Royal Ontario Museum, Toronto, Canada.

C-13. Emperor's twelve-symbol dragon robe *(ch'i-fu)*. Entire ground covered with counted darning stitch embroidery in diaper lozenge patterns with plied gold silk; accents in stem and satin stitch. Collar and cuff bands in lozenge diapers of counted darning stitch. Couched wrapped goldwork and satin stitch in water wave areas. Length, neck to hem, 53½ inches (135.89 cm.). China, Ch'ing dynasty, Ch'ien-lung period (1736-1795). Courtesy of the Metropolitan Museum of Art, purchase 1935, Joseph Pulitzer Bequest.

C-14. Emperor's dragon robe *(ch'i-fu)*. "The Hundred Cranes Robe." Bat and cloud designs in a twill binding of blues and creams on a brown satin ground. Polychrome embroidery in long and short, satin, knot, and stem stitches; couched wrapped gold and plied silk yarns; slight additions of paint and ink. Courtesy of the William Rockhill Nelson Gallery, Atkins Museum of Fine Arts.

C-16. Noh theater kosode. Gold *nuihaku* on dark brown satin ground, embroidered with incense wrappers, paulownia leaves, and trellis designs in stem, satin, and diagonal satin stitches; accents in hand-painted silver. Japan, Momoyama period, c. late seventeenth century. The Metropolitan Museum of Art, purchase 1932, Joseph Pulitzer Bequest.

C-15. Detail of wave border, "The Hundred Cranes Robe."

C-17. Kosode. Design of snow-crystal roundels and chrysanthemums in *nuihaku* and tie-dye, with satin and stem stitches and gold couching, on white *rinzu* silk. Japan, early Edo period. From *Japanese Embroidery* by Mutsuko Imai, Mainichi Newspapers, Tokyo. Courtesy of Kanebo Ltd.

C-18. Kosode. *Kata-suso* design of flowering autumnal plants. *Nuihaku* on white ground. Japan, Momoyama period. From *Japanese Embroidery* by Mutsuko Imai, Mainichi Newspapers, Tokyo. Courtesy of Kanebo Ltd.

C-19. Noh theater kosode. Gold *nuihaku* on red silk ground. Designs of peonies, phoenixes, and scrolls in polychrome silk floss laidwork, satin, and stem stitches. Japan, Tokugawa period (c. 1750-1795). Designed by Okio of the Maruyama school. The Metropolitan Museum of Art, purchase 1932, Joseph Pulitzer Bequest.

C-20. Noh theater kosode. Designs of cherry trees, phoenixes, swimming birds, and waves on red silk in long and short, satin, and stem stitches. Japan, middle Edo period. From *Japanese Embroidery* by Mutsuko Imai, Mainichi Newspapers, Tokyo. Courtesy of Kanebo Ltd.

C-21. *Koshimaki furisode.* Overall embroidery on black and red silk ground of blossoms, hat, lozenges, pine needles, all in laidwork couched with silk thread designs and contours of metal thread; swastikas in couched gold thread. Japan, late Edo period. From *Japanese Embroidery* by Mutsuko Imai, Mainichi Newspapers, Tokyo. Courtesy of Kyoto University of Industrial Art and Textile Fabrics.

C-22. Bridal robe *(hwal-ot).* Reconstruction by Ewha University, Seoul. Lotus, peony, waves, phoenix designs in long and short stitch, laidwork, satin, seed, and stem stitches; rocks in satin-stitch checkerboard pattern. Korea, Yi dynasty. Collection of the author.

C-23. Bridal robe (front view of Fig. C-24). Polychrome embroidery in satin and long and short stitches on red damask ground. Reconstruction by Prof. Joo Sun Suk, Dan Kook University, Seoul. Korea, Yi dynasty. Courtesy of the Institute of Folklore, Dan Kook University.

C-24. Bridal robe (back view of Fig. C-23). Designs of peonies, lotus, phoenixes, waves, in long and short and satin stitches. Korea, Yi dynasty. The Institute of Folklore, Dan Kook University, Seoul.

C-25. Ladies' purses. Polychrome embroideries and gold couching on silk, gauze, and satin; tassels in polychrome whippings, gold thread, coral beads, with macramé Turk's head and endless knot. China, Ch'ing dynasty, nineteenth century. Collection of the author.

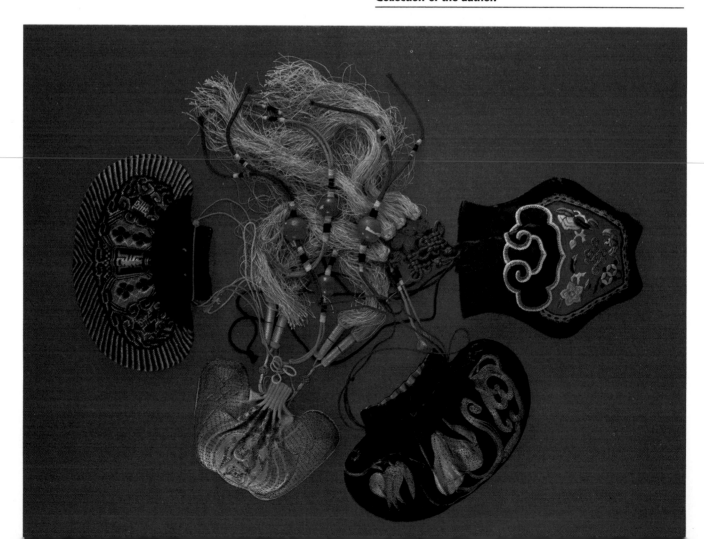

C-26. Court apron (fu-su). Polychrome embroidery in satin, stem, and long and short stitches; gold couchings on chain-link and cloud contours. Korea, Yi dynasty, fourteenth-seventeenth centuries. Courtesy of Ewha University, Seoul.

C-27. Jacket for wife of civil official, seventh rank. Scattered design of flowers, birds, and waves in seed, satin, and diagonal satin stitch on red silk ground; mandarin square in long and short, satin, and stem stitches. Collection of the author.

C-28. Matching spoon case and lady's purse. Left to right: design of Ten Longevities in laidwork, satin, long and short, and stem stitches, radiating darning stitch on pine needles; gold and silk couchings on thunder-line borders; red silk damask ground. Design of peonies in long and short stitch, with satin-stitched leaves; red silk damask ground. Korea, Yi dynasty. Courtesy of the Folk Village Museum, Seoul.

C-29. Imperial dragon medallion. Five-clawed dragon design in metal thread couching on black silk; flaming pearl in satin stitch with red thread and couched gold contours. Korea, Yi dynasty. Courtesy of Ewha University, Seoul.

C-30. Mandarin square, fourth to ninth rank civil. Polychrome embroidery in long and short and satin stitches with tightly twisted yarns on cordage base. Korea, late Yi dynasty, late nineteenth century. Courtesy of the Folk Village Museum, Seoul.

C-31. *Sun Rising Over a Turbulent Sea.* Irregular-length satin stitch, long and short, stem, and darning stitches on ocher-colored plain weave silk ground. China, Sung dynasty. Courtesy of the National Palace Museum, Taipei.

C-32. Chrysanthemums. Pedestal in interlocking satin stitch; decorative lotus flowers in satin stitch with stem stitch accents; frog designs in laidwork, stem, and satin stitches; vase in laidwork and interlocking satin stitch with flower motifs in satin stitch; gray earth areas in interlocking satin stitch; flowers in satin stitch; leaves in long and short and stem stitches; butterflies and insects in long and short, stem, and satin stitches; dark maroon silk ground. China, Sung dynasty. Courtesy of the National Palace Museum, Taipei.

C-33. Folding eight-panel screen. Tightly twisted yarns in long and short, satin, stem, seed, darning, and irregular-length satin stitches on ocher silk ground. Korea, Yi dynasty. Courtesy of the Folk Village Museum, Seoul.

C-34. *The Sea.* Ten-panel screen by the author. Long and short, stem, satin, and continuous darning stitches, padded work; on blue silk ground. Height, 9 feet; length, 15 feet (2.74 x 4.57 m.). Collection of the Presidential Mansion, Seoul.

C-35. Detail from *Rose of Sharon*, ten-panel screen (Fig. 7-7). Irregular-length satin stitch, long and short stitch, extended seed stitch, with loop couchings, padded work, textured threads on tree trunk.

C-36. Detail from *White Peacock*, four-panel screen (Fig. 7-11). Long and short, seed, stem, irregular-length satin, spaced darning, and continuous darning stitches, wrapped cordage and metallic silk thread on navy-blue silk ground. Collection of the author.

C-37. *Kwan-yin.* Interlocking satin, long and short, radiated darning stitches, gold and paper-wrapped threads, finer details in green ink; overall embroidery on tan silk. China, Ch'ing dynasty, eighteenth century. The Metropolitan Museum of Art, 1930, William Christian Paul Bequest.

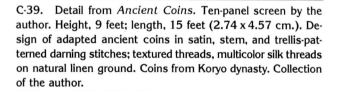

C-38. Wall hanging. Design of *shou* character, peonies, and cranes in long and short, stem, satin, and irregular-length satin stitches; tightly twisted yarns on red silk ground. China, Ch'ing dynasty. Collection of the author.

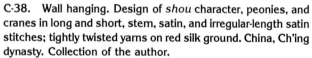

C-39. Detail from *Ancient Coins*. Ten-panel screen by the author. Height, 9 feet; length, 15 feet (2.74 x 4.57 cm.). Design of adapted ancient coins in satin, stem, and trellis-patterned darning stitches; textured threads, multicolor silk threads on natural linen ground. Coins from Koryo dynasty. Collection of the author.

Example 2: Girl's Winter Hat, Korea, Yi Dynasty (Top and Back Views, Fig. 6-5)

Top View

The central ground material of this handsome child's hat is in blue-black satin. The carefully crafted crown area has a circular medallion whose blue satin ground becomes a focal axis for the central, radial arrow design and the outer serpentine line. The circular medallion's outer edges are red cordage laid in loops at regular intervals around its diameter, which were couched at the end of each loop. (Such cordage was made by twisting many heavy threads together.) After the red cordage was couched, a white cordage was laid upon it in a second looping pattern and couched in the same way. The center arrow design was stitched directly upon the blue satin center—the red lines in stem stitch and the white areas in satin stitch.

The delightful, pastel-toned serpentine lines were done with pink, yellow, and silver cordage laid along the design and couched at quarter-inch intervals.

The brilliant orange tassels were created by looping strands of heavy yarn into successive bights; then a whipping was applied to their upper ends in a lighter orange thread, and the lower end bights were cut. Once the tassels were formed, they were couched in the elbows of the serpentine cordage.

Back View

The hanging tails, which are chin ties, are in blue, green, and orange damask, with swallowtail points and small tassels. The upper embroidery levels of the hat show a well-composed lotus design in long and short stitch, with some fine leaf figures in satin stitch. In the lower section, various conventions—deer, mountains, birds, the sacred fungus—were all accomplished by satin stitch.

A very sophisticated use of complementary colors—bright orange with bright blue, for example—and the tasteful selection of the interrelated chromatics in these and other parts of the hat denote a highly evolved degree of professional artistry, as represented by the subtly worked and dextrously hidden craftsmanship.

Example 3: Embroidered Purses, China, Ch'ing Dynasty (Figs. C-25, 6-23)

These four examples show typical Chinese color, stitchery, and design techniques in their elegant use of contrasting colors, shapes, and textures. Features to be noted on such pieces are the way space has been arranged in smooth, continuous harmonies or interesting negative space; the use of balance and balancing elements; and the incorporation of formal or informal design structures. The color work has been done in overall warm or cool tonalities or in contrasting values, while the stitchery provides additional textural richness and complementary or balancing color elements. These purses were usually made in two pieces that were joined after their embroidery was finished. Occasionally the drawstring area was made in a third, fitted piece.

Rounded Style (from left to right) The top drawstring area is in black satin, with the main body of the bag in silk gauze. The entire bag was done in diagonal counted stitch (petit-point). An outer border in the *li shui* wave pattern encloses an inner design nucleus of clouds, floral petals, and three characters for happiness, the flanking characters providing balance for the larger, more dominant central figure. This bag has a formal design.

Eared Style The yellow silk ground has been covered up to the drawstring neck with couched gold and silver thread, in a zoned pattern. The swastika figures at the left and right ears provide balance and frame the central cash and spirifloral motifs. All couching has been done in red silk thread, with violet and green accents in the lower central portion. The use of zones in the couching technique was designed in this way to create rounded surfaces and planes, which tended to increase the light-catching properties of the metal thread. The drawstring's tassels in brilliant yellow are augmented by gold thread whippings and tiny Turk's head macramé work in silver thread near their necks. The bag has a formal design structure.

Rounded Style A black satin ground with gold silk lining provides a stunning contrast for a pomegranate and scroll design in couched silver and gold thread. The red drawstrings are decorated with red coral beads and polychrome whippings in black, white, and gray-blue. This is an informal design.

Hexagonal Style The drawstring tassels of bright yellow are a complementary color harmony to the deep purple satin ground, and have been finished with red Turk's head and green endless knot macramé work. The main body of the bag shows a red silk window, upon which ground peach, peach blossom, cash, and bat designs have been executed in satin stitch. These designs encircle a central endless knot in gold thread, which has been couched with a heavy yellow thread to form bead-like accents on its surface. A gold metal thread galoon frames the red silk window, and over both a cloud lappet, done with heavy blue and white cotton thread, was finished in buttonhole stitch as follows.

A. The needle comes up at 1, about ⅛ inch (3 mm.) inside the contour. A one-inch loop is held above the first stitch with the left thumb, and the needle enters at 2 (inside the loop) at the contour. The needle emerges at 3, right next to 1, and is drawn through carefully to the right, pulling the loop to the contour and finishing one complete stitch.

B. For the second stitch, a loop is made again and the needle reenters at 4, right next to the previous stitch, but *on* the contour. It comes up at 5 and is again drawn carefully to the right. The tension on the stitches directs them in such a way that they lie next to the previous stitch. This procedure is repeated as necessary.

Fig. 6-23. Example 3: Embroidered purse cloud lappet in buttonhole stitch and zoned stitchery for light-catching technique (from Fig. C-25).

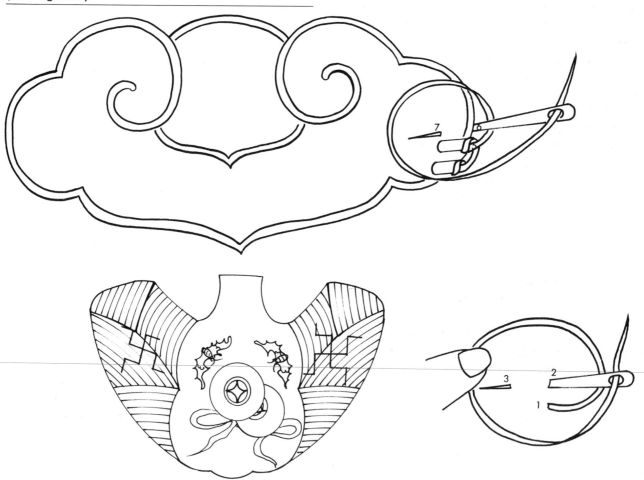

Example 4: Summer Court Jacket, China, Ch'ing Dynasty, Early Nineteenth Century
(Fig. 6-24)

This summer jacket was worn as an accessory and probably belonged to the empress or an imperial concubine. The rather abrupt ending of the wave designs at the cuffs, and a seamed area beneath, clearly indicate that the sleeves were pieced to make a full Chinese sleeve from an original Manchu narrow *ch'ao-fu* style. A rather amusing example of Chinese aversion to and subtle resistance against the Manchu dictators and the clothing styles which were imposed by them, this case further demonstrates how the Imperial *ch'i-fu* eventually came back to the full Chinese *p'ao* sleeve, even though the horsehoof cuff was retained.

The ground fabric of the jacket is in blue-black silk gauze. The dragons were done in couched, wrapped gold thread, with quite unusual body accents in a dark brown paper-wrapped thread, which may originally have been red. In addition to the woven mountains and waves above the sleeve bands and at the lower borders, embroidered motifs shown in the field include stylized cloud fillers, bats, coral, the Buddhist endless knot, and Taoist flower baskets. The Buddhist Eight Precious Things and

flaming pearls also appear in the field embroidery, with a larger flaming pearl conventionally centered beneath the main dragon. The collar, sleeve band, and lower border designs are not embroidered, but are tapestry *(k'o-ssu)* woven into the fabric, in designs of spiriform flowers and bats, augmented by a thunder line swastika. The embroidery work on this jacket was executed entirely in the Chinese version of brick stitch, the color gradation being achieved by changing the thread (color) at gradual intervals. (For brick stitch, see Chapter 2, "Home Accessory Techniques," page 36.)

The couching on the dragon's scales was done with a continuous unbroken thread, laid in symmetrical patterns to follow the form of the scales. This striking technique gave the coil's forms a more rounded, sculpturesque appearance, as well as an improved general uniformity. The couching was combined with the wrapped-thread stem stitch accents mentioned earlier.

Such court jackets became part of imperial formal wear after 1759 for public appearances. More dynamic and dramatic than lyrically beautiful, the many Buddhist and lucky symbols used on the jackets were probably politically intended to impress the people with the cosmic authority of the emperor.

Fig. 6-24. Summer court jacket. Polychrome embroidery on silk gauze. China, Ch'ing dynasty, early nineteenth century. Length, 26 inches (66 cm.). The Metropolitan Museum of Art, Pulitzer Bequest, 1935.

Example 5: Imperial Dragon Medallion, Korea, Yi Dynasty (Figs. C-29 and 6-25)

The rank of the Korean emperors was concentrated in a complex version of the dragon design, worn as the highest imperial designation on the chest, back, and both shoulders of the *gon-ryong-po,* the Korean dragon robe. This example from Ewha University in Seoul shows an extremely intricate kind of couching, which was actually done in two layers. In the first layer, the entire dragon shape, as well as the cloud figures (except for the flaming pearl), were covered entirely with couched, gold-wrapped thread. In the second layer, the scales, all of the dragon's edges, and all cloud edges are in a two-strand gold thread, which was couched closely on top of the first layer, while the scalloped edges show a double strand of heavier, gold wire thread. These techniques were executed as follows.

A. The cloud design area was completely covered with gold-wrapped thread, commencing from the center, and arranging the couching material in flat, clockwise coils that followed the outer contours. These areas were then couched with a red holding stitch.

B. The outside filament design was done in solid gold (wire) thread, one strand of which equals twelve strands of silk thread, and which is much heavier than the gold-wrapped thread used for the underlayer. The gold wire thread followed the contour of the design precisely, starting at the center. The tiny circlets on the lateral ends were made by a single loop that was couched inside. Once the first circlet was established, the contour was again followed until the second circlet was reached, which was once more created with a single loop, the movement being resumed, after this, along the contour until the starting point was arrived at.

Rather than being cut at this point, the strand was

Fig. 6-25. Example 5: Continuous and separated gold couching direction on Korean imperial rank badge.

instead couched and made to reverse itself, and to begin a counterclockwise direction along the *inside* contour line, which bypassed the circlets all the way around the design until it arrived at the inside center once more. This procedure was definitely necessary, since metal thread cannot be cut frequently; only a final cutting at the end where it is to be couched is necessary.

After the gold thread was laid and shaped along the contours, it was couched separately with holding stitches spaced one-eighth inch apart, alternating between each strand.

Example 6: Mandarin Square for Civil Official, Fourth to Ninth Ranks, Korea, Late Yi Dynasty (Fig. C-30)

Before 1505, the rank badges of Korea were traditionally three degrees lower than those of China; consequently the pheasant symbol, which was accorded the third rank civil in China, became the first rank civil in Korea. The reason for this was that Korea held the third rank in the Chinese court, and since Korea was an unofficial protectorate of China, we must assume that it signified a confirmation of her tacit liege state. Late Yi examples, such as the one shown here, demonstrate the final phase in Korean imperial embroidery, and the ultimate simplification of the Korean ranking system, where the double crane symbol now represented the first and second ranks civil. Many Korean rank badges are extremely artistic, with intense coloration and the interesting textures consistent with the typical Korean use of tightly twisted thread. In this late Yi artistic

stage, we now find a very ordered, balanced, symmetrical composition; the main Korean artistic features are still present, but a cool sophistication of line, contrasting shapes, and restrained color supply an elegant, rhythmic harmony. The stitchery craftsmanship on this example is equally excellent and, far from showing a decline at this later state in imperial history, has a superlative vigor.

The feather divisions on the back, wings, and contours of the cranes are finely executed, padded raised work. A very thin rice paper, one quarter-inch wide, was used for this purpose, tightly rolled to a wirelike strength and thickness. This padding was couched onto the fabric before the stitchery began, the paper padding being laid along the linear contours of the base design. The raised work was then couched in the same technique as metal thread, but with much tighter stitches and at closer intervals.

A diagonal white thread satin stitch was subsequently worked over the couching material. Between the corded areas, a long satin stitch provided the filling. The wings, back, and head of the cranes were all completed in this technique and strongly suggest the textures of feathers and down.

The clouds, mountains, waves, sea, and trees on this square were done in plain satin stitch without any additional raised work.

Almost as famous as costume and its accessories in the great schools of Oriental embroidery were the scrolls and screens used to beautify the elegant interiors of the home and palace, and the inspirational banners and hangings of the Buddhist temples wherein the devotions of that religion were practiced. The following chapter considers some of the historical and technical aspects of this important branch of Oriental needlework art.

7/ SCROLLS, SCREENS, AND BANNERS

HISTORY AND AESTHETICS

In the ancient and historical Orient, Western-style oil painting was unknown. When it finally arrived in the East during the late eighteenth century, it was practiced only infrequently by Asian artists, and it never assumed the important place there that it has in the West. Consequently, the hanging of framed, oil-painted canvases in the palace or home never became customary. Instead, the ages-old tradition of hangings or the use of unframed scrolls prevailed (see Fig. C-31). These were either done entirely in embroidery or painted in watercolors, although sometimes they were a combination of both, especially in the later dynasties. The scroll had the advantage of being easily portable; it could be rolled up and carried from place to place, moved with facility to various rooms in the house, or stored with a minimum of space.

The ground material for the scroll, whether it was to be painted or embroidered, was always silk, although there are a few examples from the outlying provinces of China that are made of hemp cloth. Occasionally the satin weave was used for compositions that were intended for pure embroidery, but satin was seldom used as a painting ground, for its excessive smoothness provided an insufficient tooth for watercolor. There are some scroll examples which have damasklike grounds, but these are comparatively few. Most are of fine, tightly woven plain weave, twill, or gauze silk. After the composition had received its finished embroidery, it was usually, but not always, mounted on a firm brocade or damask backing, which also served as a harmonious frame. If a brocade was not used, several layers of rice paper were affixed to the back of the picture to protect it.

The majority of embroidered scrolls and wall hangings from China date from the Sung, Yuan, Ming, and Ch'ing dynasties, with the vast preponderance from the Ch'ing, since the work of that period is younger and better preserved. There are also Korean scrolls from as early as the Koryo dynasty (A.D. 918–1392). In addition to the embroidered scrolls of these periods, there were other, related tableaux that graced the homes and palatial estates of the aristocracy, such as screens and embroidery albums. Such albums were specially created embroidery compositions on silk or satin panels about twelve or fifteen inches square and mounted on brocades, composed and bound for viewing at the owner's leisure. Also popular were pictorially embroidered lanterns, fans, and embroidered lampshades. The latter were a particularly remarkable Chinese invention. Lamplight, shining through the unembroidered sections of the picture, would cast shadows of the embroidered designs in interesting silhouettes upon the walls or ceilings of a room. Dried leaf patterns, in combination with embroidery, were used in much the same way on sliding doors, where they were embossed into the rice-paper layers of the partitions.

The embroidered scroll styles of the Sung dynasty (A.D. 960–1279) exemplify the cool elegance of that entire era, the artistic heights for which it is famous. Scroll compositions of bird, butterfly, and flower themes were popular in Sung embroidery, rendered in a variety of techniques and informal design approaches, at times simple, gay, and lyrical, at other times somewhat stern and conservative. Most examples effectively demonstrate the Sung designer's mastery of line, the subtle

Fig. 7-1. Screen panel. Design of twelve varieties of birds, with trees, flowers, and rocks in long and short, satin, stem, seed, darning stitches, and laidwork; textured, untwisted yarns on tree trunk. China, Ch'ing dynasty, Crown copyright, Victoria and Albert Museum, London.

sense of depth and airiness that is so evocative and profound, the marvelous Chinese gift for effective, dynamic pattern and the distribution of negative space.

An example of typical Sung design and embroidery is the *Thousand-Armed Kwan-yin Bodhisattva,* shown in Figure 7-2. Both the lively, vibrant design and the stitchery display the confident Sung virtuosity. The color scheme is a harmonious blend of exquisite golds, oranges, and ochers, which are capably balanced by delicate counterpoints of rich cerulean blue, jade greens, and tiny notes of black. The composition seems like a watercolor painting: The richness of its surfaces is subordinated to overall patterns, sensitive washlike tints, and a very deft use of line. If one stares concentratedly at this composition for several moments, a visual vibration is set up which gives the effect of a forward as well as circular movement in the arms and lotus base, and adds a rather floating ethereality to the canopy above the goddess's head. It is, of course, an optical illusion, conceived by the designers to add to the effect of an exalted spiritual dimension, and it does this very effectively. Kwan-yin is a Buddhist deity, her thousand arms and thousand eyes symbolizing eternal omniscience and omnipotence. The piece was executed in satin, seed, and outline stitches on a woven damask ground, which has a lovely plum branch pattern. Other important examples of Sung scroll embroidery are the magnificent *Sun Rising Over a Turbulent Sea* (Figs. C-31, 7-15, and 7-16) and the *White Falcon* (Fig. 7-17).

During both the Sung and Ming dynasties, paintings were often embroidered, or embroidery scrolls were sometimes finished with touches or accents of painting. Although embroidery purists might object to this practice, it was really only an example of mixed media developments that took place in the Chinese fiber arts of this time, especially during the Ming. Such widely ranging experimentation resulted in extensive use of the stamped gold process, much gold thread embroidery, the sewing of seed pearls and other precious stones to embroidery compositions, and the application of the lovely feathers of the peacock, pheasant, and Siamese fighting cock to embroidery scrolls or screen panels as textural variations. Some embroidery works were even stitched entirely with human hair!

While only a single dragon robe from the Ming dynasty (1368–1644) has survived, there are numerous mandarin squares and quite a number of embroidered scrolls dating from this period. The

Fig. 7-2. *Thousand-Armed Kwan-yin Bodhisattva.* Design of Kwan-yin figure on lotus throne beneath Buddhist canopy in satin, seed, and stem stitches with tightly twisted silk yarns; gold-couched contours; on a beige damask silk ground with plum-branch pattern. China, Sung dynasty. Courtesy of the National Palace Museum, Taipei.

famous Ku school of embroidery, originating in the family of Madame Han Hsi-meng and taking its name from her husband, Ku Shou-ch'ien, had its center in the Shanghai area and produced many of the extant Ming scrolls and album pieces, as well as establishing a fine tradition (the "Ku family style" or the Ku Hsiu) that was to endure for several hundred years, along with Su Hsiu, Hsiang Hsiu, and Ching Hsiu in the sites of Soocho, Hunan, and Peiping.

Ming color work is very intense, the color themes and general composition being lusher and more vigorous than the Sung manner. There is also a greater use of contrast, of dark values thrown into bold, stark patterns against lighter tones; of fawn-colored, ocher, and pale orange backgrounds registering complementary intensities against deep, rich earth browns, lapis lazuli blues, Prussian blues, and blacks. Ming scroll embroidery also tends more to purely artistic conventions, with less naturalism than one finds in Sung work. It is far more stylized, intellectual, and linear, with larger color masses in dramatic, stylized designs that are simultaneously robust, gorgeous, and opulent.

The four separate Ming scrolls shown in Figure 7-3 were designed to be seen and enjoyed either separately or as a group: Each scroll is a self-contained picture independent of the others, yet when all are shown together, the whole becomes a unified composition. This was brought about mainly through the compositional device of tying the pictorial elements to one side of the picture, the unifying use of negative space, and the rounded, inverse shape of the entire thematic structure. The last feature was accomplished by massing the pictorial components to the right side of the composition in the two left-hand scrolls and to the left side in the two right-hand scrolls. The arrangement of line, contrast, and spatial balance is thus masterfully

Fig. 7-3. Hanging scrolls. Birds and flowers with grasses in stem, long and short, satin, and seed stitches. China, Ming dynasty. Courtesy of the American Museum of Natural History.

handled, and an exquisite sense of lyrical rhythm, light, movement, and nature's airiness was achieved throughout. Repetition of the bird and flower theme and the graceful curve of the long grass further serve to confirm an overall harmony and unity. In the first and third panels a lone cardinal and a crane sit among the flowers, the strong beak line of the crane providing an oppositional thrust to the strong general movement to the right, as it points at a dragonfly placed high in the first scroll. The lovemaking parakeets and jays in the second and fourth panels add incidental romantic and spatial notes. The jays also serve the purpose of "stopping" the viewer's eye at the upper right-hand corner: Their down-thrust beaks lead us back into the picture to its main focal point, the crane. These four scrolls are all executed in varying combinations of stem, long and short, satin, and seed stitches.

The pictorial embroidery styles of the Ch'ing dynasty (1644–1912) were in many ways a perpetuation of those prevalent during the Ming but, up until about 1875, can also be regarded as their peak, their fulfilling maturity. The Manchu resistance to change, the rigid pressures imposed on China by the stagnant Manchu society, combined with other tragic events of the middle nineteenth century, finally reduced Ch'ing embroidery to a shadow of its former glory. Before this came about, however, the embroiderer's art developed into an excellence which was really the culmination of all that had gone before, and the heights of the great dynasties found their consummation in the splendor of early and middle Ch'ing needlework.

An example of the mature greatness of Chinese embroidery can be found in Figure C-37, a Tantric Kwan-yin temple banner that dates from the eighteenth-century Ch'ien-lung period of the Ch'ing. Several copies of this piece are extant, notably the example dated 1783 in the Victoria and Albert Museum in London. Such banners and temple hangings were the work of Buddhist monks in the embroidery studios of large monasteries. Typical Buddhist religious decorations, they are found in all Chinese, Korean, and Tibetan observances. Called *t'angka* in Tibet and *t'anku* in China, such banners and hangings were important means of explaining the faith and life of the Buddha to the illiterate masses, and the banners were carried forth in public processions on religious festival and holy days. Sometimes they are very large (some were gigantic), although most are similar in size and shape to Western medieval tapestries. They were never en-

Fig. 7-4. Fan leaf. Bird and flower motif in satin, long and short, and darning, stem stitches in silk yarns on silk ground. Diameter 10 1/4 inches (26 cm.). China, Ch'ing dynasty, nineteenth century. The Metropolitan Museum of Art.

tirely woven compositions, the use of the hand in embroidery being thought more devotional than the mechanical working of the loom. While Tibetan *tankas* were usually painted in vivid watercolors with only border embroidery, most Chinese and Japanese religious banners were executed entirely in embroidery and/or appliqué.

The banner shown in our example is a masterpiece of Tantric Buddhist art, and its magnificence can hardly be overstated. Kwan-yin dominates the center of this dramatic work, with six *dhyani* buddhas figured in the sky above and the Grand Lama of Peking and a disciple in the lower left and right corners. The figure of Kwan-yin stands on a lotus base, and eight of her arms are clearly depicted, beginning with the two original arms in the mudra (gesture) of prayer and the mudra of charity, the remaining arms holding various sacred objects of Buddhist iconography: the lotus, bow and arrow, vase, wheel, and rosary. The symbolic thousand arms of Kwan-yin form an aura around her, which partially obscures a flame mandala and a triangulate cloud formation. At the top center, the canopy, the Buddhist symbol of victory over the religions of

Fig. 7-5. Embroidered Buddhist scroll. Design of eagle and mon-keys, mountains, trees, flowing stream in long and short stitch with gold couching. From Jion-in Temple, Kyoto. Japan, Edo period, nineteenth century. Crown copyright, Victoria and Albert Museum, London.

Fig. 7-6. Detail from *The Ten Longevities,* ten-fold screen. Design of clouds, cranes, mountains, water, tortoises, pine tree, bamboo in stem, long and short, satin, and radiated darning stitches. Korea, Yi dynasty. Collection of Han-Dok Remedia Industries Museum, Seoul.

the world, is flanked by sun and moon circles at left and right, and the six buddhas.

The breathtaking grandeur and serenity of the design were achieved through the designer's selec-tion of a strong geometric theme: a circle imposed upon a triangle, augmented by the straight horizon-tal mass composing the upper third of the picture, and the solid base of landscape below. The triangle is formed by the cloud mass that surges over the goddess's head; the main circular form (of sym-bolic hands, arms, and eyes) is superimposed upon this important triangulate structure. The same theme is repeated in the upper horizontal motif: Each of the four Buddhas is framed by a circular mass imposed upon a triangulate cloud shape. The cloud fillers, which arrest the composition at the top of the picture, then undulate down and around the

central figure, are beautifully rendered, restful, softly moving masses. The trees and mountains in the lower two-thirds of the picture, extremely detailed, naively stylized, and lyrically spiritual, provide upward-thrusting forms that exalt the sense of sub-limity and spiritual beatitude, directing the eye and the mind upward. The two figures at the lower left and right echo the triangle-circle theme also. Stylized water lines flow between the lowest moun-tains to lead the eye to the lotus base upon which the goddess stands, and thence upward through the central figure.

Scarcely second to the dynamic design concept of this banner is a thoroughly astounding display of virtuosity and skill in the drawing and the highly complex stitchery. The composition has been done almost entirely in satin stitch, interlocking satin stitch, and split stitch. The smaller details in zigzag couching and stem stitches were worked with very fine gold- and silver-wrapped thread. Some of the smaller details in the foreground landscape were hand-painted in very fine, dark green line work. A variety of silk yarns have been used on tan silk, although none of the ground shows through the stitchery, the main color theme consisting of various shades of tan, blue, green, cream, and red, while the finished banner was mounted on a red satin brocade pattern of gilded paper, the whole receiving a backing of bright yellow silk. The amount of precise detail, the complex geometric Indian designs on the costumes and elsewhere, as well as the extreme sophistication of design, drawing, and stitchery, show this banner to be the work of a master embroiderer and his studio, and it probably took many years to complete. It may even have been added to and embellished over several generations, as was often the custom in Buddhist and Taoist embroidery. The special stitchery done on the symbolic circle of hands and eyes surrounding Kwanyin is especially impressive and deserves special mention and an exacting analysis, which will follow in the technical section of this chapter.

Folding screens (Fig. C-33) were in use in the earliest dynasties in China, and it seems likely that they were a Chinese innovation that spread to other parts of the world. Tomb paintings that date from as early as the Eastern Chou dynasty (seventh century B.C.) show that both screens and hangings were an intrinsic part of the home and palace almost from the beginning of Chinese history.

Essentially an article of furniture, the screen was used as a room divider for inner apartments, provided privacy for sleeping and dressing areas and also served as a windscreen in drafty rooms without central heating. Its silk-covered panels naturally seemed to call for some kind of decoration, and they were in fact decorated from the earliest times with a variety of materials, the most popular being embroidery and painting. Screens were made in many sizes and heights. Six- and ten-fold screens were usual (Fig. 7-7), but Chinese records show that huge thirty-six-fold screens were not uncommon in the imperial palace.

While extant examples are rare, the embroidered folding screen was in wide use during the historical periods of China and Korea. Screens were used extensively in the Japanese home and castle also, especially during the Momoyama period. Japanese screens, however, were usually painted and very

Fig. 7-7. *Rose of Sharon.* Ten-panel folding screen by the author. Design of flowering rose-of-sharon tree in shape of Korean peninsula in irregular length satin, long and short, stem, and seed stitches, with loop couchings and padded work. Earth greens, browns, white, purples, maroons, yellows, on light yellow satin ground. Height, 9 feet; length, 15 feet (2.74 × 4.57 m.). Collection of the Presidential Mansion, Seoul.

Fig. 7-8. Detail from master design for *Rose of Sharon* screen. Colored dyes and inks on rice paper. (Size above.) Collection of the author.

Fig. 7-9. The Soochow Embroidery Institute, Soochow, China. The artists are working on a large stretched silk flower composition, using arm rests on a traditional rectangular frame variation, which has its rollers in the sidebars (top edge). Photo courtesy of Mr. and Mrs. G. W. Barker.

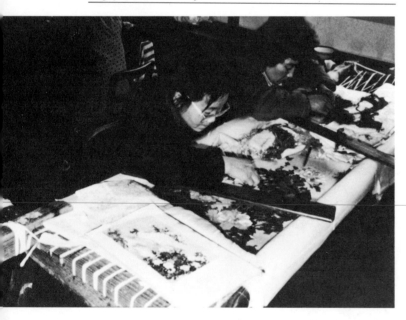

seldom done in embroidery, although they are embroidered today. The reasons for this are several and interesting: Until the great cultural influx from China during the Nara period (T'ang dynasty), the Japanese textile arts were comparatively undeveloped, and the custom of embroidering screens had never evolved there to any great extent. When the Japanese textile arts did bloom during the Momoyama period, the artistic needs of the shoguns and *daimyo* were for quickly executed screens with large expanses of gold leaf to brighten the gloomy interiors of their castles, and painting was better able to fill that need than embroidery. The Japanese sliding door, or *shoji,* also was traditionally made of undecorated white rice paper, again, a mere difference of custom and historical coincidence.

Screen embroidery has always been a specialty of Korea, and some of the finest extant examples of the historical period come from that country. The history of screen embroidery in Korea is, obviously, not as old as that of China. However, screens have been found in tomb excavations at Sagok-ri which dated from as early as the Three Kingdoms period (c. A.D. 300). Doubtless the use of screens was introduced from China during the Han expansion, since the majority of important cultural influences came to Korea solely from the south, rather than from Japan. Such cultural importation was quickly absorbed and enlarged upon by the self-sustaining Korean culture, which rose to great refinement during the important maturing epochs of the Great Silla and Koryo dynasties.

During the Yi dynasty (1392–1910) the earlier phases of imperial Korean expansion brought tremendous pressure to bear upon craftsmen to fill the many needs of the growing court. This patronage, in turn, caused the Korean crafts to develop the high levels of perfection for which they are famous. Fine examples of Yi screens have survived in preservation to modern times. Their subjects show a wide range of bird and flower compositions, scenes of the hunt, idyllic landscapes, and fabulous palaces and towers, nearly all imbued in some way with the whimsical sense of humor and vigorous quality that characterizes most Korean art.

The eight-fold Korean Yi dynasty screen shown in Figure C-33 is reminiscent of the Chinese bird and flower scroll in Figures 7-3 and C-6. The Korean screen shows eight different kinds of birds in a traditional tree-and-flower setting, the paired birds again echoing a recurrent romantic and design

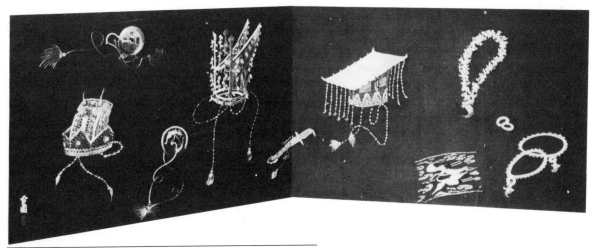

Fig. 7-10. *Ancient Korean Treasures.* Two-fold folding screen by the author. Design of ancient crowns, coins, and accessories in satin, basketweave, long and short, and stem stitches; gold couching. Ochers, reds, greens, white, gold, on navy blue satin ground. Height, 4 feet; length, 10 feet (122 cm. × 3.048 m.). Collection of the Imperial Palace, Tehran.

Fig. 7-11. *The White Peacock.* Eight-fold folding screen by the author. Designs of white peacocks, peonies, and leaves in long and short, stem, satin, continuous darning, and spaced darning stitches in silk and metallic yarns; couched silver thread, padded work. Height, 6 feet; length, 10 feet (1.83 × 3.048 m.). Collection of the author.

Fig. 7-12. Screen panels. Composition of bright-plumaged birds, flowers, trees, rising sun, in long and short, satin, seed, stem, darning, continuous darning, radiated darning stitches, and laidwork. Maroons, rose, pinks, salmon, oranges, grays, earth greens, browns, purples, yellows, blues, ochers, black and white on light silver-gray silk ground. China, Ch'ing dynasty. Courtesy of the National Museum of History, Taipei.

Fig. 7-13. *Buddha on the Lotus Throne.* Tantric Buddhist temple banner. Design of Buddha with six lamas, flowers, clouds, flame mandala, in overall embroidery of interlocking satin, long and short, stem stitches, and laidwork; with couched, paper-wrapped thread on mandala; some painted details; on tan silk warp twill ground. China, Ch'ing dynasty, eighteenth century. The Metropolitan Museum of Art, Rogers Fund, 1951.

Fig. 7-14. *Immortals Gathering Round the Buddha.* Buddhist temple banner. Central design of Buddha on lotus throne surrounded by emperors, deities, and monks in long and short, satin, stem, and couching stitches. China, Ch'ing dynasty. Collection of the National Palace Museum, Taiwan, Republic of China.

Fig. 7-15. Detail from *Sun Rising Over a Turbulent Sea* (Fig. C-31). Hanging scroll. Polychrome embroidery on silk. China, Sung dynasty. Courtesy of the National Palace Museum, Taipei.

theme in Oriental embroidery. The screen also reveals a distinct Ming influence, but there the similarity to Chinese work ends, for the rich Korean style emerges in all its humane intensity.

Classic Korean art achieved a characteristic shorthand drawing style, simplicity of design, and directness of expression that seem startlingly close to modern forms of expression. This is further exemplified by a certain flattening of the form, the use of broad, unbroken notes of color, and the intensification of stylization techniques into the most brief, direct, symbolic notes. This can be observed in the treatment of the tree and setting sun in panel 1 (at the left), by the handling of the rocks in panels 3 to 8, and by the flower and leaf techniques in panel 2. A characteristic of Korean style was the use of a bold, jagged line, which very powerfully accents the dramatic linear pattern throughout the composition. There is a great emphasis on shape, pattern, and contrast in each of these panels, and, like their Chinese counterparts, they are designed to be viewed separately or as an entire unified composition. Variety could be given the viewer by opening the folds of the screen so that the pictures could be seen in adjacent positions, or the screen could be opened to its full length to be enjoyed as a whole. The panels were always designed to present a total harmonious unit, regardless of how, or from where, the screen was seen.

Although these screen panels seem to rely less on a studied use of negative space because of a quite compact pattern in each, nevertheless the negative spatial areas are just as important and as carefully designed as those occupied by depicted objects. A distinguished use of color also greatly contributes to the screen's excellence, for the colors selected, the kinds of color used, and their arrangement in the composition are extremely lush, gorgeous, and yet in exquisite good taste. The lighter and darker Prussian blues that appear in the rocks in panel 1 are reechoed in delightful, repeating accents in each panel, an overall color harmony and sense of unity throughout the work being accomplished through this artistic device. Vibrant oranges and golds, in many shades and variations, provide a complementary counterpoint to these rich blues, as does the beige tonality of the plain weave silk ground. This brilliant color orchestration was expressed by interesting textured stitchery, the majority of the piece being done in satin stitch, with long and short stitch used for blending and gradating the various broad color patterns, and seed stitch

for some of the smaller areas. The use of these stitches in Korea during the Yi again demonstrates how universal they were throughout the Orient during historical times, most of the work being done entirely in them.

We shall now turn to some of the more unusual techniques and materials that were employed in scroll, screen, and banner embroidery, noting once more the meticulous and ingenious craftsmanship from which all Oriental embroidery art grew, and in which there were virtually no limitations.

SCROLL TECHNIQUES

Example 1: Sun Rising Over a Turbulent Sea, China, Sung Dynasty (Figs. C-31, 7-16)

This superb composition demonstrates the powerful attraction that Chinese embroideries had for eighteenth- and nineteenth-century Japanese painters such as Hokusai, for many Chinese modes of expression and artistic conventions, as in the drawing of the wave, were later adopted by Japanese artists. The subject work is, of course, a typical example of Sung embroidery at its very finest, even as it suggests the great debt that Momoyama and Tokugawa textile designers and painters owed to China.

The scroll has been worked in a variety of especially lovely and ingenious techniques. The bluish tones in the rocks presage the blues so much admired by Ming embroiderers, while the pine needles, which jut out as the fulcrum of the picture's center, are executed in a manner later used by the Koreans. Here and there throughout the piece the yellow ocher ground silk has been allowed to peek through: The sky, with the clouds and blazing red sun laid upon it, as well as the lower right area of the design, are both the ground color, and the upper and lower areas of the picture are brought together in harmony through this unifying artistic device.

A. The sea and waves were worked directly upon the ground, which shows as the yellow ocher sky color (1). Working from dark to light, or vice versa, the beige areas (2) were satin-stitch gradated in subtle changes of color and value until they met and blended with the white areas (3). The stitchery throughout the beige areas (2) was not laid either vertically or horizontally, but followed, in satin stitch, the constantly varied, undulating rhythm of the wave's upward movement; such undulating stitchery directions were intended to suggest the sea in all its turbulence. This may have been accomplished through following prepainted movement lines in the underlying ground design.

B. All of the darker movement lines (4) were carried out in stem stitch over the gradated satin stitch. These stem stitch lines reinforce the directional movement of the underlying satin stitch and contribute to the strong feeling of movement, besides adding a very artistic linear accent.

At the upper crest of the waves a swirling vortex (5) adds power and surging climax to the topmost breaking wave. Starting at the center, the vortex was done in underlying directional satin stitch, which was then accented with stem stitch, again beginning at the center. Everywhere through the sea areas this same technique was effectively used, that is, the undulating, irregular-length satin stitch accented by an equally powerful line in stem stitch.

The rocks were done in gradated satin stitch also, while the sun, clouds, and trees are in flat satin stitch. All line work and accents elsewhere are in stem stitch.

Fig. 7-16. Example 1: stitchery directions and color indications of *Sun Rising Over a Turbulent Sea.*

1. White—Satin Stitch
2. Light—Satin Stitch
3. Medium—Satin Stitch
4. Dark—Satin Stitch
5. Line—Stem Stitch

Example 2: White Falcon, China, Sung Dynasty (Fig. 7-17)

In this famous Sung piece, the embroidered body work on the proud white falcon is in a plied white silk floss satin stitch that flows with the simulated natural direction of the downy feathers. A technique of varying the distribution of thread strands further increases a sense of gleaming white feathers, through the controlled manipulation of light as it skips over the thread facets.

The craftsmanship on this piece is outstanding, even though the embroidery is less than extensive, being austerely rendered in a stark relief against the ocher-colored ground. The blue rope and braid beneath the bird's stand adds a fascinating study in color and textural contrasts, and is done in a braid stitch. The feather and wing techniques used in this composition are similar to techniques I used in the peacock screen in Figure 7-11 and crane screen in the next chapter, Figure 8-5, page 154.

Fig. 7-17. *White Falcon.* Hanging scroll (Example 2). Design of falcon, pedestal, and braided rope with tassel. Individual feathers divided in diagonal satin stitch rows, separated by stem stitch accents; braid stitch; plied silk floss on ocher silk ground. China, Sung dynasty. Courtesy of the National Palace Museum, Taipei.

SCREEN TECHNIQUES

Example 3: Flowers and Pairs of Birds, (Panel 6, Eight-Fold Screen), Korea, Yi Dynasty (Fig. 7-18)

As discussed earlier in this chapter, this screen is a priceless example of classic Korean screen style from the historical period, particularly of the Yi dynasty, with tightly twisted yarn used in a rugged bravura approach throughout. The pair of ducks in this particular panel, accompanied by their little family, are familiar Oriental symbols of connubial happiness (see Fig. C-33).

A. The blue base color of the lotus leaf was done entirely in horizontal layer stitch. Over this, the plant's veins were cleverly worked in stem stitch, and once more the versatile stem stitch served the purpose of both couching the layer stitch and providing accents.

B. The lower lotus leaf, with its curling edges, has a diagonal layer stitch that describes the interesting separation where the leaf curls over toward the greener upper surfaces, and a tawny yellow yarn was used to further delineate this effect. All four of the large lotus leaves were done in the same layer-stem combination, while all leaf contours were followed in stem stitch also.

C. The lotus and its surrounding leaves were completed in satin stitch embroidery. The nearby seed pods (which symbolize many sons) are layer-stitched and couched with a black thread diamond-trellis pattern.

D. The backs of the ducks in the water beneath the lotus leaves are embroidered in various ungradated planes of spaced darning stitch. Their belly areas are in three distinct color separations—raw sienna, pink, and white—also darning stitch without gradations, the stitched color patterns being laid horizontally and flatly next to each other. These color areas were separated by a dark gray line of darning stitch that further expressed the feather textures and created a smooth transition between the color planes.

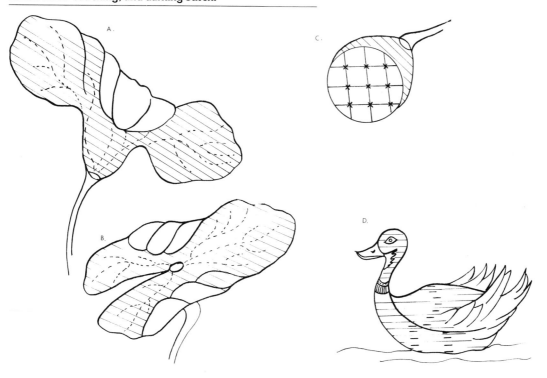

Example 4: The Ten Longevities, Ten-Fold Screen, Korea, Late Yi Dynasty

(Fig. 7-6, 7-19, and 7-20)

Longevity was a Taoist preoccupation in historical China and Korea, and it was not uncommon to find classic longevity symbols in the home on various accessories and furniture decorations such as screens. In domestic life, the traditional meanings of the longevity symbols were generally associated with wishes for a long, happy, and fruitful family life. Slightly different from the Chinese longevity symbols, the design of this screen expresses the ten most popular Korean longevity figures—the pine, bamboo, deer, tortoise, mountain, crane, sacred fungus *(bul-no-cho)*, clouds, sun and water.

A. The backs of the tortoises carry the familiar tortoise-shell designs, series of joined hexagons that are found in many variations and that were used extensively in Japan as well. The stitchery on this particular tortoise-shell motif is especially interesting and complex.

Upon the ground, the first design was applied by covering the darker portions entirely with satin stitch (1). Then the second design was filled in with diagonal satin stitch (2). In the next step, a darning stitch followed the shape on top of the diagonal satin stitch, from one point to another, and was repeated four or five times. Other areas were all done in satin stitch, while area 3 was executed in chain stitch (B).

The pine tree design in this screen is a typical example of Korean vigor in line drawing, with its undersurface rendered in satin stitch and the rough bark accents and outside contours in stem stitch. The pine's needles are the type of radiating stitchery shown in C and Figure 8-6, page 155.

The mountains have been rendered in flat, ungradated long and short stitch. The clouds, water, and bamboo were finished in satin stitch, with all contours, water lines, and accents in stem stitch, the only exception being the Manchurian crane, which shows the same technique as in our earlier example.

Fig. 7-19. Example 4: chain and diagonal satin stitch.

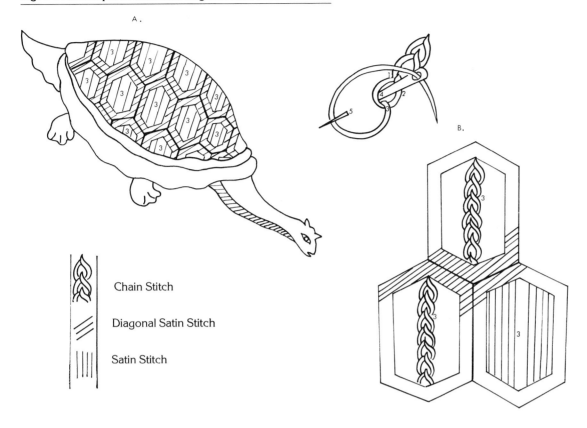

Chain Stitch

Diagonal Satin Stitch

Satin Stitch

Fig. 7-20. Example 4: radiated darning stitch — pine needle technique.

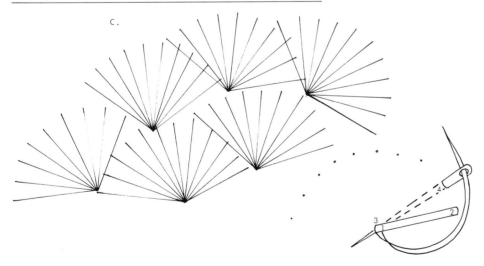

BANNER TECHNIQUES

Example 5: *Kwan-yin,* Lamaist Temple Banner, China, Ch'ing Dynasty
(Figs. C-37, 7-21, and 7-22)

This important composition, discussed earlier in the chapter, measures 19½ × 30 × 16 inches (49.5 × 76.1 × 40.6 cm.) and is dated 1784. Three copies of it are known to exist which are nearly identical in treatment and design—the example shown here from the Metropolitan Museum of Art collection, one in the Victoria and Albert Museum in London, and one in a private collection. Some of the sense of monumental power and spiritual grandeur of this masterpiece was achieved through special types of stitchery that add movement and a strongly sculptural quality that enhanced its realism. The use of interlocking satin stitch was one of the means whereby a vivid, three-dimensional effect was achieved, being used extensively on all of the cloud forms, on the lotus base, and on the halos of the small figures.

A. Interlocking Satin Stitch (Cloud Design)

The needle comes up at 1 and enters the material at 2 (between previous stitches), creating a straight stitch of even length. This step was repeated until the entire outer edge of the contour was finished,

the stitches being kept as close as possible throughout. All of the interlocking satin stitch on the cloud design was done horizontally, which made a complete textural contrast with the sky areas behind it, the latter being done in a vertical, flat satin stitch.

B. Long and Short, Stem Stitch, and Couching (Aura Design)

The beautiful, radiating circular aura behind Kwan-yin representing her thousand arms and eyes was done in a complex range of mixed stitchery techniques. Although this section of the banner has every appearance of being done in appliqué, it is nevertheless embroidered directly onto the ground fabric without any additional piecing. The rich, appliqué-like surface was achieved solely through the marvelous, intricate embroidery.

1. The beige base of the aura was done in long and short stitch, all rows laid horizontally and separately in a clockwise fashion around the diameter, about ³/₈ inch (8 mm.) apart.

2. The definition lines in the thumb and palm areas were done by couching a tightly twisted yarn of the same beige color over the irregular-length satin stitch base. The tightly twisted yarn created a line through relief and contributed much to the illusion of sculptural solidity and movement. The palms of the hands have stitched eyes in the center of each; these were done in black thread stem stitch. The broader arm areas inside the inner, secondary circle were embroidered in long and short

Fig. 7-21. Example 5: interlocking satin stitch (cloud design).

Fig. 7-22. Example 5: long and short stitch, stem stitch, and couching (aura design).

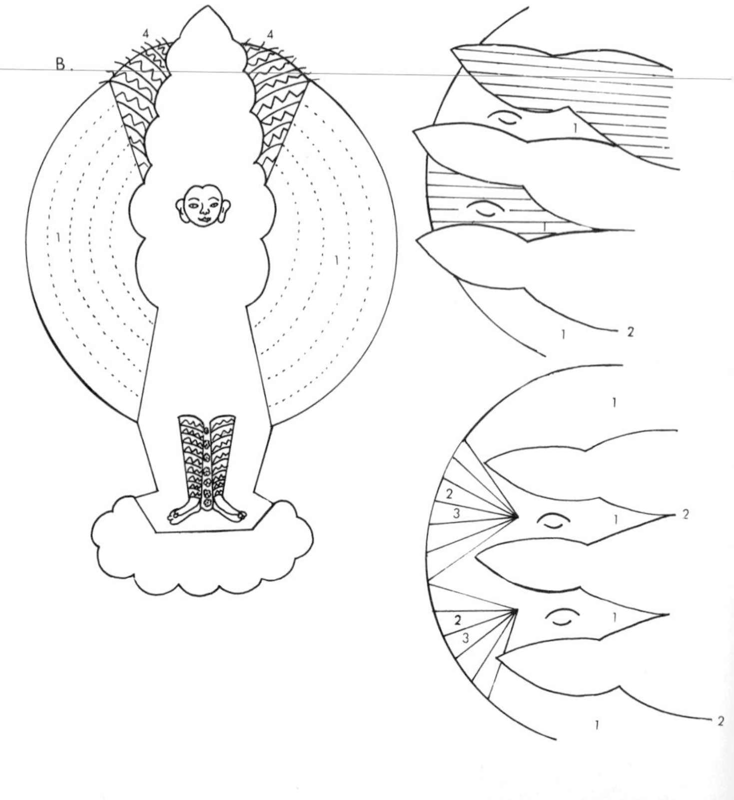

stitch in the same beige color. This created a smoother surface, a difference of texture that more fully expresses the roundness of the arms.

3. The farthest outer edge of the main circle, which is serrated by the outermost row of fingertips, was done in an umber-colored darning stitch, working from the outside and converging toward a center point in each section. In this way, the fingertips were defined by filling the areas between them with the darning stitch in a darker color than the beige.

4. The striped, inverted mandala at the top of the aura, which converges toward the head, was done in laid satin stitch, with the heavier lines in oiled, paper-wrapped thread couching and the sawtooth lines in gold-wrapped couching. These lines were allowed to continue about an eighth of an inch beyond the outermost diameter of the circle, so that they overlap and extend beyond it, thus intensifying an overall effect of a vibrating flame radiation from the mandala. The auras of the two smaller base figures (A1), and those of the six buddhas in the upper portion, repeat the same technique.

The stitchery of the Kwan-yin figure effectively adds to her mystery and subtle air of equanimity, with her eleven faces done in long and short stitch and various other head and body sections repeating techniques found elsewhere, as in the girdle area, which was done in interlocking satin stitch, the line work in couched, gold-wrapped thread; and in the design on her leggings, in the same technique as the triangular mandala above her head. The leggings show the influence of India, from whence the traditions and iconography of the theme derive, but there are also certain T'ang influences present, as in the flower designs on the skirt. A T'ang-style scroll design shows on the girdle of the Victoria and Albert Museum's example, whereas our example has a phoenix design.

Contemporary Screens

For examples of contemporary work in the modern Orient, my own embroidered screens appearing in Figures 7-7, 7-10, 7-11, C-34, and C-35 point to a free use of widely ranging stitchery techniques and design approaches that are in the modern vein, yet fully reflect and follow the traditional methods of the ancient dynastic schools. Such traditions are once more being renewed and practiced today in Korea and Japan, as well as in the People's Republic of China in such sites as the Embroidery Research Institute in Soochow. A brief discussion of the techniques used on some of my screens, which are in collections in various parts of the world, may provide an interesting perspective on the historical examples and techniques outlined in this book.

Rose of Sharon (Fig. 7-7)

The design concept of this piece is in the bold Korean-Japanese tradition, a single, dramatic natural form expanding across the main body of the screen. It has a double symbolism significant to Korea in the Rose of Sharon, the Korean national flower, and in the design of the tree in the shape of the Korean peninsula. The stitchery style is in the modern Szechwan-Soochow manner, but, unlike Szechwan-Soochow, the embroidery is not the same on both sides of the fabric. In preparing the yarns, twenty-four fibers were medium twisted for the light purple flower areas, and a thinner yarn of twelve fibers was also medium twisted for use in the darker purple areas to prevent bulging in those tighter spaces. The leaves' yarns were prepared in the same way. For the trunk textures (see Fig. 7-25), tightly twisted multicolor yarn was prepared for the edges and very roughly twisted yarns of light and dark charcoal gray, umber, and earth green for the darker, inner bark. Working directly on the yellow silk ground, I began the stitchery on the tree trunk from the bottom up, intermixing, alternating, and gradating the four colors in an irregular-length satin stitch while striving everywhere for an effect of roundness and three dimensions. This technique was continued in somewhat lighter tones of the same colors along the branches. The moss effects on the trunk were done next, in gradated satin and long and short stitches in three values of green. The flowers (see color detail, Fig. C-35) were worked next, using four values of gradated satin stitch. The satin-stitched white flowers were done last, with their maroon centers in two gradated values of satin stitch. All flower stamens have cotton underpadding, and were covered by a yellow diagonal satin stitch. The pistils are in extended seed stitch.

In all, over eight different colors and twenty-nine different color tones were used on this screen, and since I was at work on other projects at the same time, it took more than three years to finish.

The Sea (Fig. C-34)

Done in modern Kiangsu-Soochow style, which the Peking Press (in *Chinese Arts and Crafts*, 1963) characterized as "the use of straight stitches of 'irregular' length to create a texture like that of an oil painting. In the highly prized reversible embroidery, the stitching is perfectly finished on both sides of the fabric." This screen was certainly the most difficult and challenging creative problem I have ever undertaken. Its unique visual concept, a view of the undersea world, has been done occasionally in Oriental watercolors, but seldom in embroidery.

To solve the problem of realism and realistic movement, I studied thirty-six live carp in a tank in my studio, spending many days and weeks making sketches and color notes and photographing them. (They were changed almost daily and served for dinner, and needless to say, my family soon grew tired of fish!) I was fascinated by the theme—the color and movement, the shifting colors and scales of fish as they swim, their undulating shapes, and the mystical, dream-world quality of life beneath the sea all were concepts I wanted to introduce into the work. After hundreds of preliminary sketches, the master design was worked out in its finished motif: strong centripetal movements at the left and center countered by the equally strong inward thrust of the group of fish at the right, with inner circular movements in each group of fish and the sea plants massed at the left and right to create balance and unity. The master design (see Fig. 7-8) was drawn on full-size joined sheets of rice paper, the screen-panel lines included, and executed in full color. It was then traced and applied to the various panels of the screen stretched on their frames.

Unsuccessful first attempts to achieve correct color tonalities led to my pulling out the embroidery to begin again. At the second try, after a more intense study of the coloration of the fish, I mixed my own pigments and dyed raw silk fibers in these mixtures. I created four value shades of yellow for the belly areas and five shades of gray for the backs. For the red fish, I dyed four shades of yellowish brick red for the bellies and five shades of deeper brick red for the dorsal areas.

These yarns were twisted according to the size of the scales on the fish. The thickest were used on the backs of the largest fish—eighteen fibers loosely twisted together. The thinnest yarns were used on the eyes, the smallest scales, and the belly areas, and consisted of six hairlike, loosely twisted fibers.

Multicolor yellow and gray or yellow and red yarns were readied for the transitional, blended areas.

I began the complex stitchery by outlining all contours in stem stitch in the color closest to that of the fish's main body; these outlines stressed the scales' overlapping quality and added relief effects to them. In general, the treatment of the body scales was in a technique similar to that style used on silk thread dragon's scales in the Chinese historical period.

I covered the scales, each 3/8 inch (1.5 cm.), with a gradated long and short stitch, using two or three color values to each scale, and working and completing each fish separately from the tail toward the head. Those areas where the twisting or turning bodies required their characteristic iridescent quality were expressed by using darker shades of yarn in the bent or inward sections. I finished the tails, side fins, and dorsal fins in irregular gradated satin stitch, allowing the blue silk ground to show through in some places to accent their transparent quality. In the head areas, I outlined the gills in a red radiating darning stitch, which was done over a yellow laid satin stitch. The mouths are in diagonal satin stitch, while the eye areas have a white laid work base upon which the raised pupils are in satin stitch.

For the sea plants, I used four shades of earth green in combinations of stem and darning stitches (see Fig. 7-23). Generally, the lighter greens were worked first, starting from the top, and these were overlaid with the darker values, working freely up and down the stems.

Screens are always given a steaming to clean and tighten them after completion, but this particular screen was given extra steaming to further clean and puff the fish and to add sheen to the final textures. The stretching frames for this screen measured 9 1/2 by 2 1/2 feet (2.90 m. by 76.2 cm.).

Ancient Korean Treasures (Fig. 7-10)

This screen depicts important artifacts that have been discovered in various sites in Korea during modern times, and are illustrative of some of the Korean traditions discussed earlier (cf. chapters 5 and 6). They are identified with the embroidery techniques I used on them as follows: (upper left) ancient coin—satin and basketweave stitches; (left to right) crown—gold couching; dragon roof tile—satin stitch; Silla crown *(kum-kwan)*—gold couching; noble's dagger—satin and long and

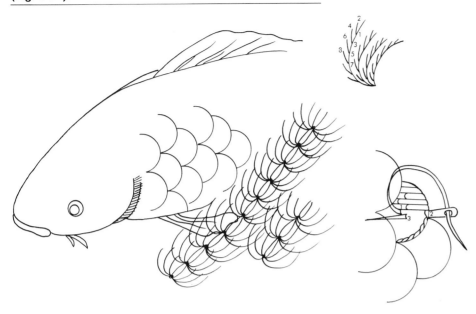

short stitches; imperial nine-tassel crown *(myun-ryu-kwan)* —gold couching; mandarin square, first rank—satin and long and short stitches; jade necklace, jade ring, and gold bracelet—all in satin, long and short, and stem stitches. All of the gold-couched crowns on this screen were done in the Kwangtung-Chaochou style.

The White Peacock *(Fig. 7-11)*

The symbol of virtue and nobility in Korean culture, the white peacocks are surrounded by a meandering mass of peonies. The central motif is balanced by dominant peonies to the left and right in a classic formal substructure, based on a triangular design.

After underpadding with cotton, I executed the peonies in maroon shades of gradated long and short stitch (see color detail, Fig. C-36), while the leaves received a gradated irregular satin stitch treatment to show difference in texture.

The elaborate stitchery of the peacocks was executed in the following techniques.

Upper Body Feathers The feathers' divisions were separated with a white stem stitch, and all the feathers themselves rendered in one shade of white satin stitch, which were then center-separated by couched silver thread. The neck and chest feathers are in white satin stitch with pink accents, also in satin stitch.

Crown and Head Area Metallic silk thread in a continuous darning stitch (see Figs. 7-23, 7-24) was used in a special technique on the crown. The orange beak and red cheek markings were finished in satin stitch, with stem stitch outlines.

Tail Area The characteristic "eyes" of the peacocks' tails first had their centers covered with a spaced, pink darning stitch. This was followed by spaced, bluish-green darning stitches, then a white layer of the same. The tails' center stems were made by cordage laid upon the fabric and wrapped with white silk, which was then couched in white couching stitches at half-inch intervals. Alongside these centers the lateral feathers were done in metallic silk thread, using the same continuous darning stitch. Pink accents in the same stitch were diffused through and in between the white laterals.

Homecoming *(Fig. 8-6, page 155)*

This screen is included in the following chapter as an example of the use of negative space and balancing elements in typical ancient and modern Oriental informal design. The yearling has been placed in a very precise position for a purpose: Even a slight deviation in any direction would disrupt the feeling of the continuity of the landscape, even though it is invisible. By such invisible forms or suggested forms, Oriental embroiderers added profound mystical and spiritual import to their work, especially in Taoist art.

A roughly twisted yarn was brought into play for

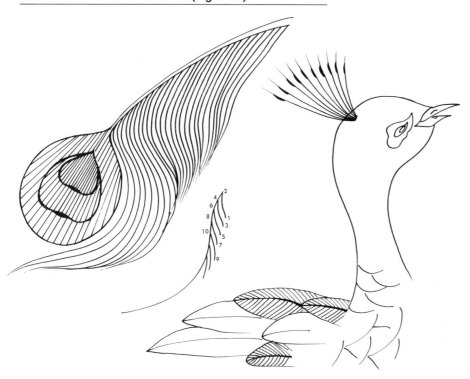

the craggy textures on the rugged pine trunk and pine cones, and these were done in combinations of irregular satin stitch mixed with stem stitch, long and short, darning stitches, and couched loops to express this rough, vigorous surface. The green pine needles were created by long darning stitches radiating from a single satin-stitched center point (see Fig. 7-20).

Irregular-length satin stitch and gradated satin stitches were again used on the entire bodies of the deer, except in the eyes. Three tones of dark brown on the deers' backs were gradated down and into three blended, radiating tones of beige on their lower bodies, sides, and bellies, with the white spots in white yarn and the fur textural accents done in dark brown. The eyes, their accents, and line work are in stem stitch.

The entire composition was completed on a pinkish-beige ground that was left untouched.

The individual panels on all of my screens were constructed according to the traditional methods for such pieces. The underlying frame is made in a manner similar to Japanese *shoji* screens; a white pine skeleton, about two feet wide and the height of the future screen, is constructed for each panel,

consisting of a center lath and crossing ribs in horizontal divisions of about one foot apart. Onto this frame, successive layers (usually five or more) of rice papers are built up through gluing and are allowed a three-month drying period or more, after which the rice paper has stretched to drum-tightness. At the same time, the finished embroidered silk is removed from its frame after steaming and itself receives a rice-paper backing of several layers to seal up and hide the back needlework. The silk panel is then rice-glued to the rice-papered panel on the wood frame, and pummeled with a soft round brush to ease out any air bubbles. This process is repeated on every panel of the entire screen.

The final stages include damask borders to trim and frame the embroidery, and a damask or plain silk backing. A border frame of cherry, oak, or maple is nailed to all sides of each panel with brass ornamental nails, and ornamental hardware is added to protect all corners. These steps are also repeated on every panel. When completed, the various panels are assembled with hidden hinges of tough linen fabric. A decorative strip of fine-quality rice paper is affixed to the back of an end panel to receive the screen's title and artist's name.

In the next and final chapter, our subject will conclude with an overview of some of the philosophical concepts, artistic methods, and techniques of Oriental embroidery design, and the various meanings of many of the most important design symbols.

Fig. 7-25. Embroidered wall hanging: *Sakyamuni Buddha Preaching on the Vulture Peak with Four Attendants.* Chain and satin stitches. China, T'ang dynasty. Courtesy of the Trustees of the British Museum, London.

8/ ORIENTAL EMBROIDERY DESIGN

The influence of Oriental design upon Western art has been significant and far-reaching, beginning with the key designs absorbed by Greece, the Han silks that arrived at Rome in the second century B.C., the Yuan textiles brought back to Venice by Marco Polo in the thirteenth century, and continuing up through the strong Chinese influences that pervaded German, French, and Venetian textiles and ceramics during the late Baroque and early Rococo and that can be seen in such collections as the Metropolitan Museum of Art and the Ca' Rezzonico in Venice. This powerful influence extended into the modern period as well, for when the Japanese print arrived in Europe shortly after the middle nineteenth century, its effect upon French Impressionist art was extreme and total. Founding the majority of their design principles and compositional structure on Japanese design (which was only the apex of the entire Far Eastern tradition), the Impressionists passed the modern torch on to their followers, the Post-Impressionists (Cézanne, Gauguin, Bonnard, Vuillard, Matisse, et al.), liberated the modern school from slavish academic traditions, and created many of the compositional devices still in use among modern Western abstract and naturalist painters, all from the original stimulus of the East.

Before the Japanese print was circulated in the Western world came the long, self-imposed isolation of Japan. And in China and Korea the same period was marked by civil conflicts, invasions, and cultural upheaval. For these reasons, and because Western painting was not yet ready for the fresh air introduced by the Impressionists, European painting before the nineteenth century had only superficially experienced, and largely misunderstood, the strange stylizations and flattened designs of the East, preferring the true-to-nature expressions of Western academic realism, although Eastern influence had long been felt in other media, such as textiles, ceramics, and furniture.

Yet it is an error to attribute all the credit for this powerful effect on modern Western art to Japan alone, for Japanese art at its peak was, quite simply, the result of everything learned and absorbed for centuries from the mighty arts of China and the prolific craftsmen of Korea. True, all that had gone before was synthesized and abstracted by Japan and translated into the characteristic Japanese way of seeing and expressing. But well before this, the fundamental artistic principles and methods had already been devised by the Chinese—complementary colors, perspective, and classic design structure—and they were used in China and Korea thousands of years before the Japanese woodblock print was introduced to Europe.

Historically speaking, Oriental design was the product of several factors: of the geographic isolation of the East from other countries and other artistic contacts; of an intense veneration of its own cultural traditions; and of an artistic evolution that began in prehistoric times with the textile arts. The utilization and exploitation of the revolutionary medium of silk contributed largely, in the early days, to highly evolved embroidery and weaving as art forms, and this early emphasis on the unique conditions associated with the decoration of silk fabrics led to many of the features of patterned design, stylization, and the complexities associated with a strictly two-dimensional expression, long before the appearance of the three-dimensional painting media in China, ink and watercolor. The early dynastic rulers were quick to learn that the production of this most beautiful of fabrics (unknown at that time in the rest of the world), and its further decoration with embroidery, would serve to vastly increase their bounty, and from this complex of production evolved very special design techniques, sometimes influenced by Persia or India, but more often completely original, to meet that demand.

Creative problems in the Chinese methods of design were met in numerous ways: by the division of space and shape into opposing, balanced segments; by directing the viewer's eye along a controlled path throughout the motif; by the use of a broadly symmetrical, cursive line (derived from calligraphy); by the simplification of natural forms into their most essential characteristics, called stylization; by the rendering of rounded natural forms into basic two-dimensional, flat patterns (see Fig. 8-1); and finally, by the use of what came to be almost universally recognized conventions, symbolic meanings, written characters, and rebuses (designs based on punning words; cf. Appendix). Behind this

Fig. 8-1. Detail from presentation cloth (fukusa). Design of cranes in diagonal satin, long and short, and stem stitches with seed-stitched crowns on plain weave silk ground. Japan, Edo period, nineteenth century. Crown copyright, Victoria and Albert Museum, London.

innovative methodology (yet subtly permeated by it) lay the combined elements of a highly evolved artistic and cosmic philosophy, inextricably linked to the formal elements of three religions, Buddhism, Taoism, and Confucianism. (To this group, shamanism, a survivor of prehistoric religions, could also be added.) Thus four main elements comprise the major segments of Oriental embroidery design: philosophical concepts; stylization; techniques; and symbolism. As important as each is to overall understanding, they will be discussed separately, as follows, under their respective headings.

PHILOSOPHICAL CONCEPTS

In the Oriental artistic viewpoint, art comes largely from the intuition of the artist, and this is considered part of a universal principle, an idea derived from Taoism. While the influences of Buddhism (especially in Japan) and of Confucianism are also very important in Oriental aesthetics, it is in *Taoism* that are found the bases which most profoundly motivate the Oriental visual arts.

Founded upon the original ideas of the Chinese philosopher Lao Tzu, of the Eastern Chou dynasty (fifth century B.C.), Taoism is essentially a cosmic religion. It is similar to other Oriental religions to the extent that it does not question the existence of a Creator, but rather affirms nature and the universe, and the human being's spiritual, moral, and ethical relationship to that universe. The meaning of the Tao (literally, "the Way") is that the cosmos is animated by a basic vital energy or magnetism (in the form of spiritual essences or principles), which is seen as the life-spirit pervading all of organic and inorganic nature—all things, including man. From this arises, further, the concept of a moral and beautiful universe: Since the universal laws are essentially good, the moral person is whoever lives most in accordance with natural law.

Taoist aesthetics perceive art as a ritual activity that unifies the artist with the cosmic or universal principle, the Tao, and gives it a defined expression on the physical and cognitive human level. The practice of art becomes the means of bringing into physical form the divine order and harmony that energize the universe, society, nature, and humanity. Where Western art sought to hold a mirror to reality, the Taoist artist saw in reality the forms of spirit and attempted to align his own spirit with the cosmic spirit, so that the Tao would be expressed through him and thus through his art. This was an effort to achieve spiritual unity with the natural order and harmony of the universe, thus making his work implicit with, and expressively reflective of, the cosmic Tao. This was believed possible through meditation, fasting, prayer, a moral life, and the special quality of artistic freedom, spontaneity of expression.

To the Chinese outlook, art was a creative ritual in which the cultured artistic perception brought a refining, educational influence to civilization, thereby contributing to the spiritual development of the latter through becoming the mediumistic realization of the cosmic principle, the Tao. Chinese aestheticians called this quality *ch'i yun sheng tung,* which was one of the most important artistic ideals throughout much of the historical period. It meant the attainment of a masterful self-discipline and a perfectly liberated, fully intuitive spontaneity of expression. From these combined moral and artistic forces the artist would achieve the highest forms of art and beauty in the work ("spirit resonance"), the very essences of nature and the universe.

Many artists (the best, perhaps) remained free spirits in the practice of *ch'i yun sheng tung,* but in time artistic ideas were conceived in the form of codifications, the conventionalization of designs, forms, shapes, lines, and symbols to express both universal and social principles, and this could be taught and handed down to artists and craftsmen without the inconvenience of spiritual discipline. Such conventions were regarded as the most propitious, if not the most ideal, way of achieving the essence of spiritual or universal meaning. Essentially artistic tools, they were thought to lead to greater efficacy and development in the artist and in society. Once the conventions became established as traditions, there was the tendency for them to endure institutionally in typical Oriental fashion. Although Taoism had to compete with Buddhism after its arrival in China, and was not greatly aided by the eccentricities of the neo-Taoist upsurge in the late Han dynasty, the old universal ideas nevertheless endured and remained a permanent part of Oriental aesthetics.

Examples of the expression of harmony, order, rhythm, balance, and unity in Chinese, Japanese, and Korean painting are too numerous to cite here. But a perfect example of this artistic philosophy to be found typically in embroidery design, particularly in costumes, was the characteristic use of symbols that expressed the unity of nature and man (see the discussion of kosode designs in Chapter 4), the universal life-spirit. All geometrical figures (stripes, lines, squares, triangles, lozenges, circles, diamonds, thunder line), as well as any man-made object (pagodas, flower baskets, incense wrappers, characters, bridges) are symbolic of man. All natural forms (birds, trees, flowers, rocks, clouds, water, animals) are, in their largest sense, symbolic of nature. The combined appearance of these two, man-made symbols and nature symbols, together in the same composition or on the same costume, expressed the symbolic spiritual unity of man, nature, and the universe—the classic Taoist conception (see Fig. C-38). The long-life and good-fortune meanings so often associated with the various emblems were really secondary to this main cosmic view of existence. Actually, costumes and textiles done in embroidery were the perfect place to express this universal philosophy, for their creators were under no obligation to supply representations of pictorial reality and could stylize and mix the symbols freely.

Buddhism, particularly Japanese Zen (Chinese Ch'an), introduced concepts of art that also had important effects upon embroidery design. Restraint, simplicity, reverence for nature—these were religious ideals, which, when translated into design, produced the disciplined division of negative space and the exquisite tastefulness of the Japanese kosode (Fig. C-17), the poetry of Chinese bird compositions (Fig. 8-4), the unfinished suggestion or formal stylization of Korean mountain designs (Fig. 8-2). Also from Buddhism came the deemphasis on the logical mode of thought that was so highly regarded in the West, the reliance on heart, inspiration, intuition, the creative act totally independent of precise steps of the intellect.

A wholly spiritual religion, Buddhism views the natural state of man to be spiritual, that is, non-dualistic, achieving true existence and ultimate peace only through living in the supreme freedom and oneness of the primary universal spirit or law. This idea affected Oriental aesthetics profoundly, in that true beauty, in the Buddhist belief, can exist only on a plane where it has no antithesis—in the unified realm of perfect spiritual integrity or Divine Original Law—and is, therefore, a spiritual quality.

Fig. 8-2. Throne pedestal screen. Design of stylized mountains, trees, rocks, water, sun, and moon. Hand-painted color on silk. Korea, Yi dynasty, eighteenth century. Collection of Chang-Duk Palace, Seoul.

However, Buddhism itself does not formulate an aesthetic concept, since making such distinctions as beauty and ugliness, good and bad, right and wrong is regarded as an impediment to enlightenment.

In the Buddhistic sense, anyone can become a buddha, one who has attained the fundamental state of grace, and the craftsman or artist who relies on spiritual grace will achieve the highest beauty in his work: It is here that the aesthetic similarities to Taoism become evident. In Zen, the distinction is made that the cultivation of one's individual abilities must be pursued until enlightenment is achieved, and in this circumstance, the reliance on grace or inspiration is replaced by self-reliance, although the goals are the same. To the Oriental designer, intuition is the work of the spirit, and it is the union of the human spirit with the cosmic spirit, in an intuitive process (feeling rather than thinking), that produces the beauty of the design.

Buddhist symbols and conventions were very prominent in Ch'ing Chinese and Yi Korean embroidery, but less common in Japan. Generally they represent significant events in the Buddha's life, or his attributes, the earliest beginning to appear in Chinese textiles shortly after the arrival of Buddhism in China in the first century A.D. The sacred number eight so frequently encountered in Chinese and Ko-

rean art embroidery and textile symbols probably originated with the lengendary eight important events in the life of the Buddha, composed shortly after his death, such as the assault upon him by Mara, the demon of evil, his preaching of the message of the enlightenment beneath the bodhi tree, the Parinirvana or his victory over reincarnation, and so on.

The concept of natural law or principle that fills Oriental aesthetics can also be traced to Confucianism to a large degree. Although Buddhism eventually yielded to Confucianism and Taoism in China as the dominant religion, similarities are found in all three, and the artistic influences, again, were profound, important, and enduring in Chinese and Korean iconography. Like Taoism, Confucianism discovered in nature the same attributes of order and harmony that existed in man and the universe—a spiritual concept. Yet the universal order was seen by the Confucian as highly rational, in which trees, rocks, mountains, clouds, flowers—all of nature—were pervaded by a harmonious moral order. This idea of a rational natural order embodies the principle called *li* by the Chinese, and includes those high ethical and moral qualities set forth by Confucius. Many of the conventions developed for embroidery design and Chinese landscape painting were devised by Con-

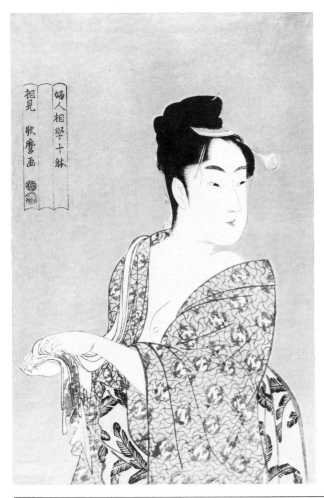

Fig. 8-3. *Inconstant Type,* from the series *Studies in Physiognomy: Ten Kinds of Women* by Kitagawa Utamaro (1753–1806). Color, woodblock print. Japan, Edo period. Courtesy of the Cleveland Museum of Art, Bequest of Edward L. Whittemore.

Fig. 8-4. *Cassia.* Design of cassia tree, birds, butterfly, flowers, and rocks in satin, stem, long and short stitches, with beadwork of seed pearls. Hanging scroll, with poetic inscriptions by Chi Huang embroidered in characters. China, Ch'ing dynasty. Courtesy of the National Palace Museum, Taipei.

fucian artists, out of Confucian ideas of the correct and most meaningful way to express the spiritual and rational essences found in natural forms. But the presence of a rational universal order in Confucian thought should not be confused with logic or scientific thinking, for it meant simply that the universe was based on a coherent and intelligent (hence, moral) structure.

Oriental aesthetics, in the main, can be characterized by a nonempirical, intuitive, spiritually motivated approach to creativity, based upon the various religious overtones outlined in the foregoing statements. The wealth of complex mythologies and superstitions that sometimes accompanied these ideas cannot, of course, be taken seriously in modern times, but should be regarded, rather, in some

cases as the effect of a lack of scientific knowledge in a geographically limited world (also true of Western mythology and superstition) and in other cases as mere spiritual allegories, which, while not having any concrete reality, can to some extent be regarded as the bearers of certain spiritual truths and modes of thought prominent in the three great Oriental religions. Buddhist thought, for example, asserts that the many deities are merely various manifestations of the sublime, original Law, in much the same way that the sun radiates many beams. This is not a demonstrable polytheism, but simply an aspect of the many complex modes of spiritual expression with which Buddhist art and iconography are so heavily permeated.

STYLIZATION

Appearing in its most extreme form in embroidery, costume, and other textiles, the artistic stylization (see Fig. 8-1) of natural forms in Oriental art has often been the source of confusion, if not of outright consternation, to persons comparing it with Western naturalism or realism, and yet it is a highly artistic, concise visual language that, in the minds of many, expresses the essence of natural forms far better than a more explicit and literal art.

Oriental stylization evolved from a period in history in which few conceptions of artistic realism were prevalent, it is true, but this was not the reason for its being. It was derived, on the contrary, from very early attempts in the textile arts and pottery to develop symbols that were effectively expressive of (1) natural forms, (2) supernatural figures associated with shamanism, and (3) geometrical patterns that had a ritual, social, and/or aesthetic significance. Additionally, designs and symbols were needed that could be readily adapted to the characteristics and techniques of those early media.

The earliest Shang masks and *k'uei* figures most certainly had origins in the cultures that preceded them in the Neolithic Yellow River Valley communities, for by the time of the Shang, stylization was already a perfected artistic technique. Clearly, such figurative stylization techniques came from either pottery or textiles, for there were no other major art forms in the Neolithic. The weight of evidence is much greater in favor of textiles as the origin of stylization, however, for geometrical motifs were more commonly expressed on the Painted Pottery examples, even as the nature of textile designing demanded the adaptation of figurative forms to fit the limitations of two-dimensional expression. (See Fig. 8-5. See also the Painted Pottery example in Chapter 1, Fig. 1-2, page 9).

By the time of the Chou, and into the Han, Taoism had already taken strong roots in China and had worked its influences on Chinese aesthetics. The stylized figure was uniquely and coincidentally appropriate to express the universal spirit or essence of a subject. All nonessentials were eliminated from the stylized form; the powers of suggestion, directness, and simplicity were found the best means to express the life-spirit of the universal Tao, the rational universe of Confucius, the undifferentiated reality of the Buddha. Order and harmony were seen in the artistic elimination of unimportant detail, the expression of the character of a thing (its essence), through its simplest structural elements (see Fig. 8-4). Eventually archetypes were developed to express the myths and legends of remote prehistory, and in stylized archetypal forms, such as the face and running coils of the dragon, were also seen the workings of natural law, the presence of the universal harmonies and rhythms.

Fig. 8-5. *Cranes.* **Four-fold screen by the author. Design of cranes and pine tree in diagonal satin, long and short, and seed stitches; pine needles in radiated darning stitch; loop couchings and roughly twisted textured yarns on tree trunk; navy blue satin ground. Height, 6 feet; length, 10 feet (1.83 x 3.048 m.). Collection of the author.**

Oriental stylization can be most readily understood as a kind of artistic shorthand, the sophisticated use of artistic conventions. What are artistic conventions? Merely technical devices that have been learned by artists (and are still used in all kinds of art) to express visual images powerfully and directly, with the most economical brushwork. Suggestion is important in this method, for a skillfully executed drawing that suggests the roundness of a form, rather than stating it literally, is often the most effective expression of that form. To show one side of a figure, for example, as Utamaro did in the woodblock print in Figure 8-3, with only the merest hint of accent on its other side, can be the most evocative depiction, in artistic terms, of the appearance, character, shape, mass, and essence of a given subject—whether it be a tree, a rock, a bird, or a human figure. Artistic conventions, and design conventions such as those found in the Appendix, are really highly charged symbols that express meaning in the most direct and simplified terms.

The deft, restrained use of accents typifies the nature of most artistic conventions. We know that the flowers, mere touches of red, in Monet's *Field of Poppies* did not look like that in reality, but how well the painter captured their spirit! This kind of suggestion is another example of an artistic convention, as is the delicate, threadlike line of the lady's chin in Utamaro's print, which so well suggests the contour and jawline of the entire face, just as the gently curving line below so exquisitely shapes the breast. We know that no nose has such a line at its side, yet how excellently the line expresses this particular feature, how authoritatively it seems to summarize the whole face! The same conventions and accents appear in embroidery design, as in the touches on the leaf, bird, and butterfly forms in Figure 8-4, as well as the rugged line accents on the rocks. Monet said aptly of Oriental art that it "evokes presence by means of a shadow, the whole by means of a fragment."

There is no essential difference between the stylization of painting and the stylization of embroidery in Oriental art, and, as suggested earlier, there is every reason to believe that the former came into being from the latter. Both feature the major characteristics of stylization: the expression of the essence of a subject; artistic suggestion and convention; the use of calligraphic, cursive accents to describe and express forms; and the deployment of line and flat linearity to describe space. To these components might also be added what is called pattern, the overall distribution of flat color areas in the composition, delineated by contours and accents in calligraphic line (Fig. 8-3). The latter, derived from the characteristic brushwork of calligraphy, is the highly skilled technique of using cursive brushstrokes to express forms; more specifically, of letting the characteristics of a particular stroke express particular forms (Fig. 8-4).

As we draw closer to pattern and flat color forms, we draw farther away from the atmospheric techniques found in tonal watercolor painting, such atmospheric painting not being stylized art at all, but naturalism, although it commonly contains many artistic conventions. It was for this reason that the

Fig. 8-6. *Homecoming.* Four-fold folding screen by the author. Design of deer and pine tree in irregular-length satin, long and short, stem stitches; pine needles in radiated darning stitch; on beige silk ground. Height, 6 feet; length, 10 feet (1.83 × 3.048 m.). Collection of Ikenobo Women's College, Tokyo.

Fig. 8-7. Detail from *Homecoming* (Fig. 8-6).

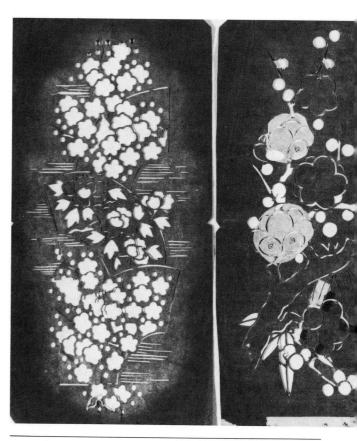

Fig. 8-8. Stencil for kimono inner collar design *(eri).* Japan, Edo period, late nineteenth century. Collection of the author, gift of Mr. and Mrs. Kensaburo Ikeda.

Japanese divided painting into two kinds, the atmospheric *sumi-e* ink styles (Kano school) in the Chinese tradition, and the fully opaque, patternized color stylizations of *yamato-e,* or Japanese traditional style.

Pattern in stylized art (embroidery and painting) means the combined visual impact of the large masses, forms, and negative spatial areas in a nonatmospheric composition (Fig. C-39). Their combined color, shape, and contours should form a unified sense of wholeness and oneness in the Oriental method, and the way this was done is part of some of the design techniques outlined in the following section. Pattern, in general, is rendered with an eye to the design as a whole, and its unified visual image can be vital to the expression of an idea or an essence; so vital, in fact, that the characteristic Oriental use of pattern has been thought to be the most outstanding feature of Oriental design and stylization, and a certain mystique has even sprung up around it.

Japanese crest designs are a good example of pattern in its most fundamental form. The dragon robe's main field is extremely patternized, as is the

Korean mandarin square. The use of flatness in a patternized composition is, again, an artistic convention. It is not intended to be naturalistic; indeed, it intentionally avoids realism and reduces forms to what is an artistic vision rather than a natural one. Yet it is the artistic vision that expresses the natural essence better than the reality itself, better than nature itself. One of the reasons for this is that forms become more symbolically laden and more evocative when stripped to their barest and most essential elements. Framed by an exquisitely conceived artistic interpretation of space, no other image is so powerful; it is the ultimate essence of both symbolism and the real beauty of nature. That it is decoration is quite secondary to this very real symbolic and emotional import.

Pattern, and Oriental stylized art in general, could be summarized by saying that it leaves things to the imagination of the viewer. These large masses and unfinished forms, these liquid contours and bold, haunting accents need the eye of an audience to complete them, to realize the goal of the symbol, and because of this, because it draws one so completely into it, it is one of the most satisfying and purely artistic kinds of art. Through such artistic conceptions we see and experience nature as it is in itself, in its purity, and we learn how to look at it ourselves. It extracts from reality the truly beautiful, and is thus more beautiful than reality ever is. In stylized art we come into contact, through our own imagination, with the real world of essences, with the artistic transformation of the real world into its purest value and meaning, and that is the experience of the beautiful, the eternal, and the universal.

TECHNIQUES

Hsieh Ho, a master designer and art critic of the Six Dynasties period (c. fifth century A.D.), elaborated the four cardinal rules of composition as "Planning, Division, Placing, Arranging." These four categories of course represent the classic problems involved in the creation of any design. They seem deceptively simple, but their execution, particularly of the last three, called for the utmost skill, good taste, and artistry on the part of the designer, in a process that was far more intuitive and creative than the wide use of conventional design symbols, repeats, and stencils would lead one to believe.

Planning involved the direction of the designer's attention to choices of color and fabric, to the size and shape of the piece to be designed, to knowing what he intended to do within a given space, to the execution of many preliminary sketches before approaching the master design. In Division, the designer addressed his attention to the conceptual patternization of space, to the layout of the various motifs and their overall effect, to the distribution of mass and line, and to the consideration of the positive and negative design elements and components. Next came Placing, the assemblage of the main motifs of the design; the decisions as to what kinds of motifs related harmoniously to the main theme; the juxtaposition, balance, order, and internal harmony of those motifs; the relationship, in terms of contour, shape, and color, to other contours, shapes, and colors, and to the negative space areas. Finally came Arranging, the careful positioning of the design elements to form the most har-

monious and pleasing pattern, the arrangement of lines and shapes until they fitted the designer's intuited vision, until every element had its balancing opposition, every line its graceful direction, every form its own symmetry.

Oriental embroidery designs were first executed on a master design drawn on heavyweight rice paper, which was then traced and transferred to the fabric through any of the methods shown in Chapter 1. In preparing the master design, the designer executed the finished conception in the same size

Fig. 8-9. Panel. Bird and flower design in satin stitch, couched textured yarns on crane and pine tree; tie-dye; on brocade silk ground in design of thunder line and flowers. Japan, Edo period, eighteenth century. The Metropolitan Museum of Art, gift of Mr. and Mrs. H. O. Havemeyer, 1896.

that the finished embroidered design on the fabric would be, an exact replica—half in finished color themes with ink outlines, and half in black line drawing on white. (See Figs. 8-10 and 3-24, page 56). Once traced and the tracing transferred to the fabric, it was posted as a guide for the ensuing stitchery. In a simpler method of preparation, the master design was still executed in the same size as the embroidered piece, only entirely in ink outline, with the colors merely jotted in, as notes, on their proper areas.

The various design motifs were usually placed on the master design through the use of precut stencils or cardboard templates, cut into the shape of the desired motifs or conventions (Fig. 8-8). This obviated the need for repetitious hand drawing, copying, and impractical loss of time. Probably every professional or imperial embroidery studio had a large library of such stencils and templates already cut into the traditional conventions and designs.

They were indispensable in the execution of exact repeats and opposite designs, and the uniformity of the motifs, especially on the dragon robe, shows that such stencils were used extensively (Fig. 8-10). Repeat designs were obtained by simply moving the template or stencil about to its various repeat locations on the master design, while opposites were created by "flopping" the stencil or template—that is, turning it over to its opposite side—and tracing its opposite image.

For purely decorative compositions, such as the dragon robe, such methods had the distinct advantage of saving the time and labor of excessive copying and delineation of repeats, easily standardized the design motif's uniformity, and gave the designer maximum latitude in placing and arranging every element of the design. The majority of geometrical figures, such as the swastika and the thunder line, were almost certainly done with stencils, as probably were the conventional symbols, such as the

Fig. 8-10. Master design for a twelve-symbol dragon robe with colors indicated. Paint and ink on silk fabric. China, Ch'ing dynasty, late nineteenth century. Courtesy of the Nelson Gallery—Atkins Museum, Kansas City, Missouri.

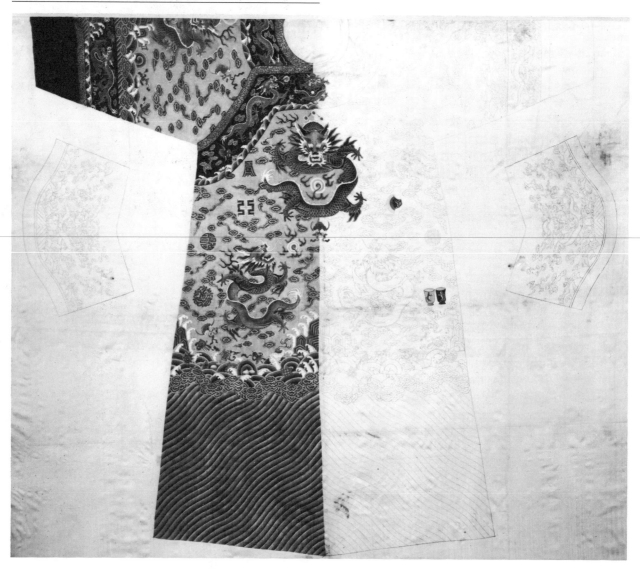

Eight Precious Things, the bat, cloud fillers, and dragons. Characters, too, such as the *Shou,* were made in precut stencil form for ready application to master designs.

Designs were also executed freehand, however, especially on works where many design conventions were not used, such as in landscapes and, occasionally, costume, as an inspection of several dragon robes in the Metropolitan Museum of Art reveals. As discussed earlier, mixing embroidery with painting, or the practice of embroidering passages or all of a painting, was not uncommon, and in such cases the designs were also painted in ink outlines directly on the fabric and were then tinted or painted in dyes or watercolors before embroidery.

Stencils, templates, tracings, freehand drawing, and other technical devices were merely the instruments the designer used to help create the complete orchestration. Although many design formats, particularly in imperial use, were codified and regulated, and restricted by tradition into conventional paths, and although the various symbolic motifs, such as the bat, the cloud filler, and the dragon, were largely dictated by convention as well, the main organization and creation of the master design's pattern still lay in the designer's hands, for the arrangement of the motifs, the division of space, and the exact placement of each component was left up to him. It was, indeed, expected of him that his artistic powers, skill, and intuitive command would so incorporate the elements that the composition would be a work of consummate beauty.

The result was, in China and Korea, the development of an exalted sense of geometrical composition based on formal and informal principles of symmetry, balance, and unity, augmented by what came to be a genius for the handling of negative space and the illusion of great depth in two-dimensional needlework media. Such classic formalism was already in use as early as the Shang, appearing on their bronzes, and had become a fixed tradition by the Chou. While some of the original design principles may have evolved as influences from the West, from Mesopotamia or India, the Chinese were one of the first civilizations to organize design into a complete artistic system, to formulate a complementary color wheel, and to discover the laws of perspective. By the fifth century B.C., the power of Chinese design had already begun to influence the West, one of the most notable examples being the derivation of the classic Greek key from the thunder line (see Appendix). Pre-Momoyama

Japan, enthusiastic for Chinese culture, generally reflected the Chinese creative tradition also, but after that epoch began, Japanese design celebrated flamboyance and the liberation of individuality, breaking with the old Chinese codes and replacing the classic Chinese tradition, revolutionary itself from the beginning of history, with an even greater revolution, that of free expression. (See Fig. 8-9; see also discussion of kosode designs, Chapter 4.)

Chinese and Korean design composition can be resolved into two main principles, formal and informal design. Formal design was characterized by the use of a dominant motif, usually circular, square, or a natural form, placed in the center of the composition, which served as a main focal point and as an axis about which all the supplementary motifs revolved (cf. Figs. 8-11 and 8-13). A variation of the formal design was the incorporation of underpinning elements beneath the central motif to form a center which was triangular in structure, the base of the triangle being the ground line of the lower elements, with its apex in the centered, main motif (Fig. 8-12). The basal figures could be equal in size to the central motif or smaller, but the principle was the same, that of a combination of formal

Fig. 8-11. Taoist priest robe. Design of yin–yang with trigrams and flaming pearls in partially embroidered and gold-couched appliqué and piecework; ground of silk brocade with chrysanthemum design. China, Ch'ing dynasty, eighteenth–nineteenth century. The Metropolitan Museum of Art, gift of Joseph S. Asch, 1936.

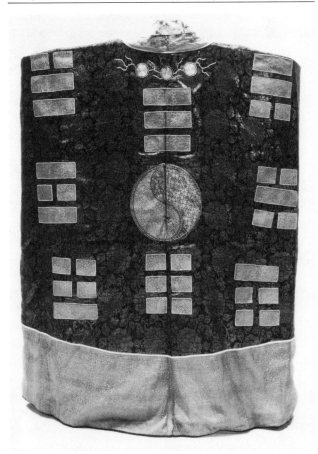

and informal features. Other variations of formal design included the introduction of four pinning elements whose corners formed a square around the central motif, as in Figure 8-13, and whose symmetry threw directional lines that bisected the center of the central figure. The use of a circle within a circle, diamond or square shapes within circles, circular or natural forms within squares, inverted triangles with the central motif at the bottom, and so on, were some additional variations (see Figs. C-14 and 8-13). However, in Chinese formal design the triangular or pyramidal type of formal composition was most popular and most often seen.

The major characteristic of informal design was balance (cf. Figs. 8-14 and 8-15). In this type, two opposing elements of equal weight, importance, and/or mass occupy space directly opposite, or in contiguity to each other, which might be likened to a pair of scales perfectly leveled in balance. Harmony, proportion, and unity are implicit in such a concept, both symbolically and artistically. Informal design was found alone as a dominant theme (Fig. 8-14), or in combination with formal design, as mentioned above. It is more restful, casual, and less

rigid than formal design, and consequently was used more often on informal court robes or costumes of nonimperial origin (Fig. 8-15). It was a typical design structure in most Oriental embroidery landscapes and painting, where objects or figures in space were always balanced by opposing elements of some kind, whether they were two birds (Fig. 8-1), a tree and a man, foreground in balance with background (Fig. 8-6), or a large mass acting as a balancing element for other parts of the picture (Fig. 8-5). Calligraphy and signature seals were even used to balance opposing masses, as Figure 8-4 demonstrates. China was one of the first countries in the world to use informal design in this way. Both formal and informal design were used extensively in the oils and frescoes of the Italian Renaissance, and they still remain one of the vital principles of modern art and design.

Japanese free expression, as it evolved during and after the Momoyama period, was really a kind

Fig. 8-14. Court vest worn by imperial concubine, first rank. Design of paired five-clawed dragons, clouds, mountains, waves. China, Ch'ing dynasty. Crown copyright, Victoria and Albert Museum, London.

Fig. 8-15. Imperial theatrical robes. Left to right: design of geometrical figures, scrolls, flowers, dragons, in piecework and embroidery; design of mythical beasts, geometrical motifs, and scrolls in piecework, embroidery, and appliqué. China, Ch'ing dynasty, late K'ang-hsi period (1662–1722). The Metropolitan Museum of Art, Rogers Fund, 1929.

of informal design, although its features were far more subtle, refined, sophisticated, and hard to detect. The use of oppositional masses was quite common, as were paired balancing motifs; repeats; larger areas of negative space; free-form masses in opposition to broad negative space or abstract geometrical masses; advancing and receding forms in space; overall patterns of minute motifs; a very bold use of line; chains of line, spiriflorals, and meanders to provide unity; understated simplicity; daring use of color in the pastel and vivid ranges; and close observance of complementary color harmonies (see Figs. C-17, C-18, and C-21.) In addition to these design techniques, the combining of man-made geometrical symbols with the figurative symbols, as noted earlier, is very important in Japanese free-expression designs, and is quite typical of many. While some formalism was still present in the post-Momoyama designs, the majority were of the informal, free-expression type, relying heavily

on the trained eye, refined taste, and sensitive intuition of the master designer.

Unity, symmetry, and balance were achieved in Oriental embroidery and textile designs through the infinite possibilities inherent in the foregoing techniques, which admitted of endless variety and were interadaptable in uses and effects. Unity, for example, was achieved by repeats, but was also established through symmetrical line and the harmonious order of balance. Symmetry, even in informal compositions, was accomplished through the unifying device of the smaller repeats, as well as in the inner agreement of corresponding lines and shapes. Balance, the weighing of shapes and masses, is but an aspect of harmony, and from harmony once more comes the sense of unity with which it is synonymous. Every design was a cosmos that expressed the cosmic order, given life by the cosmic hand of man.

APPENDIX / DESIGN SYMBOLISM

The decorative design conventions that were used traditionally in China and Korea literally numbered in the thousands and were part of a vast religious, artistic, and social iconography with which everyone was familiar. Consequently such conventions were symbolic; that is, they had a meaning that was other than, or in addition to, their purely decorative, artistic, or visual significance.

Most of the conventions were of Chinese origin, although some Korean motifs were indigenous to that country. While the Japanese never developed a complete symbolism of their own to any great extent, they had their own conventional designs, and these were used along with some of the classic Chinese conventions, whose symbolic meaning was known to them.

Symbolic design conventions were always figurative. The majority of geometric designs, such as the thunder line, have no known symbolic meaning in the strictest sense and are purely decorative in concept. The exceptions to this were the swastika, which was a prehistoric shamanist luck symbol that later became prominent in Buddhist iconography; the various characters used in design, such as the lucky *fu* and *shou* figures, which naturally still carried their semantic meaning; and certain religious geometric icons, such as the yin—yang and the trigrams. It is probable that some of the classic geometric designs are prehistoric in origin, and may have once had an important symbolism, but the earliest appearance of them has been lost to time and is unknown to us. A general, remote symbolism that was unconventional attended some geometric principles—the circle, for example, was a cosmic symbol, its unbroken line signifying the infinite and eternal; but a specific convention was seldom attached to this or any other geometric principle, other than those noted above.

The conventional symbols fall into various broad categories: imperial, Buddhist, Taoist, Confucian, good-luck emblems, longevity figures, and miscellaneous motifs of uncertain or mythological origin, such as the dragon and the *ch'i-lin*. The following list designates for the reader's reference some of the more important and most frequently seen textile design conventions and their symbolic meanings.

THE DRAGON (Fig. A-1)

The symbol of imperial authority. A five-clawed dragon *(lung)* was worn by the emperor and his immediate family, a four-clawed dragon *(mang)* by lesser nobles and high court officials of special designation. A three-clawed dragon was worn in Korea by princes for a brief period, and was used in China up to and including the T'ang dynasty (A.D. 618–906). The use of the five-clawed dragon began during the T'ang and eventually replaced the three-clawed variety, except in Japan.

Fig. A-1. The dragon.

THE TWELVE SYMBOLS OF AUTHORITY (Fig. A-2)

These symbols were commonly associated with the authority of the emperor, but they appeared as embroidery decorations on imperial textiles other than the dragon robe. Extremely ancient, traditional figures, the Twelve Symbols were derived from motifs that appeared on aprons worn with very early sacrificial robes (Fig. 3-7, page 45) and may date from the Shang or the Neolithic period. Their earliest known appearance on the dragon robe dates from the Ming dynasty (Fig. 3-7). The Twelve Symbols had judicial and cosmic significance and could be found in use alone or grouped as a whole. Represented together, they were understood to express the emperor's symbolic rulership of the universe. Each of the symbols had a specific meaning, as follows.

The Sun   The symbol of heaven and intellectual enlightenment. Usually it is depicted as a red circle enclosing a three-legged phoenix, set over stylized clouds. The phoenix was a Taoist as well as an imperial symbol of nobility.

The Moon   The moon circle shows a hare with mortar and pestle engaged in preparing the elixir of life. Its color is a pale, crystalline blue, encircled by stylized clouds.

The Stars   Three small circles joined by forty-five-degree lines form a triune symbol of the eternal unity of the sun, moon, and earth, or the cosmic universe. A Taoist concept.

The Mountains   The symbol of earth, this figure completes the elemental unity of the cosmos. When it is depicted together with the bronze cups, the water weed, fire, and grain, the five elements are represented: metal, water, fire, wood, and earth. Mountains were also symbols of steadfastness and longevity.

The Dragons   Two smaller five-clawed dragons symbolize the emperor's power of adaptability through transformation or renewal. When they are shown together with the ax, the *fu,* and the pheasant, the special judicial powers of the court are implied.

The Pheasant   The symbol of literary refinement or education.

The Bronze Cups of Sacrifice   These symbolize filial piety and, when shown with the mountains, the ores (brass, copper) of the earth. Filial piety is a Confucian concept.

The Water Weed   This plant is the symbol of purity.

The Grain   This symbolizes the emperor's responsibility to feed the people. Together with the mountains, it represents the wood, or plant, life of the world.

The Fire   A stylized flame symbolizes brilliance of spirit and intellect.

The Ax   This is symbolic of the emperor's power to inflict punishment.

The Fu   This geometric design is derived from the prehistoric character for happiness; symbolically, it is the emperor's responsibility to create a happy nation.

STYLIZED FLAMES (Fig. A-2, J)

Usually added to indicate creatures of a mystical or mythical nature, the flame motif is found extensively on the dragon robe, on the mandarin square, and in Buddhist art, where it symbolizes fire, lightning, or consuming energy.

Fig. A-2. The Twelve Symbols of Authority.

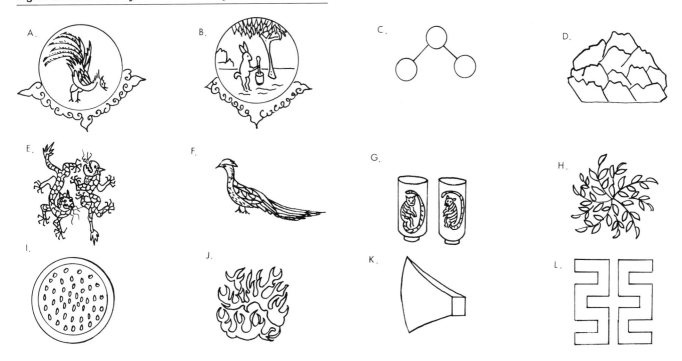

Fig. A-2. The Twelve Symbols of Authority.

THE BUDDHIST EIGHT PRECIOUS THINGS (Fig. A-3)

The first of three sets of Eight Precious Things *(pa pao)* in Chinese lore, the Buddhist conventions were also considered the Eight Emblems of Happy Augury *(pa chi hsiang)* and represented the spiritual attributes of the Enlightened Buddha. Occasionally they are shown intermixed with the eight Taoist motifs (see next section).

The Parasol   The symbol of nobility that sheds the heat of desire.

The Pair of Goldfish   The symbolic union of happiness and utility. It was also the symbol of yin and yang, to be discussed shortly.

The Vase   Called the "treasury of all desires," it was believed to contain the elixir of heaven.

The Lotus   The Buddhist symbol of divine purity and the promise of nirvana.

The Conch Shell   Called the sign of the "blessedness of turning to right," it was originally used to call the faithful to prayer, and is the Buddhist symbol of victory.

The Endless Knot   Also called the entrails. It is the symbol of the Buddhist path, the "thread" that guides one to happiness. In Indian lore, it was the mystic mark that appeared on the belly of Vishnu, and it probably found its way into Chinese Buddhism from this source.

The Canopy   The symbol of victory over the religions of the world.

The Wheel or Chakra   Symbolic of the Buddhist teaching that leads the disciple to nirvana. At times a bell takes the place of the wheel.

Fig. A-3. The Buddhist Eight Precious Things.

THE TAOIST EIGHT PRECIOUS THINGS (Fig. A-4)

This set of *pa pao* is also called the Attributes of the Eight Immortals *(pa an hsien)* and consists of symbols of various Taoist patron saints.

The Fan   The symbol of Chung-li Ch'uan, patron saint of the military.

The Sword   The symbol of Lu Tung Piu, a scholar-warrior, the patron of barbers.

The Crutch and Gourd   The emblem of Li T'ieh-kuai, patron saint of the sick.

The Castanets   The symbol of Ts'ao Kuo-chi'ui, patron saint of actors.

The Flower Basket   The symbol of Lan Ts'ai-ho, the patron of florists and gardeners.

The Bamboo Tube and Rods   The symbol of Chang Kuo Lao, the patron saint of artists and calligraphers.

The Flute   The symbol of Han Hsiang Tzu, the patron of musicians.

The Lotus   The symbol of Ho Hsien Ku, the female patron saint of housewives.

Fig. A-4. The Taoist Eight Precious Things.

THE SECULAR EIGHT PRECIOUS THINGS (Fig. A-5)

These *pa pao* were purely secular in nature, although their many literary and artistic symbols imply strong Confucian overtones.

The Pearl   A symbol believed to grant wishes.

The Cash   A copper coin decorated with ribbons, the symbol of wealth.

The Open Lozenge   A victory symbol.

The Pair of Books   Symbolic of scholarly learning.

The Painting   Represented by a solid lozenge, the symbol of art.

The Musical Stone   The symbol of musical accomplishment.

The Pair of Horns   Probably a symbol of health. Rhinoceros horns, which the symbol greatly resembles, were valued for medicinal purposes.

The Artemisia Leaf   The symbol of the prevention of disease. The artemisia was also considered a plant of good omen.

Fig. A-5. The Secular Eight Precious Things.

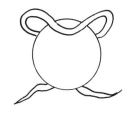   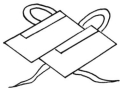

THE EIGHT TRIGRAMS

(Fig. A-6)

Called the *pa kua* by the Chinese, the trigrams were mystic symbols that were the basis of a very ancient system of divination and philosophy that began with the Chinese classic *I Ching* (Book of Changes). Traditionally they were said to have been found on the back of the dragon horse by the legendary hero Fu Hsi. They appear as decorative motifs in almost all crafts media beginning from about the fourteenth century, and they frequently appear in association with yin–yang.

THE YIN–YANG

A dualistic, cosmological symbol, the yin–yang is a circle bisected by a curving, S-shaped line. The dark side (yin) represents the female principle of creation, the light side (yang) the male principle. The whole symbol signifies the balance of opposites inherent in all of nature—male and female, dark and light, sun and moon, cold and heat, and so on. More specifically, yin symbolizes the procreative element of nature and yang the creative element. The yin–yang and trigrams form the emblem of the modern Korean flag.

THE THUNDER LINE

Originating in the Shang dynasty or earlier, the thunder line is so called because of its derivation from the prehistoric Chinese character for thunder. Used mainly as a background or border motif, it is found typically in a continuously running series of squared or rounded spiral shapes, but very close S-curves are commonly also included in this term. Sometimes used in connection with the swastika (see below), the thunder line was the basis for similar key styles in the Middle East and Greece.

THE SWASTIKA

The Oriental tribal peoples who migrated from Asian Siberia across the Bering Land Bridge about 25,000 B.C. evolved into the American Indian, and they carried this symbol with them from Asia. It is therefore one of the world's oldest known design symbols, and was probably associated with prehistoric shamanist rituals. In China it became a Buddhist luck symbol sometime after A.D. 200. It is also the shortened form for ten thousand, indicating longevity.

THE SHOU

A Chinese character meaning "long life," the *shou* was used in either its round or long form as a decorative design element, where it retained its semantic meaning. When it was found in combination with other figures such as the *fu,* the bat, or the swastika, its meaning then became "long life and happiness," "10,000 long lives," and so forth.

THE FENG-HUANG

The phoenix was worn informally by the empress in the Chinese and Korean court, and the pair of phoenixes, the *feng-huang,* was usually given to princesses and lesser female nobles of the court as a ranking emblem on the mandarin square (see Fig. 6-16, page 114). The double phoenix figure represented the male and female principle, *feng* being the male phoenix and *huang* the female.

Fig. A-6. Various geometrical and imperial symbols.

Classic Thunder Line

Prehistoric Glyph
for Thunder

Shang
Adaptation

Shou

Yin-Yang with Trigrams

Swastika

Feng Huang

THE TEN LONGEVITIES

(Fig. A-7)

These symbols imply all the blessings of a long and healthy life. They are found singly or in groups in China, and Korean designs sometimes show all ten together (see Fig. A-7). A preoccupation with longevity and immortality was characteristic of neo-Taoism, and they are thus, in addition, Taoist symbols. The ten longevity symbols are the Manchurian crane, the tortoise, the peach (also a fertility symbol in Korea), mountains, clouds, water, the sacred fungus (*ling-chih*, Chinese, and *bul-no-cho,* Korean), the sun, the pine, and the deer.

STYLIZED WAVES

Wave designs symbolized the seas and waters of the earth and were found in several types. Half-circles superimposed on one another indicate still water, while the waves of the sea were depicted by the *li shui* type, a diagonal pattern. A third form was the cresting kind, the rollers appearing at the tops of the waves. The wave pattern was usually shown in combination with the dragon, as though the mythical creature were rising from a primordial home in the sea, and almost always as a border design. On mandarin squares, wave patterns were shown with other creatures also, such as the *ch'i-lin.* As a general rule, the more narrow wave patterns date from the earlier dynastic periods, and they typically become higher and more immoderate as they approach the late Ch'ing decline.

THE MANCHURIAN CRANE

Chinese mythology attributed a lifespan of 2,000 years to the white Manchurian crane, after which it was said to become entirely black. Korean mandarin squares often show this frequently used longevity symbol bearing the sacred fungus in its beak.

THE DEER

Deer and antler motifs date well back into Asian prehistory and were probably primitive hunting totems. In design conventions the deer was a symbol of longevity, for it was fabled to attain its long life through eating the sacred fungus *(ling-chih),* which it is sometimes depicted bearing in its mouth.

STYLIZED CLOUDS

Symbolic of heaven and long life, these interesting design forms appear in endless variations in Oriental embroidery and textile designs. They could be used in any number, and on the dragon robe, as elsewhere, they served the artistic purpose of space fillers, adding a unifying element to the whole design. Seldom seen outside of Asia, their use in embroidery was probably unknown before the Sung dynasty (A.D. 960–1279).

STYLIZED MOUNTAINS

These conventions are long-life symbols, but they also appear on the dragon robe as symbolic of earth, or the world. The conventional shapes and forms are allowed a wide latitude and show many variations, following only a general symbolic type. Since they are believed to have originated with the tapestry weave *(k'o-ssu),* they probably did not appear in embroidery before the Sung dynasty.

Fig. A-7. The Ten Longevities.

Bamboo

Pine

Deer

Tortoise

Manchurian Crane

Sacred Fungus

Sun

Water Waves

Clouds

Mountains

BLOSSOMS OF THE FOUR SEASONS (Fig. A-8)

The four most important flower emblems each symbolized a blessing and a season: the peony—wealth and spring; the lotus—purity and summer; the chrysanthemum—friendship and autumn; the plum blossom—beauty and winter.

THE FLAMING PEARL (Fig. A-8)

This convention appears on nearly every dragon of the Ch'ing dynasty, usually centered in the upper coils of the main dragon. It is called *lung-chu* in Chinese, the "pearl of the dragon," and its center contains the same prehistoric character for thunder (see Fig. A-8) upon which the thunder line was based. In combination with the stylized flames that surround it, the idea of thunder and lightning was expressed, and the awesome power of the dragon, ruling the symbolic heavens, was thus intensified.

THE LOTUS (Fig. A-8)

The symbol of purity and summer, the lotus was also the symbol of the Buddha and is an extremely important motif found often in Oriental designs. Its origin in China probably dates from the arrival of Buddhism there in the Han dynasty, but its ultimate origin is usually attributed to India and the lotus throne of the Buddha (padmasana). It was assigned a prominent place on the dragon robe, although it never appeared above the dragon, perhaps indicating the emperor's symbolic rulership over religion, although the figure secondarily symbolizes nature as well.

THE BUTTERFLY (Fig. A-8)

The symbol of great age, the butterfly *(hu t'ieh)* here becomes the rebus for the character for "length of days" *(t'ieh),* and the visual butterfly convention takes on the meaning of a written word.

Fig. A-8. Various imperial, religious, and secular symbols.

Peony

Lotus

Chrysanthemum

Cherry Blossom

Butterfly

Flaming Pearl

THE BAT (Fig. A-9)

The Chinese are a people who appreciate humor, and puns on words, or rebuses, are found in various design conventions. For example, the use of the flying bat on the dragon robe and elsewhere seems inexplicable until we realize that the Chinese character for happiness *(fu)* and the final character for bat *(pien-fu),* both have the same sound. The bat figure thus becomes the means for translating an auditory symbol (a word) into a visual one (a design), and the bat design becomes the symbol for happiness.

Similarly, the swastika, called the *wan* character, was the Buddhist symbol of good luck, but it was also synonymous with the character for the number 10,000, also called *wan;* hence a swastika in combination with a *shou* design means "10,000 long lives."

THE PEACH (Fig. A-9)

A popular Chinese longevity figure, the peach was said to be the food of life and the nourishment of the Eight Immortal Taoist Saints. It is often found in connection with other symbols, such as the bat. In Korea, it is also a fertility symbol.

THE PHOENIX (Fig. A-9)

An ancient figure of uncertain origin, the phoenix signified goodness and benevolence in China and in this connection was the symbol of the empress. It was also believed to be the messenger of the Eight Taoist Immortals, and its appearance on earth to presage happy times and propitious events. Often used as a central design, the phoenix appears to be a mixture of several birds, for it has the neck of the crane, the feathers of the golden pheasant, and the tail of the peacock. It was sometimes depicted with a peony in its beak, and was then said to be the harbinger of great wealth.

Fig. A-9. Imperial and good-luck symbols.

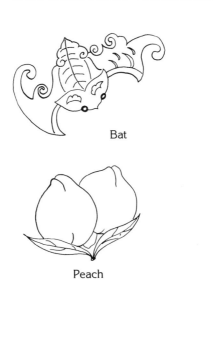

Bat

Peach

Phoenix

BIBLIOGRAPHY

AESTHETICS

Adachi, Fumie. *Japanese Design Motifs.* New York, 1975.

Lee, Sherman E. *Japanese Decorative Style.* New York, 1972.

Medley, Margaret. *A Handbook of Chinese Art.* New York, 1964.

Mizoguchi, Shiburo. *Japanese Design Motifs.* Tokyo, 1973.

Munro, Thomas. *Oriental Aesthetics.* Cleveland, 1965.

Osborne, Harold. *Aesthetics and Art Theory.* New York, 1970.

Siren, Osvald. *The Chinese On the Art of Painting.* New York, 1963.

Sze Mai-mai. *The Tao of Painting: A Study of the Ritual Disposition of Chinese Painting.* New York, 1956.

Watson, William. *Style in the Arts of China.* London, 1974.

Yanagi, Soetsu. *The Unknown Craftsman.* Tokyo, 1972.

ASIAN ANTHROPOLOGY AND ARCHEOLOGY

Andersson, J. G. *Children of the Yellow Earth.* Cambridge, 1934.

Batchelor, J. *The Ainus of Japan.* London, 1892.

———. *Ainu Life and Lore.* Tokyo, 1927.

Boas, Franz. *Primitive Art.* New York, 1951.

Cheng Te K'un. *Archaeology in China.* Three Volumes and Supplement. Vol. I, "Prehistoric China"; Supplement to vol. I, "New Light on Prehistoric China"; vol. II, "Shang China"; vol. III, "Chou China." Cambridge, 1959–1963.

Creel, H. G. *Studies in Early Chinese Culture.* Baltimore, 1938.

———. *The Birth of China.* New York, 1937.

Denwood, Philip, ed. *Arts of the Eurasian Steppelands.* London, 1977.

Fairservis, Walter A. *The Origins of Oriental Civilization.* New York, 1954.

Foreign Languages Press. *New Archaeological Finds in China.* Peking, 1973.

Jettmar, Karl. *The Art of the Steppes.* New York, 1964.

Kwang Chih Chang. *The Archaeology of Ancient China.* New Haven, 1977.

Laufer, Berthold. *Decorative Arts of the Amur River Tribes.* New York, 1902.

Li Chi. *The Formation of the Chinese People.* Cambridge, 1928.

———. *The Beginnings of Chinese Civilization.* Seattle, 1957.

Michael, H. N. *The Archaeology and Geomorphology of Northern Asia.* Toronto, 1964.

Okladnikov, A. P. *The Soviet Far East in Antiquity.* New York, 1965.

Phillips, E. D. *The Royal Hordes: Nomad Peoples of the Steppes.* New York, 1965.

Rice, Tamara Talbot. *The Ancient Arts of Central Asia.* New York, 1965.

———. *The Scythians.* New York, 1961.

Treistman, Judith. *The Prehistory of China.* New York, 1972.

ORIENTAL ART HISTORY

Doi, Tsugiyoshi. *Momoyama Decorative Painting.* Tokyo, 1977.

Eckhardt, Andreas. *History of Korean Art.* London, 1929.

Griswold, Alexander H.; Kim, Chewon; and Pott, Peter H. *The Art of Burma, Korea and Tibet.* New York, 1964.

Kim, Chewon, and Lee, Kim Lena. *Arts of Korea.* Tokyo, 1974.

Kim, Wan Yong. *Art of Korea.* Seoul, 1974.

Korean Art Center. *Korean Art.* Edited by Park Jong Wha. Seoul, 1965.

Lee, Sherman E. *A History of Far Eastern Art.* New York, 1972.

McCune, Evelyn. *The Arts of Korea.* Rutland, Vt., 1962.

Nakamura, Yasuo. *Noh.* Tokyo, 1971.

Noma, Seiroku. *The Arts of Japan: Late Medieval to Modern.* Vol. II. Tokyo, 1974.

Seton, Lloyd. *The Art of the Ancient Near East.* London, 1961.

Stein, Sir Mark Aurel. *Serindia.* Oxford, 1921.

Strommenger, Eva. *Five Thousand Years of the Art of Mesopotamia.* New York, 1964.

Swann, Peter. *The Art of China, Korea, and Japan.* New York, 1963.

Tokugawa, Yoshinobu, and Okochi, Sadao. *The Tokugawa Collection.* New York, 1977.

Willetts, William. *Chinese Art.* Baltimore, 1958.

Zozayong. *Diamond Mountain.* Seoul, 1975.

CHINESE CLASSICS

Book of Changes (I Ching). Shanghai, 1937.
Book of History (Shu Ching). Shanghai, 1937.
Book of Poetry (Shih Ching). Shanghai, 1937.
Book of Ritual. Shanghai, 1937.
Spring and Autumn Annals. Shanghai, 1925.

COSTUME

Boucher, François. *Twenty Thousand Years of Fashion.* New York, 1967.

Camman, Schuyler. *China's Dragon Robes.* New York, 1952.

Davenport, Millia. *The Book of the Costume.* New York, 1948.

Fairservis, Walter A., Jr. *Costumes of the East.* New York, 1971.

Kim, Dong-uk. *A Study of the Dress and Clothing in the Early Yi Dynasty.* Seoul, 1963.

Noma, Seiroku. *Japanese Costume and Textile Arts.* Tokyo, 1974.

Wilcox, Turner R. *Folk and Festival Costume of the World.* New York, 1965.

EMBROIDERY AND TEXTILES

Bellinger, Louisa. *Textile Analysis.* Washington, D.C., 1950.

Birrell, Verla. *The Textile Arts.* New York, 1973.

Chung, Young Yang. *The Origins and Development of the Embroidery of China, Japan, and Korea.* New York, 1977.

Korinsha Ltd. *Old Treasures from Japan's Needles and Looms.* Edited by Rokura Uemura. Tokyo, 1949.

Lefebvre, Ernest. *Embroidery and Lace: Their Manufacture and History.* New York, 1889.

Mailey, Jean. *Embroidery of Imperial China.* New York, 1978.

Metropolitan Museum of Art. *Momoyama: Japanese Art in the Age of Grandeur.* New York, 1975.

Muraoka, Kageo, and Okamura, Kichiemon. *Folk Arts and Crafts of Japan.* New York, 1973.

National Museum of History. *Chinese Costumes, Brocade, and Embroidery.* Edited by Ho Hao-tien. Taipei, 1971.

National Palace Museum. *Masterpieces of Chinese Silk Tapestry and Embroidery in the National Palace Museum.* Taipei, 1971.

———. *Masterpieces of Chinese Portrait Painting in the National Palace Museum.* Taipei, 1971.

———. *Masterpieces of Chinese Figure Painting in the National Palace Museum.* Taipei, 1973.

Paul, William C. *Old Chinese Embroideries.* New York, 1927.

———. *Chinese Arts and Crafts.* Peking, 1973.

Priest, Alan, and Simmons, Pauline. *Chinese Textiles.* New York, 1934.

Tokyo National Museum. *Japanese Textile Arts.* Tokyo, 1973.

Wang, Y. C. *The Research and Examination of Chinese Women's Gowns in Successive Dynasties.* Taipei, 1972.

GENERAL HISTORY

Eberhard, Wolfram. *A History of China.* London, 1977.

Hookham, Hilda. *A Short History of China.* New York, 1972.

Hubert, H. B. *The History of Korea.* Seoul, 1905.

Kennedy, Malcolm. *A Short History of Japan.* New York, 1972.

Koryo University. *History of Korean Culture.* Seoul, 1970.

Latourette, Kenneth Scott. *China.* Englewood Cliffs, N.J.: 1964.

Lee, Sun-gun. *Korean History.* Seoul, 1973.

Watson, William. *China Before the Han Dynasty.* New York, 1961.

———. *Early Civilization in China.* London, 1966.

———. *Ancient China.* Greenwich, 1974.

Wiethoff, Bodo. *Introduction to Chinese History.* London, 1975.

JOURNALS AND MONOGRAPHS

Andersson, J. G. "Preliminary Report on Archaeological Research in Kansu." *Memoirs of the Geological Survey of China,* Series A:5 (1925), p. 25.

Bishop, Carl W. "The Beginnings of North and South in China." *Pacific Affairs,* 1934, p. 299.

———. "The Beginnings of Civilization in Eastern Asia." *Smithsonian Institution Annual Report,* 1939–40, p. 431.

———. "The Chronology of Ancient China." *Journal of the American Oriental Society,* 1 (1932), pp. 232–247.

Camman, Schuyler. "The Development of the Mandarin Square." *Harvard Journal of Asiatic Studies,* 8 (1952).

———. "Embroidery Techniques in Old China. *Archives of the Chinese Art Society of America,* 16 (1962).

———. "Notes On the Origin of Chinese K'o-ssu Tapestry." *Artibus Asiae,* 11 (1948), pp. 95–98.

Chard, Chester S. "Archaeology in the Soviet Union." *Science,* 163 (1969), pp. 774–779.

Far Eastern Archaeological Society. "Pi-tzu-wo: Prehistoric Sites by the River Pi-liu-ho, South Manchuria." *Archaeologia Orientalis* (Tokyo), 1 (1929).

———. "Inner Mongolia and the Region of the Great Wall." *Archaeologia Orientalis* (Tokyo), Series B:1 (1935).

Kiyoyki, Higuchi. "Flowers and the Japanese." *The East* (Tokyo), 10 (1974), p. 14.

Lowry, John. "Tibetan Art." Victoria and Albert Museum, 1973.

Lubo-Lesnichenko, Evgenii I. "Ancient Chinese Textiles and Embroidery, V Century B.C.—III Century A.D., in the Collection of the State Hermitage." Leningrad, 1961.

Munsterberg, Hugo. "Dragons in Chinese Art." *China Institute,* New York, 1971, pp. 7, 9.

Vollmer, John E. "In the Presence of the Dragon Throne." *Royal Ontario Museum,* 1977.

PHILOSOPHY AND RELIGION

Chan Wing-tsit. *The Way of Lao Tzu.* Indianapolis, 1963.

Creel, H. G. *Chinese Thought from Confucius to Mao Tse-tung.* New York, 1953.

Lao Tzu. *Tao Te Ching.* New York, 1967.

Legeza, Laszlo, and Philip Rawson. *Tao.* London, 1973.

Lin Yutang. *The Wisdom of Confucius.* New York, 1938.

Pardue, Peter A. *Buddhism.* New York, 1968.

WEAVING AND TECHNOLOGY

Baity, Elizabeth. *Man Is a Weaver.* London, 1947.

Forbes, R. J. *Studies in Ancient Technology.* Amsterdam, 1956.

Mailey, Jean. *Chinese Silk Tapestry: K'o-ssu.* New York, 1971.

Reath, Nancy. *The Weaves of Hand-Loom Fabrics.* Philadelphia, 1927.

WORKS IN CHINESE

城 子 崖
Cheng-tze-yai (The Black Pottery Culture Site at Lung-shan-chen in Li-ch'eng-hsien, Shantung Province). New Haven, 1956.

中 國 古 文 物
Chung-kuo-ku-wen wu (Antiquities of China). Peking, 1962.

故 宮 織 繡 選 萃
Ku kung chih hsiu hsueh ts'ui (Masterpieces of Chinese Silk Tapestry and Embroidery). Taipei, 1971.

絲 綢 之 路 汉 唐 織 物
Szu ch'ou chih lu Han T'ang chih wu (The Silk Road: Fabrics from the Han to the T'ang Dynasty). Peking, 1973.

T'u shu chi ch'eng (The Kang Hsi Encyclopedia). Peking, 1796.

Tu ch'ing hui tien (Institutions of the Ch'ing Dynasty). Shanghai, 1908.

文 化 大 革 命 期 間 出 土 文 物
Wen hua ta ko ming chi chien ch'u t'u wen wu (Discoveries during the Cultural Revolution in China). Peking, 1972.

WORKS IN KOREAN

韓 國 古 美 術
Department of Cultural Affairs. *Han guk ko mi sul* (Ancient Arts of Korea). Seoul, 1974.

李 朝 의 刺 繡
Han, Sang Soo. *Yicho ui ja su* (Embroidery of the Yi Dynasty). Seoul, 1974.

韓 國 通 史
Han, Wu Gun. *Han guk tongsa* (A History of Korea). Seoul, 1970.

韓 國 의 刺 繡
Huh, Dong Hwa. *Han guk ui ja su* (Korean Embroidery). Seoul, 1978.

韓 國 裝 身 具 美 術 研 究
Hwang, Oh Kun. *Han guk chang shin gu mi sul yun gu* (A Study of Korean Costume Accessories). Seoul, 1976.

國學圖鑑
Il Cho Kak Publishers. *Kook hak do gam* (The Korean National Encyclopedia). Edited by Lee Hung Jong. Seoul, 1969.

韓國民畵展
KBS Broadcasting. *Han guk minhwa chun* (Korean Folk Painting). Edited by Kim Ho Yun. Seoul, 1977.

韓國服飾史研究
Kim, Dong uk. *Han guk bok sik sa yun gu* (A Study of Korean Costume). Seoul, 1973.

韓國國立中央博物館名品圖鑑
Korean National Museum. *Han guk kuk lip chung ang pak mul kwan myong pum do gam* (Encyclopedia of Masterpieces of Korea). Seoul, 1972.

韓國史
————. *Han guk sa* (Korean History). Edited by Chin Tan Hakhoe. Seoul, 1959.

韓國名人肖像大鑑
Lee, Kang-chil. *Han guk myong in chosang dae gam* (Portraits of Historic Koreans). Seoul, 1972.

韓國服飾史
Suk, Ju Sun. *Han guk bok sik sa* (History of Korean Costume). Seoul, 1977.

韓國服飾史研究
Yu, Hee Kyung. *Han guk bok sik sa yun gu* (A Study of Korean Costume). Seoul, 1975.

WORKS IN JAPANESE

日本美術の起源
Egami, Namio. *Nippon bijutsu no kigen* (The Beginning of Japanese Art). Tokyo, 1959.

絹布路と正倉院
Hasahi, Ryoichi. *Kempuro to shosoin* (The Silk Road and the Shosi-in). Tokyo, 1965.

日本の刺繍
Imai, Mutsuko. *Nihon no shishu* (Japanese Embroidery). Tokyo, 1977.

日本美の眞理
Katsura, Hirosuke. *Nihon-bi no shinri* (The Truth of Japanese Beauty). Tokyo, 1970.

着物模様の美
————. "Kimono moyo no bi" (The Beauty of Kimono Patterns). *The East* (Tokyo), 10 (1974), pp. 7, 81.

奈良佛教藝術
Kobayashi, Takeshi. *Nara bukkyo geijutsu* (Nara Buddhist Art). Kyoto, 1967.

平安時代の美術
Kyoto National Museum. *Heian jidai no bijutsu* (Art of the Heian Period). Kyoto, 1958.

絽刺と佐賀錦
Tsukamoto, Yasuko. *Rozashi to saga-nishiki* (Silk Embroidery and Saga Brocades). Tokyo, 1970.

INDEX